Robert M. Collie, ThD

The Obsessive-Compulsive Disorder
Pastoral Care for the Road to Change

The Haworth Pastoral Press
An Imprint of The Haworth Press, Inc.

The Obsessive-Compulsive Disorder

Pastoral Care for the Road to Change

THE HAWORTH PASTORAL PRESS
Religion and Mental Health
Harold G. Koenig, MD
Senior Editor

New, Recent, and Forthcoming Titles:

A Gospel for the Mature Years: Finding Fulfillment by Knowing and Using Your Gifts by Harold Koenig, Tracy Lamar, and Betty Lamar

Is Religion Good for Your Health? The Effects of Religion on Physical and Mental Health by Harold Koenig

Adventures in Senior Living: Learning How to Make Retirement Meaningful and Enjoyable by J. Lawrence Driskill

Dying, Grieving, Faith, and Family: A Pastoral Care Approach by George W. Bowman

The Pastoral Care of Depression: A Guidebook by Binford W. Gilbert

Understanding Clergy Misconduct in Religious Systems: Scapegoating, Family Secrets, and the Abuse of Power by Candace R. Benyei

What the Dying Teach Us: Lessons on Living by Samuel Lee Oliver

The Pastor's Family: The Challenges of Family Life and Pastoral Responsibilities by Daniel L. Langford

Somebody's Knocking at Your Door: AIDS and the African-American Church by Ronald Jeffrey Weatherford and Carole Boston Weatherford

Grief Education for Caregivers of the Elderly by Junietta Baker McCall

The Obsessive-Compulsive Disorder: Pastoral Care for the Road to Change by Robert M. Collie

The Pastoral Care of Children by David H. Grossoehme

Ways of the Desert: Becoming Holy Through Difficult Times by William F. Kraft

Caring for a Loved One with Alzheimer's Disease: A Christian Perspective by Elizabeth T. Hall

"Martha, Martha": How Christians Worry by Elaine Leong Eng

Spiritual Care for Children Living in Specialized Settings: Breathing Underwater by Michael F. Friesen

The Obsessive-Compulsive Disorder
Pastoral Care for the Road to Change

Robert M. Collie, ThD

The Haworth Pastoral Press
An Imprint of The Haworth Press, Inc.
New York • London • Oxford

Published by

The Haworth Pastoral Press, an imprint of The Haworth Press, Inc., 10 Alice Street, Binghamton, NY 13904-1580

Cover design by Monica L. Seifert.

Library of Congress Cataloging-in-Publication Data

Collie, Robert M.
    The obsessive-compulsive disorder : pastoral care for the road to change / Robert M. Collie.
      p. cm.
    Includes bibliographical references and index.
    ISBN 0-7890-0707-X (alk. paper)—ISBN 0-7890-0862-9 (alk. paper)
    1. Obsessive-compulsive disorder—Patients—Pastoral counseling of. I. Title.
BV4461.6.C65 1999
259'.425—dc21
                                                       99-23094
                                                        CIP

To my Masters
Dean Walter Glick, historian, Texas Wesleyan College
Dr. Albert Outler, theologian, Southern Methodist University
Dr. Bernard Loomer, philosopher, Graduate Theological Union

ABOUT THE AUTHOR

Robert Collie, ThD, is a Pastoral Counselor and a Licensed Clinical Social Worker in private practice in Fort Wayne, Indiana. Dr. Collie is also a Clinical Member of the OC Foundation, a Diplomate of the American Association of Pastoral Counselors, and a professional consultant to an obsessive-compulsive disorders support group. A prolific writer, Dr. Collie is the author of *The Confessional Prayers of a Pastoral Counselor* and a variety of articles on pastoral care and counseling issues. Dr. Collie's professional interests include theology, innovative thinking on mental health, and pastoral counseling.

CONTENTS

Acknowledgments xi

Chapter 1. Take the "On Ramp" 1

The Making of the Map 3
Clearing the Mind: Not a Bad Joke 7
But . . . But . . . But 8

Chapter 2. The Disorder of Paradox 11

Tourist from Jupiter 11
The OCD Group: A Study in Poles Apart? 12
Starting to Sort It Out 15
We Mammals 17

**Chapter 3. OCD: Hunting for the Disorder
of the Thinking Animal** 23

The Solution 24
Seeing the Problem 25
The Scent of the Hunt 25
The Hunt 26
In the Beginning: Cause and Effect 29
As It Might Have Been 30
Summary 39

Chapter 4. OCD and *Homo Religiosus*—Religious Man 41

The Emergence of Religious Feelings 41
Now We Are in Recorded History 48
For Christians, the Dividing Line of History Occurs 50
The Jewish Track of History 56
The Christian Track of History 58
Three History-Bending Saints 59
Implications for Today 68
Summary 71

Chapter 5. Now It Is Our Turn   **73**

Humility   73
Nancy: A Chain of Three   75
Marie: The Girl Gang-Tackled by OCD   79
Nanette Joyce: A Love of Beauty and a Compulsion
     to Hoard   82
Anne: Wrestling with Shame and Guilt—and Perfection   86
Mary: The Little Girl Who Wanted to Marry Jesus   88
Lou: Thirty-Five Years in the Dark   91
Paul: Poet Laureate of OCD   95
What We Can Learn from OCD   114
Summary   121

**Chapter 6. *Homo Sapiens Sapiens:* We Have Found
the Enemy and It Is Us**   **123**

The Old Brain   125
The Midbrain   127
The New Brain   133
Adding It All Up   137

Chapter 7. Theory Made Practical   **145**

Differential Diagnosis   146
Rethinking Diagnosis   147
Symptom Selection   154
Progression and Regression   157
Bagging the Game: Implications of Evolutionary Thinking   158
Personality, OCD, and Symptom Creep   161
Personal Development   166
Pathways to Change   171

Chapter 8. Learning from Effecting Change   **181**

We Have Much Experience with What Does
     Not Work   181
We Now Have Some Experience with What Works
     and Why   184
Clean, Clean, Clean Your Carpet, Gently Down
     Life's Stream   189

Step Ahead   198
Theory into Scenario   201
Planning for Practice   203
We Climbers Now Have a Good Foothold   204
Gaining Wisdom from OCD   208

Chapter 9. OCD and the Quality of Life   **211**

Loving with Your Heart   214
Loving with All Your Mind   216
Loving with All Your Strength   221
Loving with All the Soul   222
Quality of Life: The Need for a Role Model   225

Chapter 10. Theologizing in a Neurobiological Age **229**

Our Past Continues into Our Present   230
Implications for Living in the Present   234
What Then Can We Affirm?   239
The Direction of Human Potential   243

Appendix: Available Resources   **247**

Notes   **249**

Index   **257**

Acknowledgments

My thanks, first of all, to OCD support group participants and also to counselees for having taught me about the obsessive-compulsive disorder. I also owe an expression of appreciation to the OC Foundation for their fine national meetings and to those presenters who have contributed so ably to an understanding of this disorder. Thanks also to the staff of the OCD Library of the Dean Foundation who never failed to respond helpfully to a telephone call about some topic.

I would also like to thank Dr. and Mrs. David Thoma, our veterinarian and his wife—who conducts obedience classes—for a stimulating dinner conversation and suggested readings.

Those who have read the manuscript and made recommendations have done me—and the reader—a great service. Thanks to "Mary," a participant in the support group whose story you will read later, and to my son, Felix, for a perspective from biology.

Four distinguished professionals have generously given their time: Dr. Arthur Foster, who was a professor of pastoral counseling at Berkeley Baptist Seminary and for whom I had the pleasure of serving as a teaching assistant, and Dr. Henry Gerner, former director of the Buchanan Counseling Center of Indianapolis. Both Dr. Foster and Dr. Gerner are Diplomates in the American Association of Pastoral Counselors. Dr. Robert Greenlee, who is board certified in both child and adolescent and general psychiatry, and especially Dr. David Sorg, board certified in internal medicine, who was very generous with his time and suggestions.

All biblical references are from *The Good News Bible: Today's English Version.* This is a translation published by the American Bible Society with the aim, as it states in the foreword, "to give today's readers maximum understanding of the context of the original texts."

Most deeply, I am in debt to my hiking buddy and professional colleague. As my wife, thanks also for her patience in the kitchen and on the hiking trail when her husband becomes lost in thought, if not footing.

Mention should be made of Dürer, a rabbit; Penny, Pumpkin, and Pewter, squirrels; Wendell, a woodchuck; Rudy, a raccoon; Lynnet, a titmouse; and a host of lesser characters with walk- or fly-on parts. I also want to make special mention of two of my teachers: Maya, a Golden Retriever, and Frances, a yellow Labrador.

Robert Collie

Chapter 1

Take the "On Ramp"

In the book of Genesis, you will remember, the Tower of Babel was being built by an arrogant humankind who spoke one language and were cooperatively erecting a tower all the way to the sky. God became concerned, pulled a site visit, and then "confounded" them so they could not understand one another. I have a theory for how it was done. That night, God gave a formal dinner and awarded everyone a PhD. By the next morning, they were all so specialized, they could not talk to one another. Having blown it on the World's Highest Tower project, there was nothing to do but split to the five corners of the earth and become consultants. I am a descendant.

In 1972, when as a pastoral counselor I first experienced the puzzlement of a case of OCD, I never thought it would be the beginning of pulling together a lifetime of reading and experience twenty-five years later. Ten years ago, I had not even started to recognize that OCD is what we normally think and experience only magnified in some individuals ten, a hundred, a thousand times. Five years ago, I was just beginning to put the puzzle together, coming to the conclusion I share with you: *OCD is humanity writ large*. In it, streams of evolution, neurobiology, personality development, and religion begin to converge. The implications of this convergence are important not only for counselors (i.e., pastors and pastoral counselors working with persons having OCD), but also for those who suffer from the disorder. Clearly there are also larger religious and clinical implications as well.

We have all suffered from a narrowed perspective; it is the curse of our somewhat educational schooling. One of the great "light-bulb" occasions for Annelie and me was when we invited our veterinarian and his wife over for dinner to discuss OCD. If I were to identify the central learning I have gotten from OCD, however, it is not that it is partially the story of our animalness, it is that OCD helps us understand the Human Saga.

Referring again to the Tower of Babel, what is being told is not merely a story of why different groups have different languages; what is being taught is that a fundamental part of the human problem is that we cannot understand one another. In The Acts of the Apostles, the Good News—the Gospel—is demonstrated on the Day of Pentecost when persons from all the world hear that good news in each one's own language so that everyone understands what is being preached. It would be good news indeed if we could quit talking past one another and start talking with one another. I would like to have OCD sufferers discuss OCD with veterinarians, who would listen to paleontologists and who would dialogue with church historians, who would get to know those suffering from OCD. The discussion should include geneticists and psychologists, who would pass on their work to psychotherapists and pastors. It would be marvelous if church leaders would listen and comment and pastoral counselors would hear and reflect on what this means as we enter a new millennium. What is being done here is to write a text for a survey course: not OCD 101, but 201, building on what we know so we can move from learning *about* to learning *from*.

If that sounds complex, you might ask, "What do you get when you cross a pastor with a counselor?" An interdisciplinarian: a person with a professional bias for looking at a problem from a number of different perspectives. The tradition of the American Association of Pastoral Counselors is that, for training purposes, no case conference is creditable without representation from three different professional disciplines. The intention is to give the counselee the maximum benefit of diverse points of view and teach the counselor respect for other perspectives.

For a word as big and gross as neurobiology, the insights from OCD offer exceptional interest. If it is puzzling why references are made to support group experience more often than to a professional practice experience, all you need is a truly fine group. It is a magnificent advantage to be able to listen and wonder rather than hear and respond. As the professional consultant to a support group in earlier years, some evenings it is as if I could watch in imagination some little band of Not Yets/Will Be "people" on the veldt of Africa trying to stand taller so they could check, check, check. At times I could almost watch the firelight illumine the walls of the cave as a story-teller recounts How the People Came to Be or hear reflected the attempt of the shaman to heal what could not be understood. More recently, I have found myself listening to the theological implications of stories shared in the group, but that really deserves a book by itself.

In the meantime, the present chapters provide for the swing of the pendulum to extend to exploring some of the religious implications of neurobiology. I hope that sufferers with little theological back-ground may be better able to talk about their religious feelings, that mental health workers who have left the religious beliefs of their childhood may newly reconsider these in the light of the experiences of their practice, and that pastors may better understand the religious implications of what is being learned from neurobiology. It would be a great compliment if a group of seminarians might gather to discuss the theological implications of these issues, for a church school class and support group members to meet and explore the meaning of suffering and faith, or if a behaviorist feels more confident in raising religious issues with a client who has OCD.

When I was growing up in West Texas we loved to go hiking. About the middle of the afternoon, if we were feeling a mite con-fused about the best way to supper, it was a good idea to climb a windmill. The country was so flat you could see from Friday to Tuesday.

In order to get the "lay of the land," I propose climbing the windmill of religion, since the obsessive-compulsive disorder is highly charged with religious symptoms such as scrupulosity. It is a needed perspective, as one of the seminar leaders remarked at a national OCD convention in San Jose, that no one has really ex-plored that topic in any breadth. Excellent work has been done on scrupulosity and also on the lives of saints: parts are known, the whole is yet to be mapped in its outlines.

THE MAKING OF THE MAP

I had done my time as an executive director of a pastoral counsel-ing center and so I looked around for a limited practice, one that was intellectually stimulating and congruent to a lifelong religious commitment. I decided to look closely at the obsessive-compulsive disorder, having worked with a number of sufferers. If you want to be in private practice, it is a good idea to identify a group of responsible people (they pay their bills!). Combine this with a number of reliable medications and effective treatment techniques and it adds up to a pretty weighty option for how a therapist might enjoy spending his or her time.

When my wife and I went to the very first OCD national convention in Minneapolis, what impressed us was that half the group were professionals in health care and half were sufferers of OCD. There seemed to be no second-class citizens; lay or professional, all were accorded respect and everyone freely contributed. I thought to myself, "This pastoral counselor has found a professional home," and I have written this book in that spirit. Whether you have a PhD or GED, are a psychiatrist or social worker, or family participant in a support group, all are welcome to a seat at this roundtable. The conventions continue to be a feast of shared learning. My purpose in writing is to continue to broaden this. Sharing and enlightenment are fraternal twins.

We were on our way home from the first national OCD convention when Annelie exclaimed, "Heide!" If OCD ever has a registered trademark, it ought to be for such moments when a lightbulb is shown over a cartoon character's head. Heide was a dear friend who had cared for Felix on weekends when Annelie was doing continuing education as a chaplain. As so often happens with those learning about OCD, the enlightenment is retrospective, as little was recognized about the disorder at that time. Annelie's first exclamation was followed by "straightener." Every time Heide came she reorganized the kitchen. I came up with my own realization, "cleaner," when I recalled how Heide kept her apartment perfectly immaculate.

But what if we had been able to give it a name back then? So little was understood about OCD we probably would have been embarrassed to discuss it with Heide because, back then, she might have thought that having it was shameful. Even if all three of us had the wisdom and maturity to explore it, there was no treatment back then. Heide, it was so long ago and we have gone our separate ways, but if some miracle of grace should occur and you should read these lines, all of us remember you with great affection.

It just keeps on and on. We were walking our yellow Labrador, Frances, yesterday when Annelie asked me, "Do you know the name of that saint who would lead his horse through the forest trying not to step on ants?" The subject had been a vacation in the Black Forest with her mother when she was ten. She had heard the story in religion class at school and was so impressed she tried it. She said her brush with scrupulosity ended abruptly when an ant bit her. We never could be sure, but we decided it must be the medieval St. Martin, as he is always shown with his horse. I hope you have seen El Greco's magnificent painting of him. St. Martin is pictured on his horse cutting his cloak in two with his sword in order to share it with a beggar. OCD seems seldom to draw back from goodness—perhaps because of its torment of badness, perhaps because it outlines the progress of goodness.

I hope you saw the movie *As Good As It Gets* in the theater and observed that only half the show was on the screen; the other half was the audience. They mostly sat in couples, and every five minutes heads would jerk forty-five degrees toward each other; you could not overhear the whispers, but if you could read lips, they must have been saying, "Just like my mother," "Uncle Roy does that!" *As Good As It Gets* got the wrong Oscar; it should have received an award for Greatest Audience Participation Show-and-Tell Hollywood Ever Produced. The movie was great, of course, not because it was about OCD, but because it revealed aspects of the human story with which we all identify.

I had expected my move toward greater specialization would take the usual route of learning more and more about less and less, until you cannot describe what you are doing or thinking to anyone except a similar specialist. What I discovered was that the OCD knowledge explosion vitally affected the work of pastors and pastoral counselors, so I invited them to the feast. The first literary fruit of my specialization was "The Obsessive-Compulsive Disorder: The Pastoral Knowledge Explosion" in *The Journal of Pastoral Care*.[1] What I discovered was that the less and less I had been expecting became the more and more as streams of learning flowed together. What emerges now is what you see: an invitation to feast on what we can learn *from* OCD, a feast that resembles an interdisciplinary and ecumenical church dinner where everyone brings a favorite dish to share and in which a layperson feels equally accepted in commenting.

Scripture says "God is love"; as a longtime admirer, I think the subtext should add, "and a practical joker": the poor in spirit are blessed, the mighty are fallen, those wise in their own eyes look foolish—and it is the meek who inherit the earth. One of those innumerable jokes occurred while I was doing research on the incidence of OCD in a clergy group. I had counseled with about eleven or twelve hundred clergy and their families, so I had a good idea the percentage of OCD would be high: it was, about half again as much as in the general population. I also had another idea: if ministry was attractive to some with OCD, the highly practical joke was that it probably affected the problem significantly in a positive fashion. It did. Based on the level at which the general population apparently experiences OCD, the clergy rate in the study is almost 50 percent less.[2] A group having more, suffered less. The question was and still is, "What is there about the attitudes, beliefs, and practices of ministry that lessens the impact of OCD?"

You may question, however, why any author would rush into the area of OCD and religion, for it is rightly an area where many a therapist dreads to tread. You can quickly disrupt a support group when some participants get on the subject of religion. It is at the core of what brought them to the group. I have come to the conclusion, nevertheless, that you cannot understand OCD without coming to grips with religion, any more than you can understand human beings without an interest in religion. It is all so intertwined.

I think any psychotherapist or pastor who went to an OCD national conference would find it the best use of time and money ever spent on continuing education. I am not doing them a favor, either, however, in suggesting this. I know what it is to squirm over a pastoral or client relationship and realize what was missed. I did not recognize what they were telling me, but they were not exactly being completely forthcoming, either, about what they feared was their craziness.

CLEARING THE MIND: NOT A BAD JOKE

Readers probably already know a lot about OCD; some may be wishing fervently they did not. An older mental health supervisor, with a supervisee as a Bright Young Thing who storms book lists, also might have several fervent wishes as to knowing. Pastors, if asked about "scrupulosity" and admitting more ignorance than piety for the moment, are certainly not to be accused, in that they know a great deal about hoarding and cleaning and straightening from pastoral calling in homes and equally about hypochondriasis from making sick calls.[3] Most people could easily make quite a list of what they know about OCD, even if it was only from seeing the movie *As Good As It Gets*. Thinking about it and the ability to make quite a list becomes part of the problem: we know a lot *about* OCD, but until now the field has not sufficiently matured so that we learn *from* it.

The longer the list and the more you study it, the more it resembles the proverbial story of the six blind men grabbing different parts of an elephant and trying to explain it to one another. We know a lot, but the whole escapes us.

Consider the human appendix. Not only is it useless, it can get you into a fix in which the doctor is having a talk with your family, not unlike OCD. Fortunately, we know a lot about the appendix and we know how to manage it when that becomes necessary, not unlike OCD. Would it not be wonderful, however, if we *understood* the appendix? What a marvel to our minds if we could just learn from it. Its tale would unfold back to the beginnings when it must have been useful: Mother Nature does not fool around with the unnecessary. If we just understood what the DNA, the genes, and the chromosomes could tell us; if we just could read the developmental sequence; if only we could unravel the effects of stress and the dying and rebirth of cells: why, understanding *all*, we probably would even grasp the intricacies of our humanness more adequately, *not unlike OCD*.

Partially, the problem with most of us is that we do not know what we do not know. Good writing and good research are going on, but mostly we are ignorant of just how ignorant we are because we know so much more. Not too long ago, if you had OCD, you had no idea what it was. The media have done a pretty good job on that one, although you can still hear a few, "Oh, good griefs!" after some magazine article comes out. The fact that you are reading this and can make a list of "knowing about" is quite remarkable, just not entirely helpful. If you are one of those who suffer—or suffer along with—you may have knowledge of . . . but have lost all sense of wonder and consequently the potentiality of wisdom from it.

To get at that, I propose we do what we did as kids in second grade. When the chalkboard got too chalky, the teacher picked out a favored student who got to take a rag down to the washroom, get it wet, and wash the board, to the envy of the rest of us. I propose we do the same. There is a beauty about a chalkboard when it has been cleaned and is freshly ready to do its thing. Wipe your mind clean of what you *know*—even though as a sufferer you may not free yourself of what you *feel*—and appreciate the wonder of what we are yet to know. With that openness, all of us have a better opportunity to manage an awkward condition.

BUT . . . BUT . . . BUT

"Awkward condition" is enough to set a sufferer off with several "buts," especially when first into treatment, as often the person comes with the sickening thought that he or she is "crazy." "No one could think or act in such a way as I do." The idea most often comes because he or she is "hearing voices"—and you know what *that* means. Then comes the hope-filling differentiation: the sufferer of schizophrenia hears voices directed at him or her—it is an external voice. In OCD, what is happening is an *interjected* thought—one part of the brain e-mailing to another part. In this latter instance, it is an unconscious part thrusting a coded message into the conscious part where it is decoded and interpreted—but we will get into that more fully in a later chapter.

A part of the problem here is that the sufferer has been told by all-and-sundry, "Just quit it; you can if you would just really try." It is not a shocking revelation to an OCD sufferer for the federal government to issue a ruling that this disorder has a physical basis, just like arthritis or diabetes.

The natural response of anyone with OCD, of course, is "Bah, humbug," to hope for change. You cannot just wipe the slate clean in a sufferer's mind; those accursed thoughts and agitated (and agitating) behaviors will not go away, as they are biologically driven. However, once it has been established that a disorder is physical, options exist in working with it, and this is true of OCD, too. What needs a clean slate are the beliefs, attitudes, and unconscious assumptions stalling the family to get the person into therapy and, once in therapy, plaguing the efforts of a person to "hang in there." Cognitive behavior therapy usually has effective results, but it takes a lot of "hanging in there." Maintenance of gains, too, is a real problem unless there has been sufficient reprogramming. There is life after therapy, but it never ceases to need intelligently directed determination.

Just for a while, imagine your brain as a computer. A good deal of new data will be processed in reading this book; for instance, you probably have read some newspaper reports describing neurological research about there being more than one memory system in the brain. The significance of this will help in pursuing an understanding of OCD. In exploring the possibility of a more primitive memory system as the source of interjected thoughts, it will be clear why the individual's contemporary "working memory" needs all the help it can get. What needs to be done is to clear the memory of some unneeded old stuff by identifying attitudes, beliefs, and unconscious assumptions saved "back when" and for which there is no longer any use. That will give space enough to take in what veterinarians are writing on OCD.

What happens in both personal computers and our minds is that things are saved automatically. So, both models need to be reviewed periodically. With our minds, when we were young we saved some of the Big People's opinions and turned them into our unexamined beliefs, just as we did their prejudices. As kids, we very small people vacuum up facts and fiction—here, there, and yonder—from our very important people. Now that we will be exploring evolution for its significance in the development of OCD, for instance, some will find it stimulating. Others will have to deal with opinions and assumptions absorbed back when their hair was still thick and naturally curly. It is of lesser importance, though, to accept the idea of evolution than to clear enough working memory to consider it. Equally stimulating, once you know about scrupulosity, Matthew becomes even more different from Mark and Luke than John is. We all have outdated files in the personal computers of our minds that are no longer useful and need to be dumped so that we have an adequate amount of working memory for today.

If you do not have OCD, you may be deluded into imagining that clearing things out in order to have an open mind is easy, but you might want to consider The Drawer in your home where things get thrown when we do not know where else to keep them. The bi- or tri-annual Cleaning of the Drawer hangs like the Sword of Damocles over a person's head: you do not have to be a "straightener" or "hoarder" to know that feeling.

Persons with OCD, challenged to clear an open space in their minds, are looking at the same problem persons without it would have with cleaning the garage, attic, and basement, too. It is as if they were moving and deciding what they want to take and what to ask the Salvation Army to pick up. Persons—family mostly—can know how much assistance and how little criticism sufferers need with those chores . . . or how unhelpful it is to offer help when it is unwanted or to cater to a ritual in a way that sustains it.

Now, with cleared working memory, in your imagination, take the door marked "To the On Ramp."

Chapter 2

The Disorder of Paradox

To Francis of Assisi: the saint bonded to his body, "Brother Donkey."

Come with me now and be my guest. Allow yourself to be a tourist from Jupiter: if "men are from Mars and women from Venus"—and OCD does not have a gender preference—then Jupiter is a good choice as the largest planet, with its ability to accommodate all, besides being the name of the chief god in Roman mythology. A particularly good choice, considering that, of all the psychiatric classifications, OCD is most characterized by religious expressions. Be my guest; later we will visit an OCD support group.

TOURIST FROM JUPITER

It may strike some as bizarre to introduce an interplanetary guest to what might be called "Earthlings Anonymous," where some exhibit what conventional wisdom regards as strange, peculiar, and psychiatric. Perhaps. Or it may lead to a grasp of what it means to be human, with its irrepressible and inseparable religious concerns.

First, however, I would like to invite you to recover from rocket lag. Come sit in my garden. "It is," you may say, in order to indicate a good educational background, "your own little Garden of Eden." That is the appropriate way to begin the road to change.

You will enjoy studying the small creatures in our backyard wilderness. The robins and the nuthatches fly away, but they will soon return if we are still. The scurry? A mother rabbit. If you look closely you will see her baby; it is so still it is almost invisible: each thing seeking security in its own way. Over there a wren is already beginning to feed: a peck at seed, stop and check; a peck at seed, stop and check. My yellow Labrador suddenly bristles; at what, we cannot say. Startled by what? Our sensors are too unrefined to let us say.

That squirrel peeking at us will soon nibble at the corncob on the feeding tray—a cunning little hoarder who saves for hard times; tonight at the group, the memory of him will cause you to wonder. See the sunflower appearing so inadvertently? What the squirrel has stored, the chipmunk has stolen; what has been stolen, however, may be so little regarded that it will lie unused and thus renew itself another year.

Suddenly all is as if frozen. A hawk has drifted over from the neighboring tree line. His silhouette against the sky is a reminder that she who checks lives to eat another meal . . . and we are all someplace on the food chain.

Hurry. We are late as we cross the parking lot. That fellow will be even later; he is a newcomer still circling his car three times to be certain of lights and locks. The car lights! Did I remember? Doubtless a tourist from such a lordly place as Jupiter would only smile secretly that I was the only life form he had observed that did *not* check.

THE OCD GROUP:
A STUDY IN POLES APART?

Here is a group member who rarely ventures out for fear of being contaminated; sitting beside him is another who fears going out because *she* might contaminate others. Over there is a person pouring her heart out because she is so driven to exhaustion in cleaning the refrigerator that she omits eating rather than get fingerprints on the door handle. She is comforted by a man struggling with a house he has filled to the point where only trails exist and none of his children will visit. Nearby, a woman sits tapping her chair in patterns of threes, yet so inconspicuously that one would never guess she is gripped by a superstition that this behavior will prevent her house from burning down. Yet, listen to her participation in the group: she is clearly able to teach classes in Reality 101 and 202. Next to her sits a man who has earned his master's degree in spite of having to count the e's in every paragraph he reads. Hopefully he is not oblivious to the needs of the lady across from him who surrendered her joy of reading because of having to read, re-read, and re-re-read; or another woman who sacrificed her driver's license for fear she would run someone down while driving ever so cautiously.

Here is someone who cannot free herself from an obsessional thought, *plus* she pulls out her eyebrows; another person straightens every shoe and hanger in the closet and is unable to go to work until it feels "just right," *plus* panic attacks. In this so-called "anxiety disorder" there will be pluses of depression, mixed with an occasional tic of Tourette's disorder—with just a smattering of bathroom floor cleaning. There will be a fellow counting everything standing still long enough to be counted by fives or sevens, if the symptoms shift. Then (if that wasn't burdensome enough) he alienates his beloved pastor because he is such a weary-wort about his unsinful sinning. An experienced therapist will, naturally, be on the alert for adult forms of attention deficit disorder with hyperactivity: it keeps the meetings from becoming old hat.

To help stay awake there will be still another new mother's tale of a harrowing obsession in which she would turn the baby of her hopes and dreams into a newspaper story of another infant fatality. Perhaps some very gentle man will explain why he hides all the knives because of the fantasy of what he might do to his beloved wife. Another may have such a fear of having run over someone he keeps hitting potholes because of constantly checking the rearview mirror. If the group gets dull, the following week someone will explain that he, like the great English literary figure, Samuel Johnson, cannot get through doors. A woman will say that she has not been able to get out of her home because she fears germs as much as Howard Hughes.

Meanwhile, some pious elderly lady may decide to share about her blasphemies or outlandish sexual fantasies. An older and experienced psychotherapist, perplexed by these paradoxes, contrasts, and contradictions, might be excused for sitting in numbed silence, older theories such as reaction formations simply irrelevant. Another option would be to sit by the lady with trichotillomania to see if pulling out your hair really does bring relief!

If a tourist from Jupiter had a mind like a computer, he or she would be storing such contradictions as one person compulsively overeating and another undereating, along with those melancholy stories of addictive alcohol consumption and the only once-upon-a-time effective medication. By now you will, naturally, come to expect that the next story will be about someone who cannot take *any* medication because of fear. Here one's thoughts are so slow it takes fifteen minutes to write a check (so that checks are written first at home), while another's thoughts move as fast as her vacuum cleaner. There will be a would-be agnostic who cannot stop praying and a saintly old soul who cannot quit blaspheming. There may be a woman drop-in at an OCD group who is so attractive that she arouses the women and stuns the men, but has to fight with herself for weeks about coming because she is convinced she is so gruesome she would sicken the group.[1] She and the woman with anorexia compare stories of being captured and tortured in a carnival's fun house of mirrors because they have no sense of reality—just a distortion reflected back to them.

With a mind like a computer, a well-intended tourist would want to program in a "Why?" question. That is when he or she finally would feel stonewalled. The consensus of experienced support group participants is, "It Just Is." For all their questionings, "It Just Is."

Obsessive-compulsive disorder and its spectrum is like a multi-thousand-piece puzzle of a seascape that an evil genie dropped off for the family at Christmas.[2] Some OCD sufferers will exhibit genetic traces but there is no uniformity, no consistency. Its "favorite flavor" symptom may be learned within a family or it may not. It may be brought to awareness by a trauma or it may be felt as having always been there. The symptoms can be grouped and charted by a therapist, but their dynamics seemingly never can be analyzed helpfully, as "neurotic" conditions often can be. There will be sagas of futile hospitalizations—even attempts at exorcism—and acknowledgments of mental health billings that could make a congressional hearing. A interplanetary tourist might suspect he or she had been hauled off to an inner-city shop with an "Antiques for Sale" sign slouched on the window of a storefront full of generations of discards piled from floor to wall to ceiling, and not a bargain to haggle over. It all adds up to the seventeen-year gap between either the eruption or sly emergence of the symptoms and a diagnosis of the disorder.

It will come as no shock for a tourist to learn it is rumored that an effective treatment plan might entail the saintly fellow asking his pastor's permission to practice cursing for thirty minutes a day or another homework assignment entails a germ-terrorized lady sprinkling water from the toilet around the house. There will be a teenager stating proudly that he has successfully gone a week without making up his bed and he is applauded by mothers in the support group. It is, as the King of Siam told Anna in *The King and I*, "a puzzlement." This is OCD, the Disorder of Paradox, where even the doubts are doubted.

Some conclusions might be drawn: (1) If there could be a classification of what the group was sharing, it might well be "The Dysfunction of This, That, and the Other." (2) It is clear why doctors have had such a hard time diagnosing such a disorder—nobody in his or her right mind would admit to having such crazy thoughts and behaviors and certainly would never conceive that anyone else would either. (3) Given this disorder's paradoxes, it seems that these people have either too little memory or far too much. (4) Even though the school system on Jupiter is scant on neurology, this group does seem to be actively using the thinking of their *minds* to cope with the organic difficulty of their *brains*. (5) For a planet with an intergalactic reputation for being "red in tooth and claw," some talk up to that ill fame. Yet, as a group they certainly live violence down.

Given time to get to know each other, a tourist such as yourself, might well conclude that as individuals and as a group, they have lived far too long in the shadows and deserve their time in the sun.

STARTING TO SORT IT OUT

Starting from Jupiter has its advantages, such as not presupposing our classification systems. We classify things so we can better think about them, but the distinctions are rather artificially imposed by us. Our "natural laws," once thought to underlie these, often exit at the same time our space satellites leave our atmosphere. Perhaps an organized tour group from Jupiter would have a lecture series by different experts from various professions.[3] On the other hand, an individual tourist might simply enjoy inviting a veterinarian over for dinner and being free to discuss observations from our backyard Garden of Eden.

Such a dinner would provide the leisure to discuss the similarities of how the little long-tailed creature "squirrels" away its hoard against its day of need, as does the OCD "hoarder." How quickly the squirrel scampers up the tree; one could wonder about the similarities to a panic attack that a support group might discuss. A kleptomaniac in the group seems to steal no less compulsively than the chipmunk. Is the "washer" in the group so different from the ring-tailed animal the Germans call "the wash bear" who visits us? The birds at the feeder compulsively check and recheck; in what ways do their sensations of insecurity differ from those in the group? Our yellow Labrador, Frances, will stay away from tight spots if her ball has rolled there, and some group member may share his or her difficulty in going through doors.

On the patio, a rustle is heard and Frances's ears stand at right angles. If it is the rabbit, Dürer, he will beat Frances to the fence. If it is the raccoon, Rudy, Frances had better let it beat her to a tree— as many a "coon dog" has learned. Recently, an opossum has begun to visit us. It might just play dead, calculating that few unspecialized prey seekers want to eat something obviously dead—sick, dead, contaminating. It is a night for reflecting on flight, fight, and stillness.[4]

It would be fair of a visitor from afar to say, "You have shown me paradox, but I think it is a riddle. What is the difference between this behavior in animals and in humans?" An alien might solve such a riddle: in OCD we are not observing—or participating in—animal-like behavior; *it is animal behavior.* The thought of that commonality may be intriguing or amusing, or it can be disturbing.

Rightful fearing of contamination goes back to the beginnings of earth's animal food chain. The carrion feeders such as vultures, feasting upon others' kills, have evolved so that no features around the beak convey contamination. On the other hand, our germ-terrorized sufferer may throw her clothes away or pitch a purse in the garbage because it has gotten incidentally splashed by rain and—to her—fatally contaminated. Either extreme is arguably a curious direction for evolution to have taken.

The newly hatched reptiles of some species scurry away from their mother for fear of being eaten; our young have no such protective instincts, which provides us with troubling thoughts. Consider that it is not unknown for the young of the human to be harmed; ancient Rome is said to have had an island in the Tiber where infants were exposed to the elements and left to die. In an OCD population there are parents—not just mothers—whose dread is that alien feeling of doing harm to those whom they love. Having had persons with OCD own that particular dread, but *never* having heard even a whispered rumor that obsession gave way to completion, it seems a worthy—but fruitless—research project. Consider the difference between the egg-laying crocodile and the soft nipple of the nursing mother. There is as much distance between the species as there is in the way the reptile discards her eggs while the human mother prefers to cuddle her child near to her heartbeat in order to instinctively maximize the infant's sense of security.

The issue, however, is not simplistic. Reptile versus human distinctions are definable in this regard, but mammals, after giving birth, may push aside the deformed and weak. Human babies can be unwanted as well. Mammal versus human distinctions remain not merely in contention, but throw us into contemporary controversy. Today's controversy deserves a discussion covering the full span of our biological condition. In the context of evolutionary process we are pondering both the anguish of individuals and the future of our race.

WE MAMMALS

We have a range of commonalities, we humans, we mammals.[5] The young are born alive, there is milk, and there is memory. Communication is not our sole prize and logic not totally exclusive. We flee, hide when we can, fight when we must. In captivity you can observe that we both pace. Today, even the medications for the depressed patient of the veterinarian and the family physician are the same. The commonality of OCD characteristics leads one to suspect that, in the human, something, sometimes, is being inadvertently—

and inappropriately—activated in the brain; the natural has become somehow unnatural.

In support groups, the issue is recurrent regarding whether OCD is genetic. Some mention a mother, some a "this," and some a "that." Shake the family tree and a quarter of the time something recognizable falls out. It is all, not quite simply, biological. Every hair color and texture, every eye color, fingernail, and length of toe—all are conveyed through that chemical we call DNA. It is not just a couple of chromosomes pairing around in a family way and genes gone awry or aright (as in some Bach with music exploding into concertos when most boys are learning to play soccer). It is all evolved from those tiniest protein building blocks. In a way to confound a computer chip, each one's organic pattern, each record of prehistory through history, is imprinted there.

Some part of the brain does not think in language, but in pictures, as animals do. Like the animals, the human brain vulnerable to OCD will react fearfully to whatever an animal would react to fearfully. Something is not in order; the feeder has been changed—is it now a trap? The lawn has been torn up—was there a death struggle here, eater and eaten? Is that strange smell to the hunted that of the hunter? The response—the mammalian response—of the human can be similar: a rug disturbed, a book disturbed—all is not as it should be; all is not in its orderliness. A thing does not look right, *feel right.* The policeman and the combat veteran know that feeling: a sixth sense all too necessary, a sensory wavelink that *something here is wrong; it just does not feel right.*[6] What is different in the human/mammal equation is that, unlike the animals whose startle response is set off quickly but also quickly subsides, for humans with OCD there is a prolongation of obsessing, probably due to higher levels of awareness. Thus, the startle response, obsessing, and the resulting compulsive behaviors tend to persist.[7]

The "why," then, stands out more clearly. Whether the casual research is about strep infections of the youngster or brain lesions of the elder; whether it is activated by birthing or accidentally induced by a too large dose of some psychotropic medication (such as Ritalin), it is all biological. It is the activation of the inheritant. In the obsessive-compulsive disorder, what we are exploring is a phenomenon of regression.

What we are is genetic, for "what exists must house its past," as the philosopher Alfred North Whitehead insisted. Yet it all interacts with the present and exists only in the present, even as a pianist sits down to play the piano. The instrument has evolved; the music on a sheet reflects a cultural and industrial process as well. But the final choice of the music and its interpretation are the pianist's. What IS, exists in a feedback loop between the genetic and the environment, an interaction between past and present, existing solely in the present—and instant by instant extending into the future to create another pattern in that feedback loop.

The pianist, this mammal, this perpetuation of pattern in a feedback loop, is a representative of *Homo sapiens sapiens.* This Thinking Specie, lord of joy and sorrows, root and branch part of all creation, is only most recently chief of the food chain to which all living must relate and is the only one who knows he or she must die. Anxiety and depression are the price of that knowledge. "Biology is destiny," said Sigmund Freud, but we have a "say" in that destiny. To have that "say," however, is to accept the soil—"dust," as it is phrased in Genesis—which nourished our roots and which now sets the outlines for our existence.

So, from the dust of the earth into which life was breathed, to massive enlargement of the spinal column and an evolved larynx, humans have been able to name all the creatures and then go on to the capacity to discuss them. We have come some distance. When seeing a reconstructed dinosaur with its hard palate, and then running our tongue over the hard part of our palate we recognize the continuity, but when we touch the soft part in our mouth, we are rightly filled with awe as we contemplate that miracle-in-distance. We particularly bring with us mammalian baggage, with which we can account for some OCD expressions, but before we account for others, we shall be in another chapter. Then will be time enough to disentangle the pressures for irreligious prayers, of self-defeating perfectionism and inauthentic guilt. Then we will see how the realization of cause and effect bloomed into the knowledge of good and evil and the consequences of that.

We are mammals, but so much more. We are the literate mammals, able to read this. We are the aware mammals, self-conscious of our feelings as we read. We are thinking mammals, rising above our sensations into the realm of reasoning. We reach beyond the Self to grasp at context beyond what we were taught and have experienced. To use the simile of nutrition, we do well to attend to the vitamins and minerals—but the basic element is always fiber, our being as animal.

We not only can read about OCD, we can learn from it. We can reach for an understanding of it, reaching into a beyond that stretches us into more than we were, into what we can be. Most of all, we are mammals who are more than mammals—dust of the earth that aspires to be godly, but not gods. We have the capacity to be silent, and to use that silence in a way no mammal possibly could: to be *thankful*.

So to end our talk and bring on rest, it is "good enough," to use that precious phrase to brains surging with OCD, to recall that most humane of saints, Francis of Assisi, remembering how he is never seen without his beloved birds and beasts:

> All creatures of our God and King,
> lift up your voice and with us sing
> O praise ye! Alleluia!
> O brother sun with golden beam,
> O sister moon with silver beam
> O praise ye! Alleluia! Alleluia!
>
> O brother wind, air, clouds and rain,
> by which all creatures ye sustain,
> O raise ye! Alleluia!
>
> Thou rising morn, in praise rejoice,
> ye lights of evening, find a voice!
> O praise ye! Alleluia! Alleluia! Alleluia!
> O sister water, flowing clear,
> make music for thy Lord to hear,
> O praise ye! Alleluia!
> O brother fire who lights the night,
> providing warmth, enhancing sight,
> O praise ye! Alleluia! Alleluia! Alleluia!

Dear mother earth, who day by day
unfoldest blessings on our way
Alleluia! Alleluia!
The flowers and fruits that in thee grow,
let them God's glory also show!
O praise ye! O praise ye! Alleluia!
All ye who are of tender heart,
forgiving others, take your part,
O praise ye! Alleluia!

Ye who long pain and sorrow bear,
praise God and on him cast your care!
O praise ye! Alleluia! Alleluia!
And thou, our sister, gentle death,
waiting to hush our latest breath,
Alleluia! Alleluia!
Thou leadest home the child of God,
and Christ our Lord the way has trod,
Alleluia.[8]

Chapter 3

OCD: Hunting for the Disorder
of the Thinking Animal

In September, I received word that the wife of the Swiss missionary, Pelot, had fallen ill at their mission in N'Gomo. The mission was 120 miles upstream on the Ogowe River. . . . At sunset of the third, near the village of Igendja, we moved along an island set in the middle of the wide river. On the sand bank to our left, four hippopotami and their young plodded along in our direction. Just then, in my great tiredness and discouragement, there flashed upon my mind . . . the phrase, "Reverence for Life." The iron door had yielded. . . . Now I had found my way to the idea in which affirmation of the world and ethics are contained side by side.

Albert Schweitzer
Out of My Life and Thought, 1931

When I was twelve, I was at Boy Scout camp and my father visited and wanted me to row him while he fished. Naturally—if you know the inevitability of boys in camp and visiting fathers—the boat sank. I swam well; he did not. I looked into my father's eyes—in his fear they had turned from blue to yellow. An oar came up with mud on it; his eyes changed to blue again. Since then, I have never doubted the reality that animal and human occupy the same space in the brain. An observation, common to us all: no one volunteers to be in a crowded theater when someone yells "Fire!" In this context, we next begin our search.

To explore OCD as a disorder, we begin by using "reverse engineering."[1] Ordinarily in engineering, one starts with a problem and proceeds to a solution; with the brain it is interesting, however, to use reverse engineering, i.e., start with the "solution" and tear the end product down to see how it works. In this case, we start with the symptomatic behavior of a person with OCD.

THE SOLUTION

Probably the most frequently used definition as to what OCD is, is one written for family physicians:

> Obsessive-compulsive disorder is a common anxiety disorder characterized by recurrent obsessional thoughts and compulsive behaviors, and the person's keen awareness of the irrational and senseless nature of these thoughts and behaviors.[2]

Since most people have some elements of this, it is wise to divide OCD into a subclinical section and a clinical one. The difference is that at the clinical level OCD significantly interferes with a person's life. The *Diagnostic and Statistical Manual of Mental Disorders* (DSM-IV), of the American Psychiatric Association, has specific criteria for OCD, for instance, arbitrarily setting the level of significant interference of those repetitive thoughts and behaviors at an hour a day. For our purposes, we need to recognize that childhood and adult forms are similar; in fact, we shall see they are identical. The more common expressions of OCD-type thoughts are contamination fears, repeated doubts, need for a particular order, and aggressive or sexual imagery. The behaviors are meant to reduce physical distress or prevent—usually superstitiously—some dreaded event.

OCD is frequently associated with other types of psychiatric illness and has yet to yield any clues to its causation through laboratory findings. The disorder occurs in the same ratio of male and female in adulthood, but usually begins earlier in males. Anxiety is characterized by being more generalized, while worry is more specific.

To this formal list we might add informal observations that sufferers who seek treatment score higher on intelligence tests than the general population. It is known that OCD occurs worldwide, but it is expressed differently in various cultures. Northern Europeans, for example, are more inclined to express OCD symptoms through cleaning and contamination fears than third world persons. There will be more scrupulosity among Roman Catholics than Unitarians, although the percentages of those experiencing OCD will be similar. In Cape Town and Cairo, Manila and Moscow, and even Pecos, Texas, "washers" wash and "cleaners" clean in a choreographed fashion.[3]

Having been in a support group meeting, a tourist might well remark—after having thought about the relationship of animal behavior to the symptoms of OCD—metaphorically that he had seen the underwater part of an iceberg. Now, in the characteristics of OCD, he was being shown the tip of the iceberg that appears *above* the water.

SEEING THE PROBLEM

The day has been long, the frustrations high. In your mind, allow yourself to relieve the stress by turning on the television to a favorite relaxer and mind expander, a *National Geographic* special. A savanna stretches to the horizon; under a tree, a leopard lies in the shade. On a limb above is draped an African antelope set aside for future consumption. In relaxing, allow your mind to drift along the track of your genetic heritage, ten thousand years, a hundred thousand, a million, three million, like a video in reverse . . .

Stop at five million years ago. The savanna is recognizable, as is the leopard. The carcass, however, is that of a being not so different in size and shape from the elementary children playing on your street.[4] *That* is seeing the problem: from you at the top of the food chain with popcorn, potato chips, beer, and hot dog down a fast, fast escalator on the food chain to that small, but related, figure.

Now, suspend your judgment regarding "evolution" just as a tourist would do in a culture foreign to his or her own. Come, follow the trail of the "Disorder of the Thinking Animal," *Homo sapiens sapiens.*[5]

THE SCENT OF THE HUNT

Having utilized reverse engineering, it will become clear that we are "standing between times." That is, OCD reflects the past from which our specie has emerged—and continues—and may forecast what our specie will become. It will explain why the contemporary disorder should not be termed a "disease," but rather "a good born out of time," as Alfred North Whitehead characterized an evil.[6] We will explore why OCD is characterized by exaggeration and why terror, rather than anxiety or worry, is a more appropriate term for the OCD experience. We will see that religion begins to play a significant part in the hunt. This will be explored in detail in the next chapter along with its dramatic impact on our history. Moving into a discussion of the formation of the brain and how this relates to OCD in our hunt for the "disease" of the thinking animal, it will be shown, not even as a "disorder," but as a dysfunction. It only appears the person is suffering from a lack of memory—checking repeatedly, for instance, as if the person cannot remember from second to almost the next—when, in fact, the person is suffering from an excess of memory.

THE HUNT

A year never passes, it seems, when in the Arctic or Antarctic the estimated age of our earth is not revised by a new discovery. So, to put things into perspective, let us picture a twenty-four-hour clock that is set at midnight five million years ago. That seems to be about the time when our ancestors and the chimpanzees differentiated themselves from other mammals. Among other differences, the females of the other species would fight off the sexual aggressions of a male unless ready to breed. Yet the females of our specie and the chimpanzees would submit to sexual aggression to appease a dominant male. To set a perspective at the other extreme of the time span, the dog may have been domesticated as early as 100,000 years ago—our families have been denning together that long and our precise specie, *Homo sapiens sapiens,* appeared in Europe about 9:15 p.m. or so—30,000 to 40,000 years back when language similar to ours developed. About 2:15 or so in the afternoon, however, is our concern; out on the African plains there appears a small group of foragers, picking food from the ground, but walking uprightly—*Australopithecus robustus,* by classification:

> Suddenly they all freeze and raise their heads. Danger seems threatening. The mothers clutch their children as the group

draws together. Some raise broken branches to be used as clubs.[7]

They were deficient in tooth and claw and were not swift; they would need clubs and cunning to survive. In addition to the fight or flight behaviors, we anticipate that we must add stillness—"laying low," as it is sometimes colloquially expressed. By this period in time, the neurons in their brains might be identical to animals, but they would be differently organized and become more and more so.

We know a good bit about these early prehumans; this is the time from African "digs" when we have a partial skeleton of a woman whose bones show a prolonged disease. There is also the "Narioko-tome Boy," from whom we have almost a complete skeleton. The woman's bones display the evidence of an advanced disease, probably caused by a vitamin deficiency. She survived for such a prolonged time because she was cared for, indicative of a caring, *valuing* capacity on the part of a group of Not Yets/Will Be; she was regarded as having worth and stirred feelings of what, in our time, might be termed "caring."

From a somewhat later period, the boy's skull revealed a new development, the "broca area" of the brain, unseen in more ancient African skulls. This is located on the area of the left side of the midbrain.[8] It indicates a capacity for *words*, if not yet for language. At a much later time when a particular nomadic tribe, in what we now know as the Middle East, began to reflect on the origins of persons, it is interesting that they chose to tell a creation story of a man and woman, who cared for each other and who named the animals.

In the period we are reflecting upon, behavior was simple. These were foragers who gathered food, picked berries, found seeds and nuts, and dug up roots as they went across their territory. Check, check, check, all the while, as they went. Is that a lion? Is that a leopard? A snake rustling, a hissing? Ears were tuned for alarm. Survival meant to stretch taller to see danger, learn to signal if water or food was found, form a protective circle with the little ones inside. Natural selection is a stern teacher. What physical discomfort that must have been, this standing tall. What cunning must have developed for such creatures to compete with more fierce competitors when meat became a food option. The Not Yets/Will Be and hyena fought for their share. Yet, was it good to eat, or would sickness and death come? The survivors of many experiments learned to be cautious, long before plagues such as the black death reinforced the fear of contamination.

The nose we have, even though the olfactory organ in the brain has regressed since that time, can still distinguish thousands of nuances of odor. To this day, when suspecting something has spoiled in the refrigerator, we look cautiously at it, smell it, then carefully taste the tiniest piece. How much more cautious must these ancestors have been when testing an unfamiliar food source? Is it poisonous or good to eat? Then, at some later point when a capacity for observation developed, is it good for healing? Thus they lived, *doubt* making it possible to survive. *Curiosity*, its twin, made it possible to discover a new food or medicinal use that made survival possible.

They were caring, group dependent, inclined to stay in their own territory. Limited in emotions, we could yet characterize them as timid, tense, and shy. "Personality," if we might use such a word, seems to parallel recent studies in serotonin deficiency, as we will see when we enter the chapter on theory.

What difficulty of expression, in grunt and grimace, there must have been as signaling evolved. As an enlarging brain included strange and intense feelings for which there were no adequate vocal cords as yet to give expression, what symbols must have emerged for those feelings? Do we see this still reflected today when someone says, "I could pull my hair out," in times of deep distress?

In drought, when neither food nor water were adequate for the immense exertions of the trek, what fantasies must have emerged to make for survival—"I am too fat," even when starving? We know that, with a too-severe diet and sudden weight loss, the body will slow its metabolism to the point where eating little results in no weight loss. The body probably "remembers" famine and retains survival tactics. Does the body also remember needing a great capacity for exertion even when the body is so malnourished that it is ready to collapse, as in anorexia?

When wading in the water to gather food, aroused by ever emerging awareness, how long must someone have stared into the reflection as the realizations came that the reflection in the water is *me*? What sensations would have been aroused in someone comparing that self-reflection and the beauty of the water lilies! What comparisons between beauty and ugliness may have been made by some sensitive being! In the body dysmorphia disorder, does some individual happpenstance of genetics exist as a humanizing recall of that contrast? We look at petrified wood and think, "If it could only talk." Is that not also true of the phenomenon of "being stuck in a mirror"?

So we have continued our achievement of naming; today it enables us to discuss such patterns as kleptomania, Tourette's syndrome, trichotillomania, and anorexia. In their desperate quest for survival, what self-awareness an enlarging brain must have brought: what is that burning in my head? pounding in my chest? What is that swelling, that blurring, that ringing, that itching? Is this sensation a prelude to screaming pain, falling and unable to reach water? What could be more understandable than the descendants of these Not Yets/Will Be, who had gradually developed the capacity to "name," finding a descriptive word for exaggerated sensations: hypochondriasis? What is more natural to our kind than to experience a relief when we can give something a name?

In the periodic African droughts, then as now, only the strongest survived. The expansion of larger brain and shrewder mind brought new feelings, new awareness. Will I be left aside the trail as I left my mother, or father, or mate, or child? When the storytellers of a particular Middle Eastern tribe recited one of the tales of the beginnings of their People, guilt would have a place, as would defensiveness. To their honor, they formulated the most famous of all ethical questions, "Am I my brother's keeper?"

IN THE BEGINNING: CAUSE AND EFFECT

The discovery of fire about one million years ago is often viewed as the beginning of what would be our human tale. The Norse attributed it to Loki, a godling who liked to play tricks and was mischievous—and they may turn out to be right if atomic warfare becomes a reality. The Greeks attributed it to the nobleness of the godling Prometheus, who paid for his gift giving with the daily rendering of his liver to the vultures whom the angry gods sent as punishment. Since growing up in the western United States, with its prairie fires, my hunch is that it was inevitable that some animals would get caught—and inadvertently cooked—and someone noticed the meat could be safely eaten for a longer time. *Voila!* Cause and Effect, and another giant step for humoid-kind.

That Middle Eastern tribe, the Hebrews, of course, told a different creation story, but it still centered on cause and effect. Their story was of innocent fruit eaters who named the animals and to whom God spoke. This story centered on "knowing"—insight—and was such a sophisticated story, as it was developed over unknown hundreds of years, that we are still learning from it, and so we shall in the next chapter.

AS IT MIGHT HAVE BEEN

These primitives looked much like us, as we know from the Nariokotome Boy, but Alan Walker concluded that, if we looked into his eyes, they would have been the eyes of an animal. There was almost total preoccupation with survival with these "Not Yets/Will Be"; it would be millions of years until obsessions and compulsions would become not quite dysfunctional. Nevertheless, along the genetic pilgrimage, they learned to make tools and weapons, thanks to an opposable thumb. Then, with a more energy-supplying food— meat—the population increased. Most likely, awareness was pretty much limited to fear, food, sex, and—later—violence. Indeed, in that period in which the midbrain was developing, sex and violence appear grouped in the same area—an observation so common to many women that neurological research must seem redundant at this point. If a regression ever would befall the ascendants of these Not Yets/Will Be "people," such themes quite likely would prominently recur.

Some began to spread, following a migratory food supply, (i.e., game animals), and the territory enlarged. They were no longer simply prey, they could prey. They were no less fearful, but much less timid and more aggressive as they became toolmakers. At some unknown point there was some social differentiation. We see in grade B movies the story of the cowboy and the nester: open range against fencing in the Old West. In Genesis, the story is that following the fruit-eating parents, Adam and Eve, came Cain and Abel. Cain was a herder—a meat eater—and Abel was a farmer, with what we might now term a vegetarian style. Putting things in a religious context, as the Hebrews liked to do, they portrayed the man of the settlement being more acceptable to God than the nomad. The meat eater became competitive, and blood spilled.

A generation ago, in a mind-expanding work by Desmond Morris titled *The Naked Ape*, the division in Not Yets/Will Be development was marked another way.[9] The grouping was by food preference, with all the lifestyle that would entail. There were the herbivores—the fruit eaters, the earliest strand of development—then a splitting with the appearance of the carnivores—the meat eaters: Ape versus Lion, if a public relations firm were creating logos. This is a highly suggestive way of looking at human groups in the mid-twentieth century: the "hippies" favoring vegetarianism, the "straights" preferring their steaks rare and thick; the former preferring communal living, the latter, a suburban ranch house; the one parading for peace, the other supporting the cold war.

Most of these Not Yets/Will Be "children" did not long survive; even as infants still do not in many countries today. The limit of life expectancy was set by Jean Auel in *The Clan of the Cave Bear* at twenty-five, and even that was at a much later date than the little band of Not Yets/Will Be we are considering.[10] (For comparison, in Jesus' time, the average life expectancy was probably twenty-nine, by 1900, perhaps thirty-nine.) Life was indeed short; survivors passed on their DNA, but the number of traumas most experienced suggests the term "veteran" as more appropriate than "survivor." It would not be unlikely that sensations we now term post-traumatic stress disorder would be familiar to most or all who lived long enough to reproduce.

In these small groups of our ancestors, the traumas probably began early for the males. They would be taught early to hunt and fight. The girls would be sent to gather. The boys would forage more broadly and then begin to hunt. Survival of trauma would begin—when it occurred—earlier for males, going out to hunt and be hunted; trauma for girls would begin about the age of giving birth. "Nature, red in tooth and claw," however, would ensure by adulthood that both males and females had an equal opportunity to perish or pass on their genetic advantages—and what would become, much, much later, a disadvantage as we know it.[11]

Now, about thirty minutes to midnight on our scale of eons, our kind of people is thought about ready to come on the scene in Africa. This occurred 125,000 years ago and humans were migrating from Africa, according to conventional scientific opinion. Alan Walker recounts that, by this time, something new had evolved. There were several new things, as we shall see, but most particularly "our" way of birth. The woman's pelvic area has not enlarged since that time, but the human brain has.[12] An adaptation was made in order to take advantage of our greatest human asset for survival. Even with that adaptation, however, birth was a brush with death, as so many females did not survive it.

It is a wonder that, in this day and age, more women do not suffer from OCD or postpartum depression after giving birth. After gestation the human brain continues to enlarge, increasing another third in size. Thus our specie has maximized its principal advantage for survival.

Migrating out of Africa, as is now commonly thought, and into the unknown, our ancestors' midbrains must have been responding to unforeseeable demands by growing forebrains like the rings on trees. Reality was probably prosaic rather than adventurous, although there must have been heroes with a thousand different faces. All that energy sapped something; perhaps that is why the olfactory "bulb" shrank. Smell, as a primary security sense, was lessening to the extent that a compulsion to smell is rare. We still say we "smell danger," but we moderns do not smell for the game we hunt. There must have been a felt need for a supplement to the security alarm systems. Someone's cunning became sharper wits, which became thought, and a hunter came home with a couple of pups and a she-hide.

At some period, perhaps during migration, they began to count. "The third stream to cross, turn toward the rising sun. You will find a valley with much game and protected cliff for shelter." Perhaps these nomads learned to use "sacred" numbers to reassure themselves as to orientation: three—up, down, here; four—what we regard as north, east, south, west. Combinations of sacred numbers are to be found in most or all primitive tribes. Magical thinking emerged—and persists yet—at any dice table.

Perhaps about this time the "goodness of fit" began to be lost in the brain. The "hair-trigger" response of emergency signals for fight, flight, or hide from the mammalian midbrain to the reptilian old brain now became an issue of impulse control. Social organization evolved to a stage where the controlling of impulses by some individuals would eventually be an issue. Nutrition was a key factor because, as a group, the serotonin level would be too low to facilitate control over acting out, other than by ostracism.[13] The brain continued to evolve and the forehead—and forethought—grew, as did the possibility of a defective or inadequate feedback loop between the new brain (the neocortex) and the hardwiring between it and the old brain and midbrain.

Looking at human development, the forebrain probably began about 100,000 years ago, and with it the beginning of "thought," *Homo sapiens,* thinking man. From the perspective of culture, about 70,000 years ago humankind began to bury their dead and a sense of valuing and caring for the dead appears, *Homo religiosus.* Linguistically, it would not be before 50,000 years ago that humankind evolved into the use of "our" kind of language, *Homo sapiens sapiens.* In the sequence of human development, religious values and practices were crucial in the humanization of our race.

It seems logical that more primitive religious *sensations* would have emerged before the more self-aware religious *feelings.* In this period, the clan ranged over a territory and had territorial feelings, of course, but this would be a time when most groups began to return at night to a given place, with cliff dwellers giving us some knowledge of that period. On the mammalian side of their experience, we could equate their territorial feelings with similar ones of animals. When they returned at night to a given place, we could make such an observation. But. The "but" is that these Not Yets/ Will Be groups were making the transition from mammal to human. Sensations were beginning to have experiences which no animal could have. The animal would experience "nest" or "den," but these Not Yets/Will Be "people" emerging into early persons would have a more self-aware experience. When they returned at nightfall from ranging the territory by day and entered their place of retreat and safety, they probably experienced what we now know as "sanctuary."

It would have been in this "sanctuary" where they would have collected what they regarded as valuable and, hopefully, would aid in survival. Thus, it was early in our own time period that persons began to collect and to store those valuables needed for survival. So early was the collection and safekeeping of what was of any potential value. So early in the experience of emerging humanness did these sensations take on tones we would consider "religious." In their place of sanctuary they would have communal meals, births would occur, and death and burial would take place. Storytelling would become a vehicle of communication, at first graphically—by sign language, then by visual art—and later develop into oral tradition while providing continuity.

Identity would form around the place of sanctuary, such as described in Auel's *The Clan of the Cave Bear*. The "who we are" would have, however, been preceded by the earlier collecting: self-identity based on "what we have." When today we hear displaced persons talk and sing of their homeland, or when peoples feel their homelands are threatened, then the old tribal feelings are evoked and the unconscious religious sensations become visible. These feelings are very, very tenacious given their heritage.

There is no evidence of religious dynamics associated with the brain stem area. Add a midbrain to that region, however, and there is potential for an eventual self-awareness. With the evolving of a forebrain, there would appear a longing to control the forces of nature; an eventuality of magic for placating the forces of wind, wave, and fire; sensations expressing a caring for one's kind and eventually a way of cursing one's enemies.

It should not be an occasion of wonder that religion began to be a factor in the story of human development. A yearning was felt to placate the animal's spirit that had been killed; therefore, some feelings of empathy and a "natural religion" must have been arising. Now feelings, a longing, began to be evidenced by the careful burying of the dead, often in a fetal position, indicating the ability to think symbolically. The dead are buried with things of value, perhaps tools and weapons of worth to the person that might continue to be so in an afterlife—even a toy for a child. Hopes for a Happy Hunting Ground or some such afterworld arose, but always "happy" in an afterworld, shadows were sensed.

Through the agency of wonder—that child of doubt—all sorts of causes began to be explored by the agency of the ever-developing new brain. Somehow, from "an eye for an eye, and a tooth for a tooth," "love your own and hate your enemies," there arose—not a consent to violence—but a sense of guilt and a curse on violence as old as Cain. A sense of guilt so miraculous that eventually, though it may reflect the loss of goodness of fit, some persons will even stop their car after backing up in order to check and make sure that no one has been injured.

The doubt and wonder must have been gradually transformed into reasoning and logic. Questions began to arise: What is real? What is false? Those twins, doubt and curiosity, served a high purpose—and continue to do so. There would have been no survival if doubt had not alerted early humans to danger, whether exploring the meaning of a snapping twig or the question of whether the setting was one of ambush. No creative advance would have been possible from magic to science without these twins. The goodness of fit, however, has been lost for some over the eons as conditions changed and exaggerations flourished, so that even doubts began to be doubted, as in OCD. This is not to deny the kernel of truth in obsessions and compulsions, but to acknowledge that anxiety became catastrophies and exaggerations turned into absurdities. What we need, however, is to celebrate that we humans are on a search for truth, and its evaluative forms, worth, and greater worth. It is in that quest that reason peaked timidly forth in some 5,000-year-ago bracket and increasingly asserted itself boldly. It was a desire to know what is real, and to consequently live better and better.

At some point the tribes in various places began to settle down, perhaps 12,000 years ago, perhaps 6,000. The hunting was good and some weeds had seeds that were good to eat and could be planted. Reassurance became less of an obsession when seedtime and harvest became an accepted routine. With this new lifestyle, however, came new opportunities and challenges. Settled conditions, including walls around settlements, meant that constant vigilance was less needed; no longer was stop/look/listen, check/check/check the condition of existence. Anxiety had been genetically programmed, however, and persisted; it now found new expressions.

Settling down, more specializations were possible. The craftsmen of the Stone Age have left us elegant examples of their work. Now craftsmen became artists as they had both time for specialization and metals with which to work. A fascination with beauty apparently began and developed into a passion to perfect beauty.

Settling down, one could have more material possessions. Famine, as well as a good harvest, came and had to be foreseen. Storing was the answer. Don't throw away anything that might be valuable: collect, collect, collect. It made sense to those veteran survivors, made sense right down to their genes. And who more trustworthy to store them than the shaman and the priest? And where more safely than in the sanctuary. In time of anxiety, where better to withdraw than to the storehouse of plenty, the place of sanctuary? Its continuation persists in at least one American religious group.

A profound nutritional difference appeared. They had been feeding on meat for a very long time. To the feeling of territoriality for the hunter was added the territoriality of the farmer: more food, more population, more competition. At some point, the milk producers were domesticated—camels, goats, reindeer, and what would become the modern cow—so "dairy products" were first available to the nomads.

Grain was added to these permanent settlements. At least the dominant male's diet increased in serotonin with the availability of a more adequate diet rich in dairy products and grain. Given the generous breeding habits of a dominant male, who would be characteristically higher in serotonin to reach that position, one might expect that a number of offspring males would tend toward higher serotonin levels in the brain as well.

Among other tendencies, the collective consciousness of the tribe would begin to break down and individualism and competition appear. As a running mate to these developments, social competition appeared: for hunting rights, farmland, and women. Meat eaters come to killing naturally; the wall-less Minoans of island Crete were followed by the warrior Greeks of the mainland.

Fermentation was discovered. At very low levels of some archeological digs, the remains of what appears to be an antique mustache cup can be found, but with holes in the lip to strain out the barley seeds floating in the brew. Thus we have a sequence: the meat eater habituated to killing + dairy products + grain + the appearance of more aggressive individuals high in serotonin. Add to this the storability and portability of the dairy products and grain + a good weather period between planting and harvesting + fermentation of beer and/or wine to lower inhibitions = an aggressive, dominant male and more docile, obedient followers. The greater availability of glucose in the grain and alcohol meant more widely available energy: *Voila!* "My children" could become "infantry."

They were living in a chaos, so order was enhanced. The dominance of the animal world was ritualized in royalty. Kingship was modified by assassination, coup, and conquest. Heredity became an amphitheater and *Oedipus Rex* provided Freud with a good story to illustrate this conflict, as the paranoid king kept his eyes on the sons and the sons kept their eyes on the father and on each other. Out of dire need, priests set rules, a code of Hammurabi to regularize behavior in Babylon, but not only there. In other places, the dynamic to "civilize" continued as with Moses, the Hebraic lawgiver, or Ollamh Fodhla, the high king in Ireland and gatherer of traditional law.

Miraculously? Transformations bloomed. Out of the need for orderliness, out of the fearfulness of chaos, in a *boundary land* that the theologian Paul Tillich would have appreciated as the time and place of innovation. Creativity flowered. From Ikhnaton, the Sun King in Egypt, to the Old Testament prophet Samuel's conflict with King Saul over a consultation with a witch, today's higher religions began their long struggle.

Our ancestors also scanned the stars to foretell their fate and attempt to produce order by studying the lights moving in the sky, astrology. Others began to plot the heavens, and astrology progressed into astronomy; so far ago were eclipses predicted; so far ago when the sacred light of the solstice sun would appear in a slit in the temple wall. Prediction began to control the planting and harvesting. As always, there was a trade-off; some persons noted that counting relieved anxiety. So long has our kind been counting sheep so we could sleep.

Also appearing was an elaborated passion for symmetry, mathematical proportions and patterning, straightness, perfecting continued, obviously simply spreading across the world at some point. In anthropological museums, the intricacy and delicacy of gold work at that thousands of years ago period is an astonishing tribute to the fascination of some with perfection. In China, porcelains were of such perfection that pass beyond our mere astonishment. At the other extreme, pyramids in Egypt appeared, so precise in cutting tons of squared stones that to this day we admire the engineering and classic geometrical shape and marvel at their precision in the mathematical concept of "pi." The same process is probably reflected in the Inca ruins in Peru. In Athens a Parthenon was raised, so lovely we still stand in awe of its symmetrical splendor. In Greece, the perception of mathematics began and, eventually, it would be said that, "Euclid alone, has looked on beauty bare."[14]

Greek sculpture of the human figure even took on mathematical rather than realistic proportions. Symmetrical, perfection of order, these must have not been the sole possession of some elite. If there had been no stirring of souls of the multitude, the gigantic structures reared by unknown ancients would have been impossible—as would the century upon century construction of the Gothic cathedrals.

As someone who knows about OCD, however, there was a "but." There emerged in those early drawings a sense of beauty: from where, we cannot tell. Perhaps in some animal grooming, perhaps in a bird's preening of its feathers at a water hole, with the sunlight glancing on the water. It is still beauty enough to pause over, even in one's backyard birdbath. So a sense of beauty was born and became, in due time, a passion for excellence in many forms. The "but" then appeared; we know anxiety massed in the gene pool, plus some passion for order—for symmetry, line, cleanliness—and all, in sufficient combination, becomes obsessing. This, in turn, brings on exaggerations to the point of striving for perfection.

Not all organic brains were able to make the transition equally; magical thinking persisted and superstitions erupted. If I make a voodoo doll and burn it, my enemy will burn; but there was transition: if I fail to avoid the number thirteen, evil will happen to me; if I do this, that will happen. Children still make a game of it, of holes and cracks and stepping thus and stepping this. In every OCD group meeting, the *minds* of the participants struggle with biological bondage to the *brain:* if I cease avoiding the number seven, my mother will die; if I somehow walk in some certain peculiar way, my lover will leave me. Our struggle has been to regain a goodness of fit of brain to the mind, to feeling and thought, and the black side of perfectionism. It is little wonder that those who are more vulnerable to anxiety should have a need for reassurance, some asking for it verbally, others literally reaching out and touching, touching, touching; this is real, real, real.

Transition abounded: the mother animal who pushed aside a defective offspring after birth and refused the teat, became the parent who exposed an unwanted child to die or made into a sacrifice to placate a god. A Greek king might sacrifice his daughter to get a favorable wind by which to sail to Troy; a Middle Eastern parent might make his child "to pass into Molock" (among the non-Hebrews in Old Testament times, this was perhaps an idol made of iron, heated red hot). How many times in unwritten history has a baby been sacrificed and the DNA of the grieving survivors later passed into imprinted human genetic experience?

Of this period, the Greeks told different stories from the Hebrews. One story is of Icarus, who was a captive together with his father, Daedalus, on Crete. Daedalus made wings of feathers and wax with which they would escape. Icarus became so enthralled with the experience of soaring, however, that he flew too near the sun and the wax melted so that he plunged into the sea. His father, wiser, flew lower and made his escape. The other Greek story is of Narcissus. He was so beautiful—so perfect—that one day when he was walking in the forest he came upon a pool and saw his reflection. He was so infatuated with his perfection that he became "stuck in the mirror," pining away and leaning perpetually over the pool.

These are stories of "hubris" in the Greek tradition, not so much of pride and arrogance as we have tended to think of them, but of the result of perfectionism: striving too high, regressing to the depths. Thus came the Greek solution: nothing in excess.

SUMMARY

We can now see why we recognized the prevalence of OCD so belatedly. It is so widespread as to make it difficult to differentiate from the cultural norm. How do you diagnose cleaning and straightening in Switzerland, for instance? Surrounded by trees, how do you recognize the forest?

The dynamics of OCD and that of culture have evolved in many ways, perhaps none more cogently studied than in the concepts of the theologian of culture, Paul Tillich, who defined God as "the Ground of Reality" and designated religion as one's "Ultimate Concern."[15] If it is accurate to recognize OCD in early, earlier, and earliest human life forms, then it is not strange that this "disorder" has the greatest tendency toward religious expressions of all the psychiatric categories . . . and having a profound effect not only on individuals but on our history.

It may be also that some divisions, such as Alfred Adler's suggestion of grouping persons into introvert and extrovert categories, reflect this early period. What is of interest in our study is what it might say about the OCD condition. How many extroverts do you see in an OCD client population? Clearly, there are many fantasies of sex and violence, but of what actual threat to others? And what of the future? Clearly, several of the Not Yets/Will Be groupings came and disappeared, leaving only identification by skull. Of the fruit eaters and meat eaters, is one a grouping that will have come—and gone? Will the meek indeed inherit the earth, while the aggressive are destined "to buy the farm" as it was phrased by soldiers in the Vietnam days . . .

This chapter was begun with a reference to Albert Schweitzer, in which he linked the animal kingdom both to human ethics and religious concerns: reverence for life. The next chapter will begin with a quotation of Father Booth and focus on the evolution of those religious concerns. We must wonder, however, just how far we have come toward this; religion has struggled against witchcraft—and produced the Salem witch trials practically in our own time. Reflecting on this history with its struggling and suffering—in which OCD has played its role—please allow me to share a story of a member of our German family.

He is a highly decorated panzer officer who served four years on the Russian front during World War II. On the way to a national convention of the American Association of Pastoral Counselors in North Carolina, he and I were swapping stories—he of the Russian front, mine of our Civil War—as we passed historical sites. His concluding comment on human struggle, sacrifice, and suffering was, "By the end of the war, I cared for every man." That is for us the hope, as we reflect on our human history.

Chapter 4

OCD and *Homo Religiosus*— Religious Man

It all began early, as it always does, in childhood. . . . I grew up in a home divided by religion. . . . When Mother had an argument with Father, all the historical prejudice and venom were unleashed. . . . [In seminary] I learned to manipulate scripture and church history to substantiate my dogmatic churchmanship. I argued . . . thus members of other Christian religions were not worthy to receive Holy Communion. . . . As you can see, I have had my days as a dogmatic religious fundamentalist. So I do know what I'm talking about when I say that it is possible to change.

I left the hospital with a changed outlook on life, determined to be a different priest. Church ritual, the priesthood, the use of scriptural texts—I had scrutinized them all, and my attitude towards other Christians was changed forever. . . . [My purpose] is to discover the challenge and adventure that religion can provide in the here and now; not to ridicule discipleship, but rather to encourage the development of a creative relationship with God that allows for personal responsibility and change, enabling one to discover the Power that exists within each of us.[1]

Father Leo Booth

THE EMERGENCE OF RELIGIOUS FEELINGS

Anyone wishing to dismiss "religion" as a characteristic of humankind must start with the cultural anthropologists and the classification of *Homo religiosus*.[2] If a novelist would like to increase the general understanding of life in those ten years ago times, he or she would be hard put to develop the story without reference to religion. When we move into that eon we are in the time of myth making, the attempt to give coherence to the evolution from chaos into order, when the slowly emerging specie to which we belong overlapped with the slow disappearance of a prehuman specie.

Jean Auel builds on the Hebraic account in her marvelous novel, *The Clan of the Cave Bear*.[3] The story is set in the context of the transitional period from *A. robustus* to the emergence of *Homo sapiens*. The young heroine, the human Ayla, has been living with a more primitive group; Ayla has vocal language, curiosity, and daring. The primitive group has only sign language. The dominant male, Durc, hates her and forces her to "take the position" (to voluntarily sexually submit) at least once a day and often several times a day. She becomes pregnant and puts two and two together. It was the first realization of cause and effect: it may have been so, although the clan had fire. Now there is insight, knowledge, and (one would suspect) a sense of valuing the good and/or bad of a pregnancy that every female experiences. There is now an understanding of the creative process and hence the potential control of it, even as the gods must have.

What we wish to examine, however, is the emergence of religious feelings and thinking in reference to OCD. A record for this comes to us in the early traditions recounted in the Old Testament. The period we want to reflect upon has a bottom line in the Babylonian captivity; extending backward, we have Moses about 1200 B.C. (the Iron Age), Abraham at approximately 1800 B.C. (the Bronze Age), and beyond that we stretch from the historical into prehistory. Thus begins the telling of those incomparable stories we have in Genesis that shaped us all. From the perspective of OCD, they help us understand the transition from repetitious functional behavior—checking for security and fear of contamination (pre-OCD) as security measures. We then see a transitional period when some of today's symptoms of OCD split into different forms (such as fear of being contaminated and fear of contaminating others). Finally, there is a new form of the use of repetitious behaviors to cope with anxiety—in which more "modern" expressions of OCD, which are truly dysfunctional, become expressed in perfectionism. Now to our story.

Out of chaos, God the Creator introduces order and our world is born. A local tour guide in Jerusalem will even point out the rock on which God was standing when He did it. Six days and sweaty but satisfying creative labor brought Adam out of the dust of the earth, then Eve. They are set in a garden, fruit eaters in a paradise, with an ability to name the animals. They are forbidden to eat of the Tree of Life, for it brings knowledge of good and evil—cause and effect. The snake tempts Eve, saying that such knowledge of cause and effect, with the consequent capacity of *valuing,* of *knowing,* will make them as gods.

We are now in that multidimensional area of myth. Symbolically, as any giggling group of elementary schoolboys knows, the snake is a good reference to a penis. The giggling girls watching them across the school yard, of course, are psychologically ready even earlier to express their curiosity than boys. Soon enough they will lose their innocence and a parent will catch them in their nakedness. It is a story reflecting reality even earlier than the first tale of Adam and Eve. The Genesis story has an angel with a flaming sword to prevent them from returning from their expulsion: once lost, there is, in reality, no return to innocence.

Scientifically, perhaps the story reflects—without ability to be self-aware—on that time when those who someday would be fully human were forced from the fruit-rich forest out onto the savanna. There the living would never be easy. Seed gathering and root digging were doubtless felt as a "curse," as was giving birth. And woman, woman so curious, with such doubts—she was cursed with submission to the male.[4] Some biblical scholars—among others—are beginning to wonder if there are not *two* versions of that story. One can only marvel at how stories can transcend reality in order to portray truth. They are like a beautifully cut diamond whose facets flash as it is turned.

With insight, they had not merely a self-consciousness that they—we—must die, there came the capacity to inflict death: the Cain and Abel story of how brother killed brother. It must have been a horrendous period—this boundaryland of prehistory recorded in myth—when the half-animal and half-emergent humans combined to be more cunningly bestial than the beasts they had named. God became enraged with "how wicked everyone on earth was and how evil their thoughts were all the time" and was determined to put an end to it. He would cause a flood and wipe out the whole lot, including the birds and animals, so they could not start the whole thing over again, one would suppose.

Then he thought of Noah "who had no faults." We know little of Noah, other than he was married and had three sons, who were also married. He was viewed by God as the "only good man of his time." He could count, for when he loaded the ark it was in pairs but, interestingly, in a pattern of sevens. He may not have been anxious before he had his talk with God, but he must have been sufficiently so after. So when God said, "Flood," Noah said, "How big do you want that boat?"

In Noah we have a transitional figure; prior to Noah, there is myth and prehistory. With Noah we are commencing the historical. It is interesting that in Noah we have a report of two qualities, anxiety and perfectionism. He was a man so good in all his ways that he attracted the admiration of even God. This is not to suggest that Noah is a figure to be associated with OCD; it is simply to say that in this transitional figure, before and after the Flood, he is said to possess the security-seeking qualities of having sufficient anxiety to build an Ark, and the perfectionism that developed as humankind and civilization evolved. Noah is truly representative of humankind.

The Greeks and Babylonians also told a story of a great flood. In the Greek version, the boat landed near the Delphi oracle and the oracle instructed the man and woman to "throw behind you the bones of your mother." They did, soon heard a clatter, and, looking behind, saw they were being followed by a number of young men and women. In the Babylonian version, their "Noah" came out of the dark and also made a burnt offering; "the gods smelled the odor and gathered around it like flies." No doubt there must have been some sort of catastrophic flooding. It could have seemed like the whole world to the small group of migrants emerging from Africa and beginning settlements in the Middle East. As a matter of fact, it must have been quite a flood, measured by the feet of sediment between layers of settlements in some of that area's archeological digs.

One of the interesting speculations about a world-encompassing flood, in reference to OCD, is that of those characteristic human fears—such as fire, plague, war, famine—there is one missing: flooding. There seems one anxiety missing that certainly plays a part in human history, flooding. A search for the key word "flood" in the OCD Library of the Dean Foundation, only located one such case, a peripheral one.[5] How intriguing it is that it is said that God placed a rainbow in the sky, a sign that humankind should never again have to be anxious about such flooding.

In Hebraic history, we begin to see a new direction taken in the Noah story. It is one familiar to those with OCD, that of avoidance. Noah is instructed to obey a religious taboo that forbids eating the blood of meat that is too rare. A person familiar with OCD would suspect this might reflect contamination fears. He is permitted to eat certain other foods—perhaps reflecting a transitional period from herbivorous to carnivorous societies. There is also a taboo against murder. An intensification of rules and regulations became associated with survival.

Trying to be perfect has a downside. If anxiety is deep and the attempt to be a perfect person results, we recognize that alcohol once presented the only effective relief to OCD depth anxieties prior to the creation of very contemporary medications. Noah may have understood that all too well, as he was so quick to plant a vineyard. He got drunk, took off all his clothes, and passed out.

With the beauty of hindsight we might see in the flood that (1) a lot of wickedness was eliminated (along with what would be viewed today as an environmental offense against animals, given our changing standards) and (2) some behaviors often associated with godliness—the keeping of food taboos—were enacted. Again, with the beauty of hindsight, we have a view that (1) anxiety can result in moralistic overachievement, (2) overachievement results in self-abusive behavior, and (3) since he was totally naked, to the embarrassment of the two older sons and the amusement of the youngest, self-abusive behavior led to an interpersonal disruption in the family, and (4) regarding taboos, whether of food or dress, it is again possible to observe that they have no intrinsic religious value, just a value for social differentiation—it makes it easier to feel "one up" on the neighbor rather than "one down."

It all seems a strange outcome, unless you consider how many persons striving to be perfectly faultless have found themselves driven to drink for relief. That Noah was also deeply religious is not altogether strange. As any pastor knows, the most predictable person to involve in a theological discussion is an alcoholic. Compulsion and religion go far, far back; two drinks and the individual is ready to talk about God, so innate is that theme to the more primitive experience of the brain. Perhaps the next advance in treating alcoholism will be in the diagnosis of a primary condition of OCD. The failure to do so may explain many of the failures in treatment.[6] It probably is more natural than strange that the religiously oriented Twelve Steps have helped so many alcoholics and persons with OCD. It also suggests incorporating a thoughtful, spiritual approach to treatment.

The road to change had been set: there must be order. Prior to the flood, the nearest picture we might grasp would be some of the more gruesome of the Hollywood fantasies of life in the post-atomic war world. And order was imposed. The dominant male became royalty; religion played its part in setting up the rule of law and order. It was a time of Totem and Taboo, and the Hebrews were only one group among many who were allowed only certain foods, prepared only in certain ways. From these humble beginnings, both legalisms of governance and religion proliferated as fully as did the population.

If the storyline with OCD has interest, it is because its characteristics always have a kernel of truth, with a pragmatic foundation and a genuine hope. Check and survive, create order, push back chaos and thrive, have a passion for excellence, and the results can be astonishingly great. So, too, are the frustrations when extreme anxiety produces self-defeating exaggerations—but this is not to deny the aspirations or the pursuit of what is of true worth.

First came the frustration: the Tower of Babel. Humankind is unified; their ambition is endless; technology has flourished. Lines can be straight; symmetry can be perfected. "Let us build a tower that will go up to heaven." Such arrogance. Boomerang. The Bible relates that God came down, saw the arrogance, and put an end to the project, if not the arrogance. He created different language groups. Humankind grouped and went.

A marvelous moment in human history is soon recorded in Genesis. Abram, father of the Hebrew people, had to deal with what can be described as a similar obsession to those with OCD. He kept brooding about his son and whether the son was more important to him than his God. It was not unnatural obsessing: child sacrifice was all too familiar in his world. At the crucial moment, Abram had an explosion of humane/theological insight, refused to cut the throat of his son, and refused to burn him upon an altar. Metaphorically, it is an "angel" who intervenes; dramatically it illustrates that "Abram" has truly made the passage into "Abraham" as he turns around, knife still in hand, and walks away from his firstborn.

How symbolic for the passage toward the humane: this "Abram" became "Abraham." Was it happening in parallel across the world, a transition from a "perfect" obedience to some unknowable awesome power, to a sense of doing no harm? Was there a movement from a more primitive fear of being harmed to a fear of *doing* harm, so eventually even hitting potholes when driving resulted in anxiety lest harm be done? Apparently, that process was not going on everywhere, and the Hebrews saw it rightly in hindsight: God was moving uniquely here.

We see other transformations moving across time, from what we regard as quite primitive to present practices. Thus, behaviors, such as self-mutilation, are recorded in the story of the prophet Elijah in the eighteenth chapter of First Kings in the Old Testament, where the priests of Baal cut themselves in order to manipulate their god into answering their prayer for dominance. Today, self-mutilation continues as a quest for beautification, in a ring in the nose, ear, or navel. "Goodness of fit" no longer exists, however, for those who express emotions through skin picking, nail biting, hair disfigurement, cutting, or bruising. The transformation may be exhibiting itself, however, in the form of scarification for the primitive, scrupulosity for the sophisticated. Evolution continues as a slow process.

The storytellers who gave us the oral traditions that became our Bible intuitively sensed they were participants in an evolution from the "animal kingdom" to what would be much later summarized as "the kingdom of heaven." God is seen as redeciding in the flood story and later bargaining with Abraham about destroying Sodom and Gomorrah; Abraham is seen as redeciding at a time when human sacrifice was believed to be religious obedience. In Jeremiah 31, the common observation is recounted, "The fathers have eaten sour grapes, and the children's teeth are set on edge," as any social worker sees daily. Not too many years later, however, in a modification and perhaps a realization of God's own process, it is recorded that Ezekiel wrote: The Lord spoke to me and said,

> "What is this proverb the people keep repeating in the land of Israel?

> 'The parents ate the sour grapes,
> But the children got the sour taste.'"

> "As surely as I am the living God," says the sovereign Lord, "you will not repeat this proverb any more. The life of every person belongs to me, the life of the parent as well as the child. The person who sins is the one who will die."[7]

NOW WE ARE IN RECORDED HISTORY

With the Babylonian captivity—that boundary war of Jewish religious and cultural history—the preservation of culture was given highest priority, as many peoples have since done in similar circumstances. The oral tradition of those marvelous stories, such as Adam and Eve and Noah, was compiled. The Mosaic Law was codified and expanded. The Law flowered, commentary upon commentary, interpretation and expansion, even unto our day and, as in Psalm 1, the goodly person was to meditate upon it night and day. Some people get into difficulty with that, as one might expect:

> Happy are those
> who reject the advice of evil men,
> do not follow the example of sinners
> or join those who have no use for God.
> Instead, they find joy in obeying
> the Law of the Lord,
> and they study it day and night.

Psalm 1:1-2

So we see the joining of ethics and what would be a positive focus "study," but inherently carrying with it the danger of exaggeration through repetitive interpretations. Most likely, as the study of the brain would now show, brain alternations lead to "obsessing" if the trauma was sufficiently intense. Joining with the positive aspects of study and dedication to ethical behavior there is the implication of feelings well known to those who obsess: sinfulness, depression, guilt, catastrophizing, and doom.

If we accept the notion of the evolution of orderliness, of trauma and reiteration leading to exaggeration, what we would then expect to see is a Book of Laws in which behavior is impressed on persons intensely. There would be ritual washing of pots and pans and prescribed repetitious behaviors, such as touching as one went in and out of doors. There would come an exaggeration of these behaviors from generation after generation of such rules—a legalism inflating to the point of triteness and triviality.[8] Given the role it has had in shaping a good portion of world culture, it is no wonder that even the most secular person can demonstrate the dynamics of scrupulosity.

Given the ever-present condition of human existence, precariousness, and the circumstances of displaced refugees, the canonization of Scripture and the development of Law were a great blessing, a cultural necessity. It offered control: control of self and social identity, a structure to set boundaries on disintegration. Given an innate sense of checking, fear of contamination, hoarding for security, and the need for repetition through ritual and pattern, what were formerly *individual* characteristics would be easily transformed into *structural* ones. Collecting and preserving would be consciously built on latent tendencies of hoarding and scrupulosity. Given time—and chaotic social conditions that cultivated high levels of anxiety—exaggerations of these qualities would mount, each generation adding a bit, every generation interpreting a bit to keep the regulations current as conditions changed and social threats shifted. The higher the anxiety level, the greater the persistence to conserve both things and values rather than to normally discard as times and relevance changed.

It would be no great surprise to see legalistic exaggerations making for a violent confrontation, if control needs were ever challenged. This is to be seen in the time of Alexander the Great and the introduction of Greek culture into Palestine. It resulted in the Maccabees and the revolt of the Jews: few men, great violence, enormous heroism, at Masada. The First Temple, notwithstanding, became ruins. Creative energy could not be denied, however, and resurrection surged. The Second Temple was built as the Roman army and Roman culture introduced themselves to Palestine. Again, anxiety arose in response to a foreign cultural threat.

Those familiar with OCD would see a story within a story: (1) a cult of holiness arises, dedicated to purity in order to preserve the culture; (2) tradition becomes increasingly exaggerated until scrupulosity exhibits itself as masochism, that is, a willingness to personally suffer and sacrifice in order to carry out what is felt to be a noble duty; (3) as masochism and sadism are two sides of one coin, there is always the potential for the accumulation of frustrations, and a "critical mass" is reached, resulting in an eruption of anger by the scrupulous.

In sum, it is like the unfolding of a classical Greek tragedy, the climax is reached in a scene in which the frustrations of the individual with scrupulosity reach such a peak, as they accumulate in response both to the demands of the parental past and to anxiety, that there is an explosion. That explosion builds from a dynamic that is internal to that which becomes external, becoming a social contagion, if there is sufficient anxiety in the community. It is a classical retelling of the oedipal story in which the father figure is attacked and destroyed.

When the flip side appears in self-righteousness—in anger, even sadism qualities, as history repeatedly shows—we might want to give it a distinctive title such as *sanctimonious* scrupulosity. We would do well to always examine scrupulosity for its sadomasochistic dynamic. Sadly, we know how it brings about self-destruction in due time: "for God will judge you in the same way you judge others, and he will apply the same rules to you that you apply to others" (Matthew 7:2).

FOR CHRISTIANS,
THE DIVIDING LINE OF HISTORY OCCURS

Into this culture then, out of Nazareth, came a carpenter with different insights into the evolving of tradition: not as dedicated to preaching purity, as compassion; a vision of God as love rather than holiness. Given the stress of Roman occupation and threats of a cultural invasion, it was inevitable that the integration of defenses against anxiety and the structural integration of these coping mechanisms into religious commitment would be brought into motion. It is, however, highly uncomfortable to read how it unfolds. Follow then the story outlined in that most Jewish gospel, Matthew.

Jesus seemingly was not looking for a fight. Both he and the "elite" believed in the same God. Like Abraham Lincoln, who told his cabinet that if you wanted to carry a bucket of water when riding a horse, you had better carry two in order to balance them. In the fifth chapter of Matthew, we read Jesus' words:

> Do not think that I have come to do away with the Law of Moses and the teaching of the prophets. I have not come to do away with them, but to make their teachings come true. . . (Matthew 5:17)

He appears to be ambivalent about the law; perhaps he understood the necessity of a politician in the primaries to straddle a few fences. The challenge is there and the message is "get the big picture" rather than the proliferations, the perfecting, the exaggerations. They were practicing "the Politics of Purity," and he was preaching "the Politics of Compassion," as Marcus Borg phrases it in *Meeting Jesus Again for the First Time:*[9]

> You will be able to enter the Kingdom of heaven only if you are more faithful than the teachers of the Law and the Pharisees in doing what God requires. (Matthew 5:20)

Then come the illustrations of "You have heard that people were told in the past. . . . But now I tell you . . ." followed by

a. anger
b. adultery
c. divorce
d. keeping a promise
e. revenge

the things about which people so easily obsess (Matthew 5:21-42).

Following these illustrations of obsessions, there naturally follows in the sixth chapter illustrations of repetitive behaviors that would serve to relieve the anxieties reflected in the obsessions:

a. public display of charitable giving
b. public praying—and do not use a lot of meaningless words
   (as the pagans do, he seemingly added tactfully)
c. fasting
d. storing up riches (Matthew 6:1-24).

By the eighth, he starts to meddle with what we will term "basic family values" in a later chapter: he heals the servant of a Roman officer, adding insult to injury by observing that he had not seen that quality of faith in Israel. He followed that up, as told in the twelfth, by condoning his disciple breaking the Sabbath laws by picking some grains of wheat and eating them. He followed that with breaking the Sabbath by healing a man with a paralyzed hand. He did not even have the common decency to respect male superiority: imagine going around talking to *women*—even a loose-living Samaritan one—as if they were real persons.

In the fifteenth, the storm is brewing. The Pharisees and teachers of the law ask, "Why is it that your disciples disobey the teaching handed down by our ancestors? They don't wash their hands in the proper way before they eat!" This causes Jesus to come out with "You hypocrites . . ." Then on to Tyre and Sidon and he does it again: pouring fuel on the fire as he heals a Canaanite woman this time. Jesus uses the metaphor of the "yeast" of the keepers of tradition to warn his disciples. It is an apt word choice to illustrate proliferation and exaggeration.

Jesus, retold in the twenty-third chapter, is still trying to balance, to harmonize:

> The teachers of the Law and the Pharisees are the authorized interpreters of Moses' Law. So you must obey and follow everything they tell you to do; do not, however, imitate their actions, because they don't practice what they preach. (Matthew 23:1-3)

Then come the denunciations:

> How terrible for you. . . . How terrible for you. . . . How terrible for you, teachers of the Law and Pharisees! You hypocrites! You give to God one tenth even of the seasoning Herbs,

> such as mint, dill, and cummin, but you neglect to obey the
> really important teachings of the Law, such as justice and
> mercy and honesty. . . . How terrible for you. . . . How terrible
> for you . . . (Matthew 23:23)

How many parish priests have heard guilt-flooded confessions concerning whether the Mass was appropriately celebrated because a tidbit of food may have been inadvertently swallowed in saliva during the preceding hour. Meanwhile, both know full well that the kids had been harshly and unfairly treated the day before.

In the twenty-third chapter, beginning with the thirteenth verse, there is a section filled with "lawyer talk." A discussion of religious hairsplitting and nitpicking ensues regarding what constitutes a valid oath and so forth. The point to be considered is this: if rules and regulations have become exaggerated and, in effect, scrupulosity structured into the organization of religious faith, how is that to be maintained? The answer is that it will not be, over time, unless a sufficient number of individuals interact with those scrupulous practices out of their own scrupulosity. In this case, knowing what we do about the emotional torment underlying scrupulosity, given sufficient stress for the torment to go from being internalized to externalized, we have the potentiality of a truly murderous "public show trial."

To the guardians of tradition, grounded in mammalian insecurity and reinforced by historical anxieties, the threat Jesus posed was felt as real, if not realistic. Apparently it was rationalized as a threat that the Romans would come and destroy the nation. That proved prophetic in 70 A.D.—but as a projection on Jesus' ministry was brought to fulfillment by the way in which tradition was guarded. Jesus was silenced, however, and assassination was as real a possibility as it was later for the apostle Paul. The Romans, however, could be manipulated into doing it, and so it was done.

It can be observed that scriptural citations about OCD involvement are all from Matthew, the most Jewish of the four. Remembrances of Jesus' ministry in the other three gospels reflect little of possible OCD dynamics, as these gospels were more oriented toward the Gentile world. This pattern lends credibility to the thesis that the dynamics we identify with OCD were present in Jesus' time and place, rather than that we are now reading back into the first century from the late twentieth. The dynamics then have implications now, both for those having OCD and for religious understandings.

It is easily noted that Matthew differs from the other gospels, each having its own audience and, consequently, its own emphasis. Each drew upon oral traditions being circulated about what Jesus did and said—essentially independent "sound bites." These sound bites— the technical name is "pericopae"—were collected by various authors of the gospel for use in addressing a particular audience. Matthew obviously was addressing Jews and recorded stories reflecting their relevant social and religious customs, as we have seen. Interestingly, Matthew added sound bites, such as "being perfect," from the Christian oral tradition that would be received favorably by a Jewish audience.

Today, a person with OCD might go through Matthew and pick out several passages that would sound, in his ears, as if they were "OCD friendly." I believe not. What are questionable exaggerations in some passages of the fifth chapter of Matthew, in the light of today and our grasp of OCD, were simply an appeal to a particular audience in a particular setting: a practice validated not only in politics but in evangelism.

If the thesis has creditability, this will be reflected in what comes after the death and resurrection of Jesus, when the reports of the Early Church would again reflect a pattern in which themes typical of OCD would be differentiated between the Jewish and Gentile scenes.

Enter Saul of Tarsus, a young Jewish student from Tarsus sent to Jerusalem for further study. He might have been fifteen and then probably would have studied for about four years. He would have been perhaps in his late teens when he participated in the stoning of Stephen, the first Christian martyr. It leads one to wonder what was implied when "Paul" the Christian, writes of his years as "Saul," the Jewish student: "Being extremely jealous for the traditions of my fathers," he advanced beyond many others of his years. It seems justifiable to wonder just how perfectionistic he was. Many of those in the pharisaic tradition would have married early, but there is never a mention of a wife. If he was a religious perfectionist perhaps he would not have considered marrying.

Regarding this period, in which he advanced far beyond others in his study group, one scholar has written:

> Approximately 67 percent of all legal pericopae governed the fitness of food for pharisaic consumption. . . . Observances of the Sabbaths and festivals are a distant third.[10]

A few pages later, the same author notes:

> The mild Hillel is reported as saying, "he who does not learn (the Law) is worthy of death," whereas the strict Shammai merely counseled, "make your study of the Law a fixed habit," and Gamaliel I proffered the practical advice "provide yourself with a teacher and remove yourself from doubt."

What we do know is that Saul must have felt some trauma in the stoning death of Stephen, as recounted in The Book of Acts. Not too long afterward, he had an experience on the way to Damascus that was at least as striking as Martin Luther's "fit in the choir." It is not unusual for epileptic episodes to be experienced by those who suffer from scrupulosity.[11]

If Saul was indeed rigid, perfectionistic, religious, and moralistic—characteristics sometimes associated with seizures—it is not beyond understanding that he might be struck blind by a sudden insight, truly a revelation. Like Oedipus, when he discovered he had killed his own father and then possessed his mother, blindness resulted: Oedipus gouged out his eyes; Saul fell from his horse and was blinded. Oedipus went out to wander the world and Saul retired to the desert for three years.

He then emerged essentially as we know him today. Paul, the greatest of the Christian missionaries, ready to preach and highly focused on freedom in Christ in relationship to any legalism. On behalf of his Gentile congregations, he took on the Jewish Christian "establishment." In Galatians he recounts that he even faced down Peter: freedom in Christ from the rules and regulations of religion was Paul's passion.

In his travels he certainly demonstrated that he was a robust man of enormous stamina, by surviving beatings, stoning, imprisonment, and shipwrecks. Yet, of himself, he wrote of "a thorn in the flesh" that tormented him and about which he was so secretive it has puzzled every scholar who has pondered his writings. Whatever it was, he knew how to keep a secret. Most scholars have speculated that he was depressed, but secret it was and mystery it remains. He simply describes it as "a messenger of Satan"; that would be an apt interpretation of repetitive, intrusive thoughts directly counter to his understanding of who he was in Christ. Considering the diverse background from prehistorical ancestors to some of the disreputable characters everyone has hanging from their family tree, it certainly could have felt like the Devil!

Paul exhibited a strange split. On one hand, he fought fiercely to keep the Jewish-Christian-handbook-of-religious-rules-and-regulations from being imposed on his Gentile recruits. Then, quite to the contrary, he determined to return to Jerusalem to perform a ritual in the temple. Everyone told him it was illogical, but he felt compelled to go. Compulsively so?

Whether or no, we do know that late in his career he wrote the words to the Romans that have given great comfort and strength (even if without curative power) to many religious persons we do know had OCD: "The just shall live by faith alone." This may well be the summation of not only his theological thought, but reflected his personal experience as well.

THE JEWISH TRACK OF HISTORY

During the same period, the Jewish need to be secure in religious and cultural identity climaxed. The Romans burned the temple in Jerusalem and scattered its stones and ashes, but in the Diaspora the Law continued to flourish and be embellished. What followed over the centuries is a story, not only of religious value, but of the greatest adventures of all times. Jewish merchants had begun to set up trading posts along a route we associate with Marco Polo extending even into the farthest Baltic states.

As the centuries passed, rabbinical traditions expanded through comments on commentaries. Within the hypothesis that reiteration deepens learning—given enough trauma—and also affects the chemistry of the brain, imprinted chemically in some similar fashion to flashbacks. It would affect the DNA transmitted from generation to generation so that such scholarship not only produced a wealth of wisdom, but it would confirm a tendency to hoard tradition and sometimes become scrupulous in religious practices.

Judith Rapoport, in her book *The Boy Who Couldn't Stop Washing*, cites a clinical case study of a young Jewish student, "Daniel," whose troubles illustrate the "side effects" of an obsession with washing. Rapoport points out that in medieval times there was a ritual to deal with such situations. Rapoport, a wise Jewish rabbi, and two synagogue officials utilized it for the relief of Daniel.[12] Paralleling this in Catholicism, a process was also being developed to relieve scrupulosity, a process that we will explore in the section on the lives of Ignatius of Loyola and Martin Luther. Before doing that, however, let us continue trekking along the Jewish trail.

In 1492 Columbus sailed west to reach east. Ignatius and Luther were young. The Renaissance was at flood tide and overflowing in university and artistic expressions—as was cultural shock. With the resulting extreme anxiety came the all too understandable dramas, such as the expulsion of Jews and Moors from Spain. In Toledo, the dreaded Torquemada practiced the scrupulous examinations of the Inquisition.

In Jewish history, the trail forked. On one path, some of the Jews (perhaps to be more fortunate in DNA) would migrate to a potentially freer society, such as England and also Brazil, and eventually to America. There some would experience greater freedom of religion—and lessened anxiety—and many would take a different and reforming direction. Some, adrift in boats, as refugees so often have been, were rescued by a Muslim sultan in Constantinople who, upon learning of their plight, sent out his fleet to their rescue.

Another path, we might suspect, might reflect imprinting on the most insecure, reinforced by pogrom and Holocaust. The stamping of anxiety into collecting/preserving/hoarding might even deepen: apparent in the individual and more and more structurally integrated into both culture and religion.

As one would expect, epidemiological studies of persons in various nations and of different religious backgrounds have found data indicating that among the Orthodox Jews in Israel, there is an unusually high incidence of scrupulosity.[13] Indeed, there was an article in the *Los Angeles Times* titled "Overzealous Cleaning Often

Precedes Passover." In it are stories of Jewish women going to absurd lengths—by non-Orthodox standards—to find bread crumbs that might contain leaven, even dismantling an oven. Anyone familiar with OCD would understand a quote from David Hartman, an Orthodox rabbi:

> The Laws are supposed to be instrumental to larger values, but they become an end that destroys the purpose of the thing. On Pesach, we worship a God who is a liberating God, but often women are so dead there's no time for symbolic reflection.[14]

THE CHRISTIAN TRACK OF HISTORY

A similar cultural shock and coping process seems to have gone on in Christianity. In the three centuries after Christ—and persecutions—churchmen went into politics and politicians were into being churchmen. It was a movement *in* and *of* "the world." Highly sensitive, dedicated men, and probably women, began to move into the desert. The written records they left indicate they were tormented by "streams of thought" and "visions of the dancing girls of Alexandria," certainly not beyond the understanding of persons who also obsess. They retreated into the far places where they hoped to escape contamination. It would seem a bit much though, even for someone with OCD, to empathize with someone's fears causing him or her to sit on top of a stone pillar for a couple of decades. Withdrawal, as a familiar dynamic of OCD, occurred in ghetto and desert and continued in monastery and cloister. Some persons must have been drawn into such a vocation by contemplation of God, some by the push of "religious" OCD into a life of avoidance. In a prior world lacking effective treatment, who would second-guess that?

For some sufferers with the severest forms of OCD, self-mutilation occurs. We know that sexuality is a common obsession. We might perhaps permit ourselves to wonder if those factors played a part in the decision of Origen, one of the early Church fathers, to castrate himself. We might suspect that an extraordinary fear of sexuality, more than just the desire to have male soprano voices for the choir, also made possible the practice of castration. This continued well into the nineteenth century in one form of the Christian Church, with the last professional castrato, Alessandro Moreschi, dying in 1922. It is reported that this practice continues in some other world religions.[15]

Not all withdrew who suffered from severe anxiety; as we see things now, some suffered, functioned, and grew saintly. Some appear to have suffered from anorexia. One saint was overheard to repeat all night, "My Lord and My God," perhaps meditatively, perhaps compulsively. Saint Ligouri is remembered in the Ligouri Press and a monthly publication, "Scrupulous Anonymous." Ignatius of Loyola founded the Jesuit Order. In the interaction of OCD and religion, there has been boiling and bubbling. In *The Doubting Disease*, Dr. Joseph Ciarrocchi cites studies from a generation ago in which 25 percent of students in Catholic schools experienced some form of scrupulosity.[16]

With Protestants we know less. My conclusion is that the role of OCD among Protestants is similar to that of Catholics and Jews, but the number of studies added together equals about as much as we know regarding the black hole in space. There is so much to learn from contemporary deeply religious sufferers, but first let us turn to understanding the influence of OCD on Western history.

We will briefly explore what we can learn from three classical leaders in the Christian tradition who had OCD. We will also learn how our history may have been influenced by their standard-setting work and OCD, and, finally, implications for contemporary religious issues that we can learn *from* OCD.

THREE HISTORY-BENDING SAINTS

Martin Luther

The first time I heard Martin Luther's name linked with OCD was at the 1996 OCD national convention in a lecture by Dr. Ian Osborn.[17]

Hearing that Luther suffered from scrupulosity in his monastic period, I was able to do 2 + 2 = 4 easily enough; multiple daily confessions + the whip he used on himself. It seemed appropriate to get out Erik Erikson's *Young Man Luther*.[18] It was the well-marked copy of a doctoral student, with one problem. Everything I underlined then makes almost no sense now. It is reminiscent of a quip that goes the rounds in medical circles. Two medical professors were talking. One said, "You know that half of what we teach today will be regarded as false twenty-five years from now." "Sure," said the other, "but which half?"

All those things that Erikson had to say about identity and personality development are valid points. But, while Erikson kept writing about Luther as being "compulsive," you can examine the text in vain for "scrupulosity," although this term was accessible to him in church literature. The truth was—and still is, to some degree— few mental health personnel at the time knew much more.

Just to take one illustration: Erikson makes several references to "the fit in the choir." This was apparently some type of sxizure when Martin was a monk and during which he cried out something like, "I am not!" Considerable speculation has been made about the episode. Current authors, such as Yaryura-Tobias and Neziroglu, can be easily researched on the association of seizures and OCD. After 350 years of panning for gold, scholars ought to find a mother lode in such knowledge and be able to correlate it with the dynamics of Luther and the Reformation period. There are quandaries yet to be resolved, such as Luther's relationship to sexual thoughts. Perhaps the "doubting disease," as the French sometimes call it, may yet throw light on other episodes related to Luther's suspected clinical depression or about a midlife crisis.

What is commonly known by Protestants about Luther starts with the nailing of the ninety-five theses to the door of the church in Wittenberg in 1517, and that high moment when he read in Romans 1, "The just shall be saved by faith alone" and, in the margin of his Bible, emphatically wrote *solo, alone.*

From what we know of recovering from OCD and learning to manage one's life instead of being managed by OCD, many factors led to Luther's dramatic grasp of salvation. He was part of a supportive group, the Augustinians, and continued to be surrounded by a supportive group after he left the order. He had a mentor in his superior, Dr. Staupitz, and thus an authority to whom to refer and measure doubts. In a letter to Luther, Staupitz inferred that he was not permissive regarding confessions of the trifles of scrupulosity.

What Staupitz *did* offer was humor. For example, when Martin (doubtless the perfectionist) complained that his mentor was "killing him" by demanding that he go for a professorship, Staupitz is reported to have replied, "That's all right; God needs men like you in heaven, too." The role of humor is not to be underestimated in working with the hamfisted, blustering bully we call OCD. Luther's therapeutic mentor won his trust and did two behavioral things that functioned as homework: he found ways to put him to work teaching and preaching. Neurologically, Martin's new career shifted him from the overintensity of the right hemisphere of his brain to the analytical and verbal left hemisphere.

In the chapter on theory (Chapter 7), more will be written about the potential effect of the evolution of the two hemispheres of the brain. This point is something to consider, knowing what we do about their functioning, and taking into account something else. Staupitz sent Luther to Rome (1510-1511) with a message as part of a delegation of two. My suggestion is that Luther was well on his way to successfully moderating his OCD prior to the trip to Rome. The trip functioned as a homework assignment to help confirm a process of effective treatment. Luther only spent a couple of weeks there, but what a couple of weeks they are likely to have been! The Renaissance Italians were reveling in color, forms, and shapes. It was a magnificent flowering of sensuous culture.

Luther apparently did the tour when he was in Rome. Tradition has it that he went to the steps taken from Pilate's palace where Jesus had trod, and murmuring a repetitious prayer on each step, he reached the top, straightened his aching knees (and probably psyche), and said under his breath, "The just shall live by faith alone."

This came at the time that is widely accepted as the low point of the papacy, the reigns of Sixtus IV, Innocent VIII, and Alexander VI, followed by the pope of Luther's time, Julius II. The popes had mistresses, and nephews were appointed cardinals. There were military adventures launched and assassinations carried out.[19] We may assume that Luther, like most clergy, had some ties to a church rumor mill; there was gossip. We cannot know what Luther's obsessions might have been, but the usual ones in OCD have to do with sex and violence. Perhaps someone with OCD can help those without it to understand what that visit would mean to Luther.

Under Sixtus IV, the Spanish Inquisition was established and scrupulosity given a rack and thumbscrews to use. Now there was an attempt to bring the Inquisition to Germany. With OCD, the "doubting disease," we can only empathize with what this must have meant to Luther.

Luther's visit came at a time when three popes had spent lavishly. The city of Rome had been vastly improved; the Vatican Library reorganized and expanded and the papal archives begun. Now the visual arts were magnificently patronized. One can stand in the Sistine Chapel and fantasize what the impact must have been on this Augustinian monk from "outback" Germany. Perhaps those with OCD who are compulsive shoppers and collectors can empathize with popes who, in effect, were buying with credit cards with what seemed an unlimited credit ceiling. Yet it all had to be paid, one way or another. One way was the sale of indulgences.

Luther the Scrupulous was in town with Pope Julius II, the Collector. As a big fan of Michelangelo and Raphel, Julius needed money for collecting. Indulgences were sold, big money for big guilt, real guilt. Luther had known guilt, a ton of tidbit here, tidbit there, tidbits of guilt everywhere, on his way to hell for every tidbit of sin. Those with scrupulosity can only attempt to describe this feeling to those who do not have it. He had beaten himself bloody and passed out on the monastery cell floor over those sensations of guilt. Here in Rome, forgiveness of guilt was on an international commodity market to cover the cost, among other things, of collecting. He had worked on his anxiety through years of homework assignments. It was enough to make a man start obsessing intensely again.

Looking at the last ten thousand years, it seems safe to assume the right brain is the older of the two hemispheres, dealing more in feelings and relationships. The left brain developed less quickly, reflecting its functioning in the service of reasoning, but it was highly developed in some admired thinkers in the world of the classical Greeks. After 1,500 years, with the fall of Constantinople, Greek scholars flooded into the West, bringing a rediscovery of "scientific" thinking. Universities were founded and flourished, scholars traveled, a printing press was invented, a merchant class grew. The European world was ready for an eruption of men of the left brain—given someone to lead them.

So this priest, who was dominated by the left hemisphere of the brain, returned to Germany to preach and to analyze theology. This pope, who was dominated by the right hemisphere of the brain, remained in Rome, loving and collecting beautiful art. A collision course was set, perhaps compulsively.

Ignatius of Loyola

For those first recognizing their OCD following some trauma, it will be easy to empathize with Ignatius of Loyola. He was in a military hospital; a physical wound led into a neurobiological one.

After Ignatius left the hospital, he entered a time of religious struggle. In his period of scrupulosity, he avoided stepping on straws that had fallen in the shape of the cross. Ciarrocchi regards this as a "transitory" type of scrupulosity, such as new converts sometimes experience. Yaryura-Tobias and Neziroglu regard Ignatius as more concerned with obsessions and as having a thought disorder or affect.[20] They interpret his obsessions as the sufferer's constant questioning of life. In his recovery from scrupulosity there was no reported use of Scripture; rather, he was able to make use of the traditional pastoral "standard operational procedures" developed by the Church.

Probably little has been written about how his OCD helped shape the Jesuit Order, but it undoubtedly did. Knowing that persons with OCD have above-average intelligence and avoid intense feelings, we might speculate that one dimension would be in the Order taking a distinctly intellectual direction. To an outsider, so many centuries later, it would be interesting to know if, in the formative years of the Order, there was an avoidance of our contemporary psychological query, "And how do you feel about that?"

Ciarrocchi summarizes Ignatius's treatment for scrupulosity as: (1) "do the opposite" (do what the OCD drives the person to avoid); (2) use a conscientious person, or persons, for a role model; (3) follow the guidance of a single spiritual director; (4) place yourself directly in the situations that trigger scruples; and (5) do not do the repetitious prayers or rituals or give in to compulsions.

To this it might be added that Ignatius divided the "touch-minded" and the "tender-minded" into distinct groups, for distinct approaches. One thing we learn from OCD is the tender-minded have loaded themselves already with a thousand guilty fantasies. It is spiritually distinctly unhelpful to them to load them with more, as Jesus remarked in condemning religious leaders who placed burdens that are hard to bear on struggling persons.

A mass-media preacher berating the "touch-minded" with the fires of hell is undoubtedly heaping those coals of damnation on the "tender-minded" at the same time. This is an outcome that, for most such preachers, would be quite unintentional. It would be an interesting piece of research to try to determine if more of the touch-minded are turned toward purity of heart or the tender-minded are plunged deeper into obsessing. Take, for instance, Jonathan Edwards, the colonial preacher and his most famous sermon, "Sinners in the Hands of an Angry God." We know what terror does to those vulnerable to anxiety, and he dangled people indiscriminately over the flames of hell. What effect did Edwards' preaching have on the people of his day? Is it possible to estimate how many "had the hell scared out them," or just *into* them?

As we close with Ignatius and go on to John Bunyan, let us note that both men were veterans of military service as well as sufferers of scrupulosity. The loss of a leg illustrates Ignatius's experience, while Bunyan offers only silence of serving for three years under Oliver Cromwell, but this is a silence a lot of combat veterans share. Three years under Cromwell in the English civil war of "Roundhead" against "Cavalier," resulting in Charles I's beheading, could give a man a lot to be silent about.

What a science fiction story it might be, however, if only veteran and OCD sufferer John Bunyan could have been transported from Bedford jail back in time to Ignatius's hospital. The two veterans could have shared and debriefed their combat experiences. Perhaps then they would have talked about their struggles with OCD. Perhaps they would have shared, as fellow Christians do in support groups, and maybe our civilization might now be different . . .

John Bunyan

To place these church leaders in perspective, Luther and Ignatius were contemporaries who lived during the period when Cortez was conquering Mexico. Luther initiated what became the Protestant state churches of northern Europe, with their nationalism and later capitalism. Ignatius was a Spaniard and his history is integral to the Roman Catholic Church and southern Europe: Protestant Reformation was followed by Catholic Counter-Reformation. Bunyan was English, a Puritan, someone we regard as a Free Church type, an early Baptist or Congregationalist. He spent a long time in jail because of the same opinions that brought a great number of folks to New England.

Without giving way to "the great man" philosophy of history, it should be noted that John Bunyan lived during a crucially formative time of Western history. It was the time of the murderous Thirty Years War (1618-1648), when church and state were as one and the rule was, as the prince went in regard to religion, so went his people. Colonists came to America for the same reasons some Americans went to Canada or Europe during the Vietnam War. Those new Americans had a core conviction: the separation of church and state. In many of their homes Bunyan's *Pilgrim's Progress* was on the shelf next to the Bible.

These immigrants evolved into a nation in which their descendants would shoot one another over slavery, but not over sacraments. Over the last 400 years the Europeans have worked out an accommodation between the political state and the established (and free) church. Americans have not. The discussion of the proper role of values in public school education and the ability of the religiously oriented not-for-profit social services continues to perplex our civic body. John Bunyan—seventeenth-century soldier under Cromwell, imprisoned for his faith—continues to influence the issues of our political campaigns. Of all the books in the world, the Bible is the most read; Shakespeare's plays and Bunyan's *Pilgrim's Progress* vie for second.

In Bunyan's *Grace Abounding to the Chief of Sinners,* the autobiographical first chapter makes the connection to OCD sufferings continually clear. On the whole, there are fewer possible allusions to his OCD in *Pilgrim's Progress,* until amost the end. It is interesting, however, to speculate on Christian and Faithful in Vanity Fair. There the merchants want to sell them various things, but the sole interest of Christian and Faithful is to "buy" the truth. If a person is afflicted with "the doubting disease," that is understandable. When Christian and Faithful refuse to buy—or buy into—other things, they are imprisoned in a cage. Their torment is interesting; Bunyan's time was a period of innovative means of torture. Christian and Faithful's torment was to be "besmeared" with dirt: a rather innocuous way of being tormented—unless the person has contamination fears. At length, they are faced with three accusers, one of whom is Superstition, that old enemy of those with OCD. No less an enemy would be Envy—or "normal" people, and of Pickthank, who robs the sufferer of appropriately being thankful for blessings.

It does make fascinating rereading of *Pilgrim's Progress* to go through the section on Doubting Castle, which seems to reflect experience with the doubting disease. In the index of one commentary, there is a subheading in which the imprisonment in Doubting Castle is listed as "a near-comic episode." Probably the commentary was written by one of those individuals who likes to say to someone with OCD, "Why don't you just snap out of it?"

Imprisoned in Doubting Castle by the character Giant Despair, we encounter the depression so frequently associated with OCD. Despair thoroughly beats Christian and Hopeful and even encourages thoughts of suicide. Despair's wife has an interesting name, "Diffidence," which may easily be equated with "unwillingness," "hesitation," "reluctance," and/or "doubt." It is she, however, who suspected that Christian may have a pick to the lock.

It is fascinating that a commentator on this escape from Doubting Castle, with absolutely no clue about OCD, should describe it as "when Christian obtains for himself and Hopeful their escape from Doubting Castle by simply remembering that as a convinced believer he has had the means of release from this spiritual malady of despair all the time in his possession." That the sufferer from OCD already has a lock pick by which to make his escape is an insight that lay and religious therapists who use the exposure/response technique will affirm.

> "What a fool," quoth he [Christian], "am I, thus to lie in a stinking dungeon, when I may as well walk at liberty! I have a key in my bosom, called Promise, that will, I am persuaded, open any lock in Doubting Castle."

The creaking of the gate as they open it awakens Giant Despair,

> who, hastily rising to pursue his prisoners, felt his limbs to fail, for his fits took him again, so that he could by no means go after them.

On escaping, they are almost immediately in the Delectable Mountains, cared for by waiting shepherds and almost to Jordan River (natural death) and entrance to the Promised Land. Prior to all of us having that experience, let us learn from Bunyan and his OCD.

It is interesting to read in Bunyan's *Grace Abounding* that the first hopeful passage has to do with promises. Unlike *Pilgrim's Progress*, where the role of "promise" comes late in the tale when Christian's trials and tribulations are almost ended, the hopeful promise is recounted in passage 65 (out of 264 numbered passages in the autobiography). Ravished by doubts, he was tormented by various Scriptures, but it was in the Apocrypha, the pragmatic Ecclesiasticus 2:10, that relief was initiated.

The explanation may be related to the forebrain's right and left hemispheres—of which we have heard and will hear more. Essentially, what we have in the most newly evolved portion of the brain, the forebrain, is a continuation of a differentiation of function into feeling and thinking. The right section may be said in a general way to deal with the subjective, the left with the objective. The person with a dominant left hemisphere would prefer a realistic painting; the person with a dominant right hemisphere would prefer an impressionistic one.[21]

Bunyan's OCD illustrates the conflict between the two hemispheres. On one hand, he would read about the love of God and salvation through Christ and logically come to a peace-giving decision. Then he would experience torment images from Scripture, such as his life was similar to that of Esau who had sold his birthright to his brother. Then he would cycle in doubt, a pendulum between the two hemispheres. Relief was initially begun, not through what he regarded as sacred Scripture, but with a quasi-authority, a pragmatic part of the "wisdom literature" such as Ecclesiasticus, appealing to right hemisphere and setting a counterweight *within* that side.

Next, several passages following, his wife serves as an ally. A pastor, Mr. Gifford, is mentioned and also a wise friend, only referred to as an "older Christian." Scriptures begin to be helpful as he centered on the commentary by OCD cosufferer Martin Luther in his work on Galatians: Paul seemed to know a lot about tormenting feelings. Now comes a new image, a right hemisphere image, that of the Cities of Refuge created to give sanctuary to those fleeing from retribution. It comes late in *Grace Abounding;* just as one would expect in OCD treatment.

The great relief is shared in the passage numbered 224 and it reads almost as if it were taken from St. Ignatius's *Manual* as the criteria for dealing with scrupulosity:

> And touching that in the twelfth of the Hebrews, about Esau's selling his birthright, though this was that which killed me, and stood like a spear against me; yet now I did consider, First, That his was not a hasty thought against the continual labour of his mind, but a thought consented to and put in practice likewise, and that too after some deliberation. Secondly, It was a public and open action, even before his brother, if not before many more; this made his sin of a far more heinous nature than otherwise it would have been. Thirdly, He continued to slight his birthright: "He did eat and drink, and went his way; thus Esau despised *his* birthright."[22]

This is the reasoned analysis so characteristic of the left hemisphere; it is a reasonable clinical hunch that what happened is that the two hemispheres were now allied in the struggle against the tormenting sensations of a primitive portion of the brain. More of this, of course, when we come to the chapters on theory and treatment.

IMPLICATIONS FOR TODAY

When we look at the seemingly insolvable problem of religious conflict in the Middle East between Arab and Jew (and no small conflict between Reformed or secularized Jew and the Orthodox), it may well be insolvable, just as we see similar difficulties in Bosnia and Northern Ireland. If the issue is like an iceberg, with politics above the water and neurobiological issues beneath, the structuralizing of hoarding and scrupulosity in religion, bonded to anxiety that has grown enormous through events of living history, perhaps there is no resolution. It is not just a matter of geriatrics, a new generation having a fresh opportunity; it is not just a matter of learning theory passing on custom and tradition; it is a matter of genetics. One issue is: Will the destruction of Jerusalem be recycled once again?

In the ecumenical dialogue between Lutheran and Catholic, a sticking point is the doctrine of justification: saved by grace or by works—reflecting institutionalized dynamics of an unresolved conflict between scrupulosity and hoarding. Perhaps God might play a little practical joke on both sides. In the June 1998 issue of *Scrupulous Anonymous* in the Dilemma Department, a letter writer raises a question:

> I was under the belief that I had to earn my salvation, I had to avoid mortal sin and live by the ten commandments. Your answers to previous questions have left me with the feeling that we can do what we please and God will give us salvation anyway. Have the rules changed?

The editor, a priest and expert on scrupulosity, responded:

> St. Alphonsus Liguori taught us, "Love God, and do what you please." In a sense then you are correct in your insight. However, what I was trying to point out is that salvation comes to us as a free gift from God. There is nothing that we can do, since we are not God, to claim a gift from God that is freely given. We can, however, follow God's Law and try to live our lives according to God's direction as a free and grateful response to God's gift of life and grace. We are not "earning" our salvation but we are gratefully participating in it. God bless you.[23]

Would not it be fun if such an expert in theology and OCD could chair the ecumenical debates? The proper question is, "What influence did Bunyan's OCD have on the course that Protestantism has taken?" It would seem there would be a shaping toward individualistic concerns at the expense of a sense of community. Obsessive-compulsive disorder scripted him to a preoccupation with spiritual self-exploration; *Pilgrim's Progress* was, intellectually, extraordinarily well done, but we need to ask, "At what expense to community, to *ethical* sensitivity, and not just personal rectitude?" Has the direction for some been of a vision of God as holy—a judge—over that of a vision of God as love—as compassionate?

I wish to offer a conclusion as to what I, at least, have learned from OCD in settling a historic theological controversy. When I was a boy, there was a continuation of an ongoing argument between Methodists and Baptists about "going on to perfection" versus "once saved, always saved." It can now be definitively said from the perspective of neurology and OCD—and a demonstration of the advantage of "neurotheologizing" as in Chapter 10—that *both* are true. There is no "cure" for what ails humans, and treatment is a matter of progressive modifications, of which there is no ending. On the other hand, once treatment has been successfully initiated, there will be lapses, but never going back as far as the original condition. Completion of theological discussion.

Finally, a note on the role of anger. We know obsessions come both in secular and religious forms. In the days of the Roman Empire, Cicero would close every speech with, "and, in my opinion, Carthage must be destroyed." So it is with scrupulosity; usually we observe it in its religious cloak, but not always, as we see it expressed in Cicero's politics. The period of early childhood will be associated with OCD in a later chapter. It begins with weaning, moves to concern with punishment and with rules; from there it moves to a need to please and perfect, and then to the oedipal period. It goes from basic family to a concern with the peer group, from internalization to externalization.[24] Then it is likely to be true, that what Cicero wants, Cicero gets.

When there is an intensity of feelings sufficient to produce scrupulosity, we have the potentiality of a profound shift in the feeling of torment: from self to others. We have heard the proverb, "Hell hath no fury like a woman scorned." I offer you an equal: "Hell hath no fury like the scorning of the self-righteous." The household of faith—or any other religion—is not immune at any time or place to the compulsion to become violent.

The public Show Trial has many historical examples, although twentieth-century media have made them highly visible, as in fascist and communist instances along with variations in Chinese "People's

Courts" and Kafka's novel. Each instance, whether in Elsewhere or Washington, can be recognized by its torturous obsessing over details in the effort to obtain emotional relief from compelled behavior; in all the play's the thing in the script of "Perfecting the Accused." In their *Oedipus Rex* subplot the settings range from the tawdry to the magnificent to even the Olympian. No religion seemingly is immune, and perhaps some contemporary fundamentalist regimes can be deemed spectacular. In the Show Trial scrupulosity across the world reveals itself most completely in its advanced and terminal form. In it the combination of the externalization of scrupulosity and the oedipal drama routinely reenacts the destruction of some father figure.

SUMMARY

Will Durant's section on civilization in his massive *The Story of Civilization* is magnificent in its grasp of the issues we are exploring. In describing the reasons for the decay of civilizations, he writes:

> Civilizations are the generations of the racial soul. As family-rearing, and then writing, bound the generations together, handing down the lore of the dying to the young, so print and commerce and a thousand ways of communication may bind the civilizations together, and preserve for future cultures all that is of value for them in our own. Let us, before we die, gather up our heritage, and offer it to our children.[25]

When we face up to the inferences listed here, they may well prove overwhelming. However that may be, when it comes to obsessive and compulsive repetitions, people with OCD have expertise in assessing what treatment can, and cannot, accomplish. In the next chapter, as we explore the lives of religious people with OCD, we will raise the issue of hope and what can be learned *about* OCD, but also what we may learn *from* it.

Chapter 5

Now It Is Our Turn

HUMILITY

I know. It is not easy to explain
Why should there be such agony to bear?
Why should the whole world be full of pain?
But then, why should her hair
Be like the sudden sunshine after rain?

Turn cynic if you will. Curse God and die.
You've ample reason for it. There's enough
Of bitterness, God knows, to answer why
The road of life is rough,
But there is glory in the sky.

I find it ever thus. I scorn the sun,
I con the book of years in bitter rage.
I swear that faith in God is dead and done,
But then I turn a page,
And shake my sides with laughter at His fun.

If life were only tragedy all through
And I could play some high heroic part,
With fate and evil furies to pursue,
I could with steadfast heart,
But my fine tragic parts are never true.

God always laughs and spoils them, and for me
He sets the stage to suit a human fool,

Who blunders in where angels fear to be,
So if life is His School,
I trow He means to teach Humility.

Rev. G. A. Studdert-Kennedy
British World War I chaplain
from *The War Poets* (1918)

When life is hard, depression often rises like fog when humidity and temperature are just so. The illusion of being far from God is as natural as the feelings of pessimism and hopelessness. Bunyan felt it, Luther, Ignatius, St. John of the Cross, and Jesus on the cross: the whole role call of the saintly. When you are down, however, if you are a believer you are not outside the Household of Faith, you are in it. Studdert-Kennedy wrote about it; you are about to read about it; about the time you are ready to give up, God gifts you a laugh. Given these factors, it seems likely we can learn *from*, as well as about, OCD. This is quite different from Karl Marx's "religion is the opiate of the people"—but then I suspect that, when his followers discussed this saying, the room was so filled with cigarette haze you could hardly see the vodka bottles.

Please use your experiences to compare with these stories. They are offered so you may give your considered judgment and form your opinions. For instance, this is obviously a self-selecting group who have chosen either to work with me or with whom I have related through a support group. They have representational qualities although many factors enter in: choosing me as a therapist, or willingness to come to what some would consider a WASP church to meet as a group, physical ability to come to sessions, and the opportunity to do so.

The seven persons asked to tell their stories were chosen based on the fact that they are genuinely religious. There are numerous case histories of OCD: Judith Rapoport[1] did a marvelous job of examining religious factors in this regard. Ciarrocchi[2] and Van Ornum,[3] from a Roman Catholic perspective, have added to this their studies of scrupulosity; persons suffering in this way, however, may or may not be religious. I have chosen a group differently: genuinely religious people struggling with OCD—some with, some without, other religious symptoms. I have taken care to present persons with a span of factors with regard to age, sex, and socioeconomic status. The stories are arranged in an order based on an evolutionary hypothesis of OCD.

The group starts with certain obvious advantages, if you regard them as "patients." They have resolved the issue Erik Erikson described in his works on personality theory as trust versus mistrust, so that all who are willing share their stories. They wrote their stories with little revision by me; obviously each is literate and intelligent. They have resolved the issue of "hope versus despair," as each has participated in treatment; each is able to relate to a peer group. Some would see in them a "wanting to please" and a "wanting to help." These elements seem to me to be presented as a "calling card" of their OCD. In their lives outside of their OCD experience (and given consideration to the effect of "symptom creep"), they live the main part of their lives in various developmental stages that do not reflect their obsessions and compulsions. I suggest the first thing we may learn from "wanting to help" reflects their religious commitments rather than a developmental stuckness.

NANCY: A CHAIN OF THREE

I proposed a draft outline; she returned hers. I had intended one direction, she took another; I think you will prefer her direction to mine. I met "Nancy" after her days of snorting "coke" were over, but another crisis had erupted; the last time we had met was when I called on her for Twelve-Step work some time back when we had a person with kleptomania come to the group. When I called her this time, she had just finished teaching Vacation Bible School at her church. When I received her draft, there was a note that began, "Thank you for the opportunity. It was a cleansing experience to pour out my soul . . ."

Nancy's Story

I first showed signs of OCD when I was about six or seven years old. I got into my mother's makeup like so many young girls do. I

[had] put more than my fair share of mascara on my lashes when I heard my mom pull up. I quickly put things away and tore at my lashes frantically to remove all traces of makeup. Well, since mascara is such a sticky substance, it caused my lashes to come out also. Needless to say, I got in a lot of trouble. My mom panicked when she saw that I had pulled nearly all my lashes out. The doctor reassured her that they would grow back in time. As they began to grow back, they were very stiff and caused a great deal of discomfort. I pulled them out again. I was obsessed. My parents tried everything: doctors, bandaging my hands, soaking my fingernails in Tabasco sauce, humiliating me in front of my family and friends, spanking—you name it. Nothing worked.

My mother was an alcoholic and eventually gave up on me. I was raised a Catholic and went to a Catholic school until fourth grade, and then my parents converted to Jehovah's Witness. A drastic change! I was a skinny child, anemic, frizzy hair, bad complexion, and no eyelashes! My childhood was a mess. I began using drugs at an early age.

I married at age seventeen, had my first child, and divorced, all in a very short time. I married again a few years later, this time to a man who quickly became a heroin addict. He was mean and abusive. We had two children and my ex-husband kept my first child in his care. My life got worse as time went by. By this time I knew I had OCD, but still hadn't linked it to other areas of my life. I had been stealing things for as long as I could remember. Usually things I didn't even want. I remember filling my empty purse with pencil top erasers and stealing them. Most of the time I would throw away what I had taken. As my second marriage fell apart, I began to use cocaine. It was always available since my husband was dealing drugs. Having OCD made it very easy for me to be addicted almost instantly, not to mention all those addictive traits my mother and her family handed down.

I remember vividly handing my four-year-old son and one-year-old daughter a peanut butter and jelly sandwich for supper and realizing that I had been feeding them the same thing for over four days. You see, cocaine is a powerful appetite suppressant and I wasn't hungry, so I didn't cook. I knew right then that I had to quit for my kids' sake. It was obvious to me that after three thirty-day rehab stays, my husband wasn't going to get clean. I had to get myself clean quickly, leave him to deal with his own addiction, and it appeared to me that I would have to do it alone.

As it turned out, I didn't do it alone, after all; God was with me the whole time. I got my own apartment, separated myself from everything and everyone that was linked with my old life, and devoted myself to being a better mom than my mother had been. After a couple of months I began to miss things—friends, companionship, and cocaine. I was cleaning house on a Sunday morning and ran out of cleanser. I packed up all three kids and went to the store. My kids were still in the clothes they slept in the night before and I was in my "scrub the toilet" sweat suit. I passed a small church and felt an overwhelming desire to stop in. I thought for sure I would get lots of dirty looks, but I didn't. I was welcomed by almost everyone. They told me of all the activities and programs for the kids and before I could say "Born Again," I was an official member of the Church.

That was the first chain of events that saved my life (and soul). My mom, the world's biggest hypocritical Jehovah's Witness, was not pleased. She had stopped drinking, thanks to hypoglycemia, Antabuse, and my dad by her side. She was a non-practicing Witness who would not come to my house during the month of December because I had a Christmas tree, as this was against her religion. Our relationship has always been rocky and I think it always will. My church filled a lot of empty spaces in my heart and made me realize that if I was sorry, and I turn to the Lord, I will be forgiven of my sins. In the following months, I did a lot of praying.

I still stole things all the time and the guilt consumed me. I never told my pastor of my problems because I was too embarrassed. In 1989 God sent me an angel. This began the second chain of events that changed my life—my husband, "Roy." Always understanding, never judgmental, loving, and good. My oldest son continues to live with his father most of the time but we have a very close relationship. My other two children lost contact with their dad as he was sucked into a fatal life of heroin. Roy adopted both children a couple years after we were married. I've been on a couple kinds of medications for OCD but before they had a chance to work I would go off them for financial reasons or because I was pregnant or nursing. Roy and I now have a total of ___ (thought this too identifying), plus my oldest son. Through all this, I had been stealing and still not linking it to OCD. Right after my marriage to Roy, we moved to a small town that he was from. I got a nice clerical job with a local family-owned business and Roy began to work for his father. It was a refreshing new beginning for me. We began to attend the church his father went to and it was like going home. I've never felt so comfortable.

Shortly after this, I began to steal money from my job. I would do it unconsciously, many times not even knowing how much I was taking. One day I found $1,200 in my purse. All stolen. I wrote my pastor a letter explaining everything. It was a huge weight off my shoulders. He called the next day and we began a plan to get help for me and also to return the money, even if it took five years. My pastor referred me to Dr. Collie, believing that I had kleptomania. Before too much could progress, I got caught stealing at work. It was the third chain of events that changed my life. As I awaited my court date, I continued my therapy with Dr. Collie and turned it all over to God. I couldn't handle it anymore on my own. My husband, the angel, stood by my side, as did my church. Dr. Collie helped me realize that my stealing was linked with OCD. In fact, I found out through my mother, my biological father, who died in a robbery when I was four, had left behind a warehouse full of stolen merchandise. Things he had kept for years and had no use for. I guess I got it honestly—pardon the pun! Dr. Collie and my pastor wrote letters to the court on my behalf. Dr. Collie explained the medical aspect of OCD and Pastor D explained that I had confessed to him prior to my arrest and was planning on repaying all I had stolen.

Well, to make a long story shorter, I got the maximum penalty. Weekends in jail, house arrest, probation, community service, restitution, court fines out of the ears, and worst of all, I had to face the family I stole from. The family that had trusted me and truly taken me in as one of their own. I did not try to get out of anything. I pleaded guilty and took what I had coming to me. When I finished the last of my punishments Roy and I had our last three children.

Between pregnancies and nursing (my youngest is now ___ months old), I am still not on medication. I still pull my eyelashes and still do things in threes, but I never steal and I never do drugs. I'm hoping to conquer all my tics eventually, but for now, I'm happy with the progress I've made. I never put myself in tempting situations. I don't know if I actually believe that this should all be blamed on OCD. I do know that it is my reason, not my excuse, for bad behavior. And I know that I have the Lord on my side. I pray with all my heart that my children never have to battle this demon but, if they do, we will win the fight together with the Lord, and maybe a little help from my friend, Dr. Collie. I'll never be on the cover of *Vogue,* but in a spiritual way I have never felt more beautiful. I'm a good mom, a faithful wife, and a grateful Christian. And after all, isn't that what it's all about?

*   *   *

In Nancy's story there are such mega-layers of meaning written that we can only wish William James were alive and ready to do a new edition on "conversion" in his *Varieties of Religious Experience.*[4] As for ourselves, we can merely bring to such a story whatever experiences each of us has.

There is, however, one issue for a considered opinion. In a fantastically rich country, by what stretch of mean-heartedness do we arrive at a national health care situation in which a mother cannot afford medications?

MARIE: THE GIRL GANG-TACKLED BY OCD

The federal referee who rejected Marie's appeal for Social Security Supplemental Income was not impressed by her combination of OCD and Tourette's disorder or by her father's medical disability. The teachers in Marie's school were much impressed when she submitted this essay in a national contest.

Marie's Story

When I was five years old, and was in kindergarten at Nebraska School in Mrs. Ford's classroom something different began happening to my body. I was not in control of my body anymore. I then knew I was different from the other kids in my classroom.

Mrs. Ford and my mother talked and decided it was best for me to visit my doctor. That really scared me because I did not know what was happening to me, or why.

My mom took me to my doctor, and he sent me to see a special doctor. The new doctor checked me out and then told my mom that I had Tourette's syndrome. He said I had no control over my body. He said my shakes were "tics" and this was something I would have all the rest of my life. He gave my mom a lot of books to read about Tourette's and gave me medication to take daily. What I remember most was my mom crying and knowing I would be different the rest of my life.

The next year my "tics" got worse. The kids in my class all noticed. They began to make fun of me, which made me sad and made my tics even worse. By now I had tics all over my body and I was taking a lot of medication and my new doctor told my mom of a hospital out of town that I was to go to.

That night my mom and dad told me that I was going on a small trip with them to Indy. The hospital was only for kids and the name was "Riley." My mom said they had doctors that treat kids for Tourette's and other illnesses, also. It was scary, but medication was not helping and I just wanted to be like the other kids in my class.

The next week was my trip. We woke up early, about 5 a.m. It took a long time to get there and I was carsick and my tics were very bad. My mom babied me and held me close so I could not hurt myself. We both said prayers in the car and when we got there.

My doctors were nice and I got to see other kids with Tourette's for the first time. I got new medication and that was the first trip of many more to come.

My schoolteachers were all very nice to me. They knew I was different but that was all right with them. I missed a lot of school and the kids were still making fun of me. I prayed nightly and my mom and I read a lot of books on Tourette's.

My mom and my doctor in Indy decided I needed to see another doctor here in town. He was a doctor I could talk to and tell him things that I only told my mom. His name is Dr. Bob Collie. He told my mom I also have OCD. He is a very nice doctor. He even comes to school every year to talk to my teachers. He talks to me a lot and is a very good friend to me, too!

My best year was when I was in grade three. Mrs. A. helped me so much. The kids still made fun of me but that's okay because I try not to let that bother me. I not only have Mrs. A. but I also talk to

Mrs. Neville at school, too, when I am having a bad day. (Mrs. Neville is the principal and always made time.)

My school has been very good to me and Mrs. A. and Mrs. Neville will always be special to me.

This year I am in the fourth grade. I once again have a good teacher. I still have my tics but I accept them now. My family and I have been through a lot but we pray every night. I know with God, my doctors, and my great teachers that I can do almost what I want. I try to control my life and not let my tics or OCD control it.

This is my story, my life. It happened to me. Thank you, Nebraska School.

* * *

There are several things to be added to Marie's story. One is that I was privileged to be a participant in the field trials of Dr. John March's "How I Ran OCD Off My Land."[5] Mapping was very useful, as was nicknaming Marie's OCD. She chose the "Devil" as the nickname and although I questioned that theologically and wondered about it psychologically, she wanted it and we used it. I was disappointed that Marie was rejected for the Social Security Supplemental Income (SSI). I suspected food stamps might not have always reached to the end of the month, but Marie never mentioned it and her mother never lost her dignity. Marie's father has since died. An unfortunate treatment reality was when we worked on the Tourette's the OCD went up and when we worked on the OCD and got that down the Tourette's went up.

The last school classroom visit helped a great deal. The peer relationships were bad and a concern both to faculty and family. It was decided that I would visit the classroom, both the present one and the class Marie would be in the next year. I did a talk on Tourette's such as you might see on a PBS-TV science show for kids. Marie sat on a high stool by me and answered questions. I explained what I needed as a therapist and asked for their help; they made a highly positive response and still are carrying through with it.

Marie's tics are in remission, but she checks; she and the family accept that. Her grades continue to be up.

As with many conditions, there is no cure. With all conditions *healing* is a part of the human potentiality, but how do we achieve this?

NANETTE JOYCE: A LOVE OF BEAUTY AND A COMPULSION TO HOARD

Her earrings were apparently chosen because they were strikingly pretty; they obviously hurt her ears. She was a person who, in school, had tested above the ninety-fifth percentile nationally in IQ. But, Nanette needed monthly help to balance her checkbook.

Nanette Joyce's Story

There was a stronger need than to keep it: when a person had no other place to stay, together they filled seven dumpsters from her two-bedroom home. Professional and carefully groomed, when she consulted a doctor about hoarding and shopping, shopping, shopping, he assured her she did not have OCD. She did not have OCD, rather, she was depressed. This was unquestionably true, as she was understandably reluctant to invite anyone inside her front door.

Childhood offered a zoo of issues. Adulthood was flooded with marital conflict; job changes were many. The vocational conflict was obvious: in a profession necessitating absolute attention to detail, the industry was pressuring for production. Consumers wanted it done right and done right *now*. The perfectionism and compulsive slowness were there to be seen; literally not seen were important papers at home because in hoarding everything is important—and consequently nothing is important. Nanette's life seemed like a soap opera to her, and it began early in life.

Nanette Joyce could never decide whether her mother was ineffective because she was so disorganized or disorganized because she was so ineffective. She could change any subject in midsentence. Nanette Joyce got the nonverbal command, Be Perfect. In retrospect, she thought it was part of a part of a message that said, Be Normal. Nanette's mother literally told her she was crazy, specifically, like one of the parents' sisters who was the one she regarded as the only person she would like to resemble. Jesus, of course, was perfect, and you had to be like Jesus.

What was not debatable was that she was abused. Nanette Joyce grew up with two images of her father: drunk and swearing that he was going to kill somebody, or sober with both of them loving their long, intimate conversations about how electricity worked and how the planets moved. Her family counted on her to be a peacemaker. She was valued as a good rescuer, with anxiety for a companion. The family was like a five-pointed star of adults, but fortunately for the little girl, at the top of the star was an aunt who loved beauty and who had money—enough money to send a favorite niece to college.

School life was not easy; she was brilliant but staying hidden was a lesson mastered. Consequently, the other kids thought her arrogant—farm kids who wanted to go to work, get married, have kids. She loved opera—she was her aunt's niece—and theater and good grades. High school was straight-line A's, but college was a zig and zag of A's and D's. She could not take notes fast enough and was too exhausted to get all the work completed.

She made it into a profession. Then disasters: one, then two, then three abusive husbands. "You've got to quit marrying these men!" said Mother. In retrospect, Nanette Joyce wondered how she came out alive. When all else failed, she could shop. And shop. She still has five hundred earrings, mostly unworn. She just stuffed *things* at home, stuffed *feelings* at work. Her boss could always count on a day off because a rescuer was always available to work an extra day. That kind of "stuffing" may be hidden at home; eventually not at work. There is an inevitable explosion of feelings.

Professionally it was, of course, very ragged. She would do very well, then get bored, and descend into chaos and job change. Two issues dogged her: having to be perfect so that no trite deed was left undone and the changing demands of the job market. Compulsive slowness and the ability to learn changeable computer systems are not compatible. Overworked themselves, bosses pressed for cost-cutting. Overworked and needing a day away, they called on overworked workers. It was a pattern that produced an explosion of anger that could astonish everyone, including herself.

Next came therapy. It was a time when sensitivity training and growth groups were in vogue. Middle-class therapists wanted to liberate themselves and others from what they perceived as stultifying middle-class values and customs. Nanette, however, as many others from a "low-class" background, did not need to "get in touch with her feelings." She was readily overwhelmed by them. The result was a hospitalization.

Procrastination slipped in slyly and seductively. It usually took the form of one of the "good old days" movies with large rounded skirts and lovely bonnets and lovely manners. . . . The fear she would be left with nothing—again—feasted on bags and boxes. The excitement of learning sent her the challenge that every paper and magazine has something interesting, if only there was time; "When I retire I will. . . . " "Insight does not produce change with me, but it was, with a jolt, that I realized that, if I am in a bare room, I get anxious; with all my clutter I feel more secure, strangely more like me if I keep all my old clothes as if they were somehow an identity. I love beauty, I need clutter. I want to do art; I have no time. . . . "

Procrastination is a seduction to be countered with the self-message: *Just do it*. It takes a stiff determination to march out to the dumpster with a bag. A support group asks about that sort of thing, you know. Perfectionism can be fought with a rational "good enough," balancing carefulness with turning out the work. Compulsive slowness was once considered; here the Americans with Disabilities Act becomes relevant, but one hint of that and she was gone again. . . .

In the midst of such a story, there is an underlying theme that unifies it, but which does not appear readily in the telling of it; it is in surviving and struggling that there is a deep sense of the religious. It is, however, as if this appears in parentheses, a nonverbal reality.

Nanette wrote her story in the third person and later added to it:

> People are always telling her [that] her thinking is wrong, yet that's the only thing she can really believe in. Despite her illness, she has survived; and other people's ways of doing things don't seem to work for her in her world. They bring disaster and undermine her self-confidence. Her eccentricity makes her feel unique. Most artists are eccentric!

* * *

To read this case story is to be overwhelmed by what we have known, what we already know, and what we will know: there are just so many stories in which the circumstances are unbelievably complicated. Not the least of these is when collecting/hoarding/shopping/procrastinating/love of beauty/intelligence/abuse (did something get left out?) are coexisting with, paralleling, developmentally higher religious feelings.

One of our difficult tasks is to learn to differentiate religious feelings from pathological dynamics in such a way that those feelings become religious commitments. These commitments can then enhance mental health rather than coexist with the pathology.

Referring to the developmental sequence identified with OCD, that of the child from age two to before being "school ready," this period is characterized by children who seem to be playing *along side of, rather than with,* each other. You will see this in a marriage where the couple are at this developmental level, as if they were two railroad tracks held together by the children acting as railroad ties. At about age three, a developmental stage appears that can have religious characteristics, but this religion appears as a separate role that coexists with other characteristics rather than being integrated with them. If the person has OCD and it exhibits itself at a developmental level earlier than three, religious potentialities will largely be submerged by the symptoms of the disorder. The person will have difficulty in verbalizing religious beliefs even though perhaps regularly participating in religious services. In the developmental stage of ages three and four, a lack of intimate interaction will occur with persons in reference to religion, although they will sometimes defer to religious authority figures. Whatever religious dynamics do exist, they lack integration by the person. Outside the OCD experience, however, the person may have a much more highly sensitive and developed religious belief/behavior system.

One of the techniques of a cognitive approach to this developmental level, in the context of OCD, is to help the person more adequately verbalize religious feelings, particularly in a group setting.

ANNE: WRESTLING WITH SHAME
AND GUILT—AND PERFECTION

The first time Anne came to group, she announced that she had a problem about "being stuck in a mirror." All the men in the group who did not suffer from scrupulosity could see why. Then she was quiet for weeks. I think she was deciding if she could trust the group.

Anne's Story

When I was little, I had a fantasy that I was an angel; the reality was that I was abused. Mother took us to church when she could; you may have assumed the next phrase was "and Dad drank." He didn't; he merely perfected bitterness as a lifestyle. I was quiet until the sixth grade. Years later, I experienced the frequent consequences of early abuse and I *really* experienced shame. When I married I know now what is called "mate selection" had all the unconscious motivations you read about, but I had no awareness then. It worked out about as you would suppose.

In the meantime, my father slithered gradually into a debilitating, insidious illness. None of the other kids were near, so I did my duty. His last week in the hospital part of that duty was getting a will signed. Everyone agreed how it read—and agreed I was to take it in to him. He took one look and demanded to know why I wanted him dead! Would you believe it, one of the sibs asked me later the same thing? Well, when the doctor thought I was well enough to get out of the hospital . . . but that is rushing ahead of my story.

I never feared death; when my father passed away I was there and felt God had answered my prayers he didn't have to die alone. Then the anxiety, phobias, and self-doubt spiraled in. We weren't Catholic but he died in a Catholic hospital and I had picked up prayer cards and used them. It began a habit and I would start the day with them. If it said "pray this prayer nine times and your prayer will be answered," I would; from that I started having fantasies about being a role model for peace and joy and serving humanity. . . . I really felt close to God. I was in church every Sunday morning and thought if I didn't repeat the Ten Commandments three or four times I would be condemned. Fortunately I started going to a women's Bible study group and began to learn about a loving God.

Then too many things happened. I had health problems. My best friend died. I felt God had let me down. I read the story of Abraham going to sacrifice his son, Isaac. How could a loving God . . . ? I began fearing for my daughter's life. What if God wanted me . . . ? I knew I wouldn't, but. I remember being in church and seeing the statue of Christ start to bleed. I was *so* frightened; I choked at communion.

I can remember praying for many months after that, "Please, God, let me get well." I kept going to church and to study groups: nothing was going to rob me of my soul or my understanding of One greater than myself. I had a fine woman therapist who walked me through, one who grasped spirituality. She taught me a technique I have never encountered since. When I feared a kitchen knife, in my imagination she taught me to turn it into a flower. It worked! It was she who also encouraged me to come to the support group. I will always be grateful to such a fine therapist.

If someone in the group asks about a medication, I usually have an opinion. If a newcomer shares a compulsion and if it seems appropriate to share, a dismaying amount of time I usually have an experience to offer, too. Ongoingly feelings erupt and they are there to be worked through; life is a learning tool.

In my woundedness, I have played my share of rescue games; I can separate those out now and I have found out in my woundedness I have a talent—and an independent confirmation—that I am good working with a particular kind of woundedness. What I have found is a purpose—wife, mother, worker, conqueror—but not a perfectionist. My OCD still kicks in some with the perfect person stuff. The "stuck in the mirror" thing? I've thought it over and discussed it with the group; it really is my style. It never makes me late to anything, just takes some time, but it is my style and I look good in it and feel good about it. Recently I just started going to my hair dresser a couple of times a month.

In fact—and this is what I have learned and for which I thank God: *I like me.* I have learned to differentiate inauthentic guilt— which was heaped on me by my family—from real guilt; some of this I learned from a therapist, some I learned from my church, some I learned as I have shared with the support group: *I like me and so do they and I like them.*

*   *   *

All too frequently we find "good" people getting into abusive relationships. One of our tasks in the Church is to help persons differentiate between being good and being masochistic. This will appear again, in the theological issues raised in the closing chapter.

MARY: THE LITTLE GIRL
WHO WANTED TO MARRY JESUS

No one would easily miss Mary in a group: tanned, tennis player, not a hair out of place, and sitting with poised perfection. She is The Wife of the CEO. Apply here for entertainment at dinner when corporate wheels need greasing. She carried it out *perfectly*—until her husband retired.

Mary's Story

As a child I was quite the performer: violin, dance, piano, and lots of the etc.

But I was different. I wanted to marry Jesus; from as long as I can remember religion has been important to me. My father was an alcoholic, never abusive, but he drank. Mother, I now realize after all these years, had OCD; she was a straightener. Today I know my OCD is genetic, but I learned how to express it from her, learned it very, very well. I grew up with applause, but never an "I love you."

It was natural that I sought approval as a teen. I wanted desperately to belong. By the late teens I had found my man to marry. A fine man, he carried himself like an officer and gentleman. Soon I was having babies and I loved it; the housekeeping was neat, but not overdone; it was a home where babies could grow up laughing. Then came promotions; an introduction to the corporate world and demands to be a well-functioning corporate wife. I could entertain and I could decorate. He did his thing well; I complemented it on my part.

Then came the perfectionism. It went from checking, to hand washing, to . . . to . . . the symptoms shifted. I can relate to lots of the stories in the support group. He was a great provider and later in life I could shop as one relief from stress. No one knew, however, I endlessly vacuumed the rugs. There could not be a line left on it, but that is getting ahead of my story, the part that finally came to light when my husband retired.

It was my need to be perfect that got me in trouble. I was a supermom; worse: I really was a Super Mom. I also was a professional volunteer and "did my thing" in the right charitable organizations. I began to feel crazier and crazier—not that anyone would know. I was a high energy person and everybody knew that; as my aunt would say, "Mary, you sure like to always have your dance card filled up!" I finally began to go to counseling. He tried the standard exposure/response blocking things, although he had no idea about my OCD, as I think back on it. I remember once he had me wear mismatched colored socks. In retrospect, I didn't stay in counseling long enough. He wanted me to go on some kind of medication; that wasn't for me—still isn't. I have always been a reader and I began to pour into the self-help books. I lost any interest I may ever have had in blame and shame. I still read and I have developed a great reading list. It is a poor group night that I don't have a title to recommend to someone.

Part of the corporate lifestyle is moving, moving on, moving up, another house, another chore of decorating the perfect house. Eventually I wearied of the social round and felt the need to be more open and vulnerable in a positive way. It became clearer to me God had a plan for my life and that He was in charge.

I was listening to the radio when I heard of an interdenominational women's Bible study group. I participated in it for over five years. It was so intense and magnificent I still have trouble describing it. The retreats were miracles of answered prayers in women's lives. There were peak experiences, mythical experiences, spiritual experiences. . . . I have had my "peaks," but I have had my share of the "valleys" of hurt feelings and resentments, too. I am determined not to camp on those.

I changed from the decorative wife and started being an outspoken, straight-on person. I may have turned off my religious radio programs before he came home from work, but there was no turning off the changes in me. Looking back, I believe I was guided and guarded from being overwhelmed by what was to come.

Part of that guided and guarded was a song on the radio, "It Is Well with My Soul." I heard it when I first heard of the women's group and continued to hear it. Once, when visiting my very difficult mother on vacation, I just had to leave. I rejoined my husband and he was beautifully supportive. Then I turned on the radio and—was it providential?—they were singing.

> When peace like a river, attendeth my way,
> When sorrows like sea billows roll,
> Whatever my lot, Thou hast taught me to say,
> It is well, it is well with my soul.

Another time, there was a terrific storm on a lake when we were in our cottage and I panicked. Was it providential that I turned on the radio? I began to have a sense of Providence, of acceptance and peace. The song never spoke to my OCD, but my mother and I reconciled.

When my husband retired, it was a shock to him to discover what I was doing. I had been the kind of housekeeper that a loving gift for Valentine's Day would have been *two* vacuum sweepers; I could wear out that many a year. I did it without having missed a point in all the other things: fixed the kids' problems, solved the friends' marriages, volunteered for this and that—and just made up for it by working the two-vacuum-cleaners-a-year system in and around that schedule. . . . Retirement was, shall we say, "a problem" with a husband off The Board Of and The Commission For and around for lunch.

We moved to be close to the grandkids. Then the deaths in the family began. It climaxed with a tragedy worse than I could have ever imagined. The teenage grandchild was killed who was the closest friend to me in all the world. Fortunately, I had been in the support group for a year and had developed a real bonding or I probably would have followed my grandchild and friend to the grave.

In the year that followed, I was not troubled by my OCD, but I needed the group and they were always ready to hear me. I probably ranted and raved and I certainly gave God a piece of my mind! I kept active in my church as always, but it was with the group I could pour out my heart. So many others just kept intimating, "Aren't you over it *yet*?" After all, it had been weeks and even months. . . . My temper was pretty bad. Thank God for the support group!

I'm back doing some OCD expose/response blocking work again in the group. I love to paint, but I have to clean my pallet again, and again, and again. I spend more time cleaning than I do painting! So my focus group self-assignment this last week was not to clean the pallet until I had finished art class. The group joked and someone told me I probably ought to frame the pallet, it might be prettier than my painting . . . those folks are just terrible.

So tonight is the Academy Awards and I need to get gone so I can phone my granddaughter on the Coast. She and I are going to watch the Awards together while on the phone. . . .

*   *   *

OCD is such an attention getter. It is hard to keep in mind that it does not eat up twenty-four hours a day; if a person does needle-point, that would make a good framed saying to hang above the fireplace. "Life is not only more than OCD, it is larger. Life goes on, and you may be sure it will call your attention to its larger reality."

The task of managing OCD so that it does not manage you requires that you maintain your perspective, the larger values we have. No one can afford to win the battle of symptom suppression while losing the war for developing the qualities of mind and heart needed to meet the inevitable larger challenges.

LOU: THIRTY-FIVE YEARS IN THE DARK

Walking past his table at a national OCD convention "Lou" is an easy "read": iron-gray hair, smooth conversation, with an after-dinner cigar. Businessman, manager, good family man, taxpayer, churchgoer, undoubtedly voted by upper management as least likely to get downsized by anyone who values customer relations.

Lou's Story

The Church has always meant a lot to me; I was an altar boy. Growing up, my mother was distant and my relationship to my father was bad enough I hated him. In retrospect I can't identify a trauma or buildup of stressors that led to the outbreak of OCD, as most group members can. I was a sophomore in college. Suddenly I was obsessed with the hand brake on the car. I released it, tested it, released it; I couldn't believe it was really off. That was the beginning of thirty-five years in the dark of what was tormenting me. I was bewildered between feeling I was crazy and knowing I wasn't.

Scruples came next. I couldn't look at the picture of a woman with a plunging neckline without going to confession. When I was in the service the others nicknamed me "Bishop," little wonder because I was always throwing the girlie magazines in the trash when I found one. A casual glance at a television commercial with a beautiful woman would become torment. My wife regarded me as a saint.

Not so for me. I had a compulsion causing me to spend twenty minutes in the rest room testing whether my zipper was up before I could come out; it was misery. I went to a psychiatrist, paying big bucks for those days. He sat there for five sessions and never said a word. That was enough for me; he didn't have any more idea what was wrong than I did.

There was a book that did begin to help me. I found a review of it in "Our Sunday Visitor" and ordered it. It was a self-help book by a Jesuit priest written in Nicaragua, of all places. He wasn't writing on OCD, but he was writing on the theme of religion and behavioral medicine in the treatment of fears: and that was the early fifties! He quoted St. Ignatius' "do the opposite" again and again. He combined it with "conscious sensations." I practiced them and disciplined my sense of reality with them. I slowed my hand as I checked: I moved my arm slowly, I felt my fingers as they touched the gas turn-off on the stove; I looked and I listened and I felt . . . slowly, slowly, striving for full awareness by all my senses. If that strange OCD distress came over me as I walked, I deliberately became conscious of every step, aware of the ground as I stepped, the sensation of feet and of leg muscles. I observed the clouds in their whiteness and the sky in its blueness. I intensely listened to a train whistle or the passing of a car. I smelled the air.

This Jesuit taught me to use my mind to draw imaginary figures in the air and I would spend real amounts of time drawing those figures in my imagination or with a pen in the air: tracing the outlines of a house or a star or some other illustration he provided, disciplining my mind. I have read St. Ignatius' *Manual,* but it didn't help me, but when that Jesuit priest combined aspects of it with behavioral modification techniques, it did.

Earning a living was tough: a salesman on the road with a compulsive need to check whether I had run over someone every time I backed the car up. There were mouths to feed, though. Today, however, when I go on the road I enjoy the driving.

There was a priest at Seton Hall who was a big help to me with my scrupulosity, although I still was in the dark as to what was wrong. He told me to take his conscience and make it my own when I was in doubt as to the right and wrong, to act and believe as he would.

The biggest help to me, though, was the tradition of the Church as to what constitutes a mortal Sin: (1) it has to be a serious matter, (2) sufficient reflection, and (3) it has to have the full consent of the will. I found the intrusive thoughts might be of a "serious matter" and sometimes preoccupied my mind, but they *never* had the "full consent" of my will, and therefore never a *mortal sin.* I have shared those criteria many times with members of the Support Group and I feel it has been very helpful.

A helpful thing I have done is I volunteered to be the reader at the worship service in my local church. It was both a challenge to my fears and doing something I have always enjoyed, worship. I do a good job as a reader and people in the congregation tell me so and that means a lot to me.

It was Dr. Rapoport's book *The Boy Who Couldn't Stop Washing* that finally closed my thirty-five years in the dark. I knew other people had these kinds of trouble, too! It was a marvelous relief . . . half the battle. My doctor and I talked about my OCD and he knew a counselor who was hoping to start a group. I was one of the first members of the OCD support group here. Since then I had never stopped reading about OCD—but I still keep that book by the Jesuit priest by my bed. It's so worn you can't see the title on the cover, but I still read in it: Irala Narciso, S. J., *Achieving Peace of Mind.*

Dr. Collie asked me to join another OCD sufferer, a pastor, and himself in giving an interview for the newspaper to help for a support group. Then it was a television interview; I left the office thirty minutes early to make sure I got there. I've had some experiences with lateness and my OCD! These were just the first of a number of experiences of going public.

Some people have asked me about my experience with this. I had shared with my wife all along about what I was experiencing; she shrugs and says she doesn't see how it has mattered. I did get her to come to a support group meeting once, but Dr. Collie told me she said to him she didn't know why she had come, as I was the world's best husband anyway! I told my kids about three or four years ago; they didn't seem to know how to respond; one or two have said they remember some incident when they were young that puzzled them about me. At the office, they all know now.

I used to worry that I might have passed my OCD on to the kids, and it has shown up in one. When she said she had multiple clocks in the bedroom, I knew. I went down with some books and a video I borrowed. She will never be in the dark; she also responded with relief to the video that she wasn't *that* bad off.

I have thought maybe I've missed a promotion or two in my years with the company, but from my perspective today, it doesn't matter; I'm satisfied with how things have turned out. In fact, they have asked me to stay on after retirement. I live a pretty normal life now. If a pretty woman walks past, I notice; I don't think I would be normal if I didn't. But I don't sin.

What have I learned? Just what I have said many times in the support group: *it is the behavior modification that does it.* Bite the Bullet!

*   *   *

All parents with OCD dread that it will be passed on to their children. What we have to learn is how to respond to this fear—and perhaps this reality—in appropriate ways.

PAUL: POET LAUREATE OF OCD

Norman Rockwell would have achieved a classic piece if he had sat in a group with Paul. Tall and thin, wearing a baseball cap and scuffed tennis shoes—semiretired and straight from his job—Rockwell would have done a cover for *The Saturday Evening Post,* bringing joy to all. It was not the visual image, however, that authenticated Paul to the group. It was the voice, vibrant with the straight-on, relevant lore of Alcoholics Anonymous applied to a sufferer with OCD that riveted attention. Here was an empathy coming from years of struggle and spirituality, climaxed with a wit that soared group laughter to vertical and horizontal dimensions.

Paul's Story

Like many who have found themselves with OCD, childhood for Paul was pleasant:

> Time was
> When we were young
> On Third Street,
> And you and I
> (Brown as berries)
> Ambled down the avenues of summer,
> Watching tall clouds
> Perched on green hills,
> And we dreamed dreams
> Of things beyond those hills.
>
> Time was
> When we were young,
> We scuffed our way
> Through wet November leaves
> (Tucked deep in fuzzy new sweatshirts)
> Dreaming turkey dreams;
> Dreaming mince pie dreams,
> Fingers numb,
> Tossing the cold football.

Time was
When we were young
We whizzed down our alley hill
Through December depths of snow,
Old Silver Streak creaking
Laughter rang
In this icy plenitude of white.
Hours whipped by
Swift as sleds,
Until at last,
Twilight,
Yellow windows,
And snow,
Icy blue with shadows,
As we two,
Painted white,
Trudged home to hot chocolate,
When we were young.

Time was
When we were young,
It was spring,
And we picked our way
Down alleys full of light,
Looking for precious junk
To build things.
Bumblebees and hollyhocks,
And feet
Scraped raw by cinders,
But we cared not
For it was spring
And we
Could not die
Or grow old
When we were young
On Third Street,
Time was.

As many persons retrospect their childhoods, however, there were stressors, although not associated with OCD. Even when young, Paul had a sense of the sacramental:

> Healer of sore throats,
> Number of toothaches,
> Quieter of fevers
> And other vague ailments.
> Ah,
> The power of ice cream!
>
> Hail to thee, Peach Melba,
> Butter Brickle, Pistachio,
> And 33 other flavors.
> Another scoop, another nickel.
> Lick it up, let it trickle
> Coolly down your throat.
> Ah,
> The power of ice cream!
>
> I remember once when I was four,
> I was going to kill myself,
> But Mom said, "First have some ice cream"
> And I did,
> And I decided not to kill myself.
> So I'm here today,
> Saved
> By the power of ice cream!

Paul remembers parochial school with pleasure:

> Is the chalk still squeaking there,
> Dust upon the teacher's chair?
> The clock slow ticking on the wall,
> As children dreamed of playing ball.
>
> Boy in knickers, stiff and straight,
> Spring fell down, we could not wait

> For the chime of recess bell,
> Penny candy, and the smell
> Of lilacs from old Norman's yard.
> Hit the ball, Tom, hit it hard!
>
> All the girls of memories,
> I recall on gentle breeze.
> Ah! First love as bright as snow,
> From dusty recollections grow.
>
> Now I grow old, and I grow lame,
> The final inning of the game,
> And as I tread this silent hall,
> Bright pictures pasted on the wall,
> Sweet memories, I now recall
> Of brighter days; the Golden Rule,
> And of dear friends at P.B. school.

Those who have read *Brain Lock,* Jeffrey Schwartz's fine book on OCD, will recognize his "fourth step" at work, "What's it all about?" as Paul reevaluates his life and celebrates the values he learned in a parochial school.[6]

But all was not well. Scrupulosity came and with it such sensations as stealing dirt on his shoes from the yards he walked across. Later came self-medication with alcohol because of the cyclical torment and finally recovery. Then came retirement and the eruption of his OCD. Paul and I came to know each other as a referral from partial hospitalization. As part of his treatment Paul was encouraged to join the OCD support group, and especially to continue writing poetry about his experience with OCD as a way of exercising both hemispheres of the brain. Paul's humor is not for the fainthearted:

> On Sunday nights we go to Church,
> On Tuesday nights we're free.
> On Wednesday nights it's bowling time,
> But Monday nights it's OCD.

On Thursday nights we watch TV
And drink a little beer.
That's what we do on Thursday nights,
But Monday nights we're here.

Each Friday night we mow the lawn
Or shovel snow, my dear.
We're always busy Friday nights,
But Monday nights we're here.

Saturday it's time to howl.
We stay out too late, I fear.
It's party, party, party time,
But Monday nights we're here.

Why do we come on Monday nights?
There's no ifs, ands, or buts.
We gather here on Monday nights
'Cause people think we're nuts.

So you may call us weird,
But we're really not too crazy.
Sometimes we may grow too tense,
And even sometimes, lazy.

Some of us can't stand
To look too close in a mirror,
But though we have a busy week,
On Monday nights we're here.

A few of us pull out our hair;
Do other things that are queer,
Like counting cracks in sidewalks,
So Monday nights we're here.

Some people stare at us,
In fact, they really leer
When we try to lock our cars,
So Monday nights we're here.

And when we sit and listen
To each other's talks of woe,
A way of hope will glisten
And we bask in friendship's glow.

It's awfully nice to be here,
To rid ourselves of fright,
So don't forget to come here
Every Monday night.

The poems were partly autobiographical and partly poetic license, of course:

Boris Becker was a really nice guy,
He loved kids and dogs and Mom's apple pie.
He went to church, put money on the plate,
And for appointments, he was never ever late.

But he had a problem, did our Mister Becker,
For you see, Mister Becker was a checker,
And he never had time for girls and such
For he was checking, checking too much!

He checked in the morning, at noon, and night;
Checked the dog's teeth, making sure they could bite.
He counted all the weeds, the stones, and a boulder;
Made sure thermometers would tell if it's colder.

He checked the locks and the socks
To be sure they were working,
And even the coffee pot
To ensure it was perking.

He then went to the bank
To check all the checks,
And down to the market
To count chicken necks.

Then he sailed to Hong Kong,
Did our Mister Becker,
Where he became famous
As a Chinese checker!

He checked all the foodstuffs,
The children, the ham,
And down by the river,
Checked cracks in the dam.

He checked and he checked
Each cranny and nook,
And wrote it all down
In a large leather book.

Poor Boris was tired; really worn out,
And soon it was time for him to check out.
But the diggers made an unseemly blunder,
For Boris the checker was just five feet under!

Each week's meetings became the inspiration for next week's poem:

Mary McBride just didn't like germs
That dwelt on toilets or inside of worms;
That hung in the ceiling in awful gray clumps,
And hid in the corners in messy brown humps.

She fretted and worried
They'd make mankind sick,
Destroying each Harry
And Tom and poor Dick.

So she got a scrub brush, some Spic and Span,
Saying, "I'll save each woman and man."
She cleaned every corner of every room;
Even washed ceilings down with a big soapy broom.

But the broom got dirty so she took it outside
And the wind blew the germs, really gave them a ride
All over the lawn, alas and alack,
From the front yard to way in the back.

Then she had to wash the flowers and trees,
And even behind the ears of some bees.
She cleaned cats and dogs from their head to toes;
Even squirted some birds with a garden hose.

But she didn't stop there, no she did not,
For the germs had spread to a nearby lot.
They kept on spreading, billowed and curled
'Til they infected our entire world.

By now Mary was tired
But she wouldn't give up.
She said, "I'll clean those germs
From each saucer and cup.

And those germs left over, I'll send to a planet
That's far, far away and made mainly of granite."
Then she loaded those germs on a very big rocket,
Even one last little germ that had hid in her pocket.

But this story has no happy end
For you know what Mary did, my friend?
She started to worry about the big planet
Thinking that folks might live 'neath the granite.

The moral of this story is you can't escape dirt.
There's germs in your pants and germs in your shirt.
So don't flee from those germs on the table or wood,
For germs are like people, some bad and some good.

Group members began vying for whose favorite flavor of OCD
got the next poem:

There once was a man
Named Barnaby Cox
Who had obsessions
With all kinds of locks.

"Look here, my dearie,"
He said to his wife.
"This lock is so strong,
It will last all my life!"

Now Barnaby smiled
But it didn't last long
For he thought to himself,
Those crooks might be strong.

So he thought till he knew
What he really should do.
He got one more lock;
Lock number two.

But Barnaby fretted
And said this to me,
"Two locks are good
But better, is three!"

And he didn't stop there.
Oh, no, he did not.
He kept adding locks
'Til he was tired and hot.

And the locks were so heavy
They pulled down the door
And squished poor Barnaby
Quite flat on the floor.

Now Barnaby lies
In the ground, cold and still,
Alone by himself

> On a bare windy hill.
> And now all the weeds
> Much higher have grown,
> But you can still see
> The locks on the stone.

Special occasions were special opportunities for Paul to exercise his gifts:

> 'Twas the night before Christmas
> Full of candles and holly,
> And the OCDs were waiting
> For their friend, Dr. Collie.
>
> While I in my kerchief
> Checked faucet and lock,
> And looked for some holes
> In my red Christmas sock.
>
> Susie was checking
> The reindeer for germs,
> For parasite fleas,
> And even earth worms.
>
> Others were outside
> Washing the lawn,
> Working quite hard.
> They'd been there since dawn.

Of the qualities that make for maturity, perhaps the chief is a sense of humor.

> All of us sickies
> Were really quite busy
> Running about
> 'Til we were dizzy.
>
> When out on the lawn
> There arose such a clatter,

I sprang from the couch
To see what was the matter.

When what to my wandering
Eyes did appear,
But one old psychiatrist
With rented reindeer.

And he gave them a nod
And a twist of his head,
And said to all of them,
"You've nothing to dread,

For I've brought you some Luvox,
Some Prozac and stuff
To give you Christmas cheer
If you're feeling too rough."

Then he passed out the presents,
The pills and some clothes,
And giving a nod
Up the chimney he rose.

But I heard him exclaim
As he drove out of sight,
"Just take all those pills,
and you'll sleep well tonight!"

Self-pity gets little tolerance in a support group, naturally:

If only my wife was a bit better looking.
If only she'd take some more classes on cooking.
If only she'd have sex every night.
If only hornets and bees didn't bite.
Then I'd be happy.

If only morning didn't start so darn early.
If only my boss wouldn't be so darn surly.
If only the world would just wait on me.
Then I'd be happy; happy as can be.
If only!!

If only my kids wouldn't make such a racket,
I could get through the day; I know I could hack it.
But they don't seem to know I need peace and quiet,
And I can't take a snooze when they're starting a riot.
And I'll make a point when I stop to say,
What's the matter with those kids today?
If only!!

If only my dog wouldn't poop on the floor.
If only my cat wouldn't scratch on the door.
If only they'd all just sleep thru the night.
If only they'd not give the mailman a bite.
Then I'd be happy!!

If only my kitchen and bathroom were clean.
And if only God weren't so darn mean.
If only my wife would write me a letter.
If only I'd lived my life a lot better.
Then I'd be happy!
If only!!
If only!!
If only!!

Group process is easily identified in Paul's poetry as in this poem he wrote on hypochondriasis:

Oh, there's a nasty rumor
That you likely have a tumor,
And they say your tongue is red
So you'd better go to bed.

Here, I brought you this begonia
'Cause I heard you have pneumonia,
And I thought a gift of flowers
Would cheer you through these trying hours.

What's that? You say you have bad sinus.
Well, that surely makes you feel minus
'Cause it likely hurts when those things drain,
And it always happens when it rains.

You say you're scared of getting pregnant.
Well, here's what my good doctor said.
He told me, "Just take these two aspirins
And never go to bed!"

But hey, you think you've got it tough.
Look at me, my lot is doubly rough.
Last week I had to battle
A virus from Seattle,
And then some mangy cattle
Gave me hoof and mouth disease.

Then my kids came down with mumps,
And my skin had funny bumps,
And the rats came from the dumps
Carrying a load of fleas.

And some germ through strange osmosis,
Gave me hives and halitosis,
And grass pollen made me sneeze.
So even though you have a tumor,
And it's really not a rumor,
Put those pills back on the shelf
And don't think just of yourself.
I've said it once, I'll say it twice,
Compared to me, you've got it nice!

One poem seemed to catch the spirit of a number of meetings:

> There's a recession in Hell,
> For evil's not selling,
> And even the brimstone
> Is getting good smelling.
>
>
> They're gnashing their teeth
> 'Cause they closed the strip joints,
> And larceny's down
> By almost twenty points.
>
> They're wailing and weeping.
> They're really feeling glum
> 'Cause some nice old lady
> Gave dough to some bum.
>
> So they ponder sadly,
> Wringing hands and lament,
> For nobody's stealing;
> Not hardly a cent.
>
> So perhaps you could help
> Those devils in Hell,
> And just sin a little,
> They'll say, "Gosh, he's swell!"
>
> For recessions cause grief.
> They make you perspire,
> Especially when sitting
> On top of a fire!

Part of that "recession" was a good priest with whom I had worked for many years. He addressed the scrupulosity in an effective and classical form with Paul, but, naturally, with this spin doctor of lay theology, it would come out like this:

I used to be God,
But I'm not anymore,
For to tell you the truth,
It made my brain sore.

It was always a hassle
From Tom, Jane, or Dick,
Who nagged about weather,
Or their dog, Rick, who got sick.

They blamed me for fires,
Windstorms and flood,
And all of the germs
That invaded their blood.

They all prayed for big cars,
Big houses and such,
But did they strive for them?
Well, not very much.

So I said to myself,
"Being God's a hard task.
They're not very grateful,
And mainly they ask."

So I decided to put
My crown on the shelf,
And quit playing God
And just be myself.

And I'll say it again,
As I did before,
"When you try to be God,
Your brain gets too sore."

The control of others is, of course, as much an issue as control of
oneself and concerned him:

When your judgment time has come,
What will your Maker say?
Will He total up the sins
That plagued you every day?

Will He add the sums of money
In your collection basket,
Or will He fix you with His eye
And go ahead and ask it;
A question that we all should know:
Did you let another grow?

Did you back off just a little?
Did you give your family space?
Did you let your children run
Through life at their own pace?

And though you gave them many jobs;
To cut and prune and mow,
Did you hold the reins so lightly?
Did you let your children grow?

Did you spend a little time
With your husband or your wife?
Did you take the time to hug them
And thank them for this life?

Did you touch them with emotion
As you did once long ago?
Did you listen to their questions?
Did you let your spouse grow?

For in giving, we receive;
A fact that's really so,
And when you give your love away,
You'll find that you will grow.

Self-esteem is always a group, as well as a personal, issue:

> Look at that building,
> So great and so tall,
> With fine looking bricks
> A-lining the wall.
> Those fine looking bricks
> Way up in the air,
> But somehow, you see,
> It doesn't seem fair,
> For nobody mentions
> The bricks on the bottom,
> But think for a bit;
> Be glad that you got 'em.
> For without the bricks at the bottom,
> Those down in the earth,
> The whole building would topple,
> And it wouldn't be worth
> Very much, and the whole thing would fall,
> Then those top bricks
> Wouldn't stand very tall.
> So each brick is vital
> In its right space,
> Doing its job,
> Secure in its place.
> And we are like bricks,
> A foundation for others,
> Supporting our sisters,
> And holding our brothers.
> So it's not important
> Where you are on the wall,
> If we all do our job,
> Then the building stands tall,
> So rejoice in each brick,
> Be glad that we got 'em.
> And be sure you recall
> The bricks on the bottom.

While religion is not often a formal theme in a group, the theologizing is clear:

> I've made lots of lists
> Of things that I missed,
> But I never made
> A gratitude list.
>
> I've writ' grocery lists
> For carrots and lettuce,
> For cookies and cakes
> That mother would get us.
>
> Each Christmas I penned a list to Saint Nick,
> Of gifts that I hoped
> He'd bring really quick.
>
> So it's plain to see
> That I've been rather rude,
> Not making a list
> That expressed gratitude.
>
> So I say thanks for food,
> For peas in a pod,
> For steak and for cake,
> And, of course, for God,
>
> For puppies and children,
> For sunrise with dew,
> For roses in Summer,
> And, of course, for you.
>
> Now I'll stop today
> But I really insist,
> You should never finish
> A gratitude list.

A great many could echo "We":

> It's nice to see the rain this morn.
> It's pelting hard about,
> For all the lanes were dusty,
> And the flowers had a pout.
>
> But now the birds are wheeling
> Thru a sky washed clean and blue.
> See the tomatoes and the roses.
> Let's take a walk, we two.
>
> There's a splotch of crimson color
> On the maple tree next door.
> Oh, come and call the kids to see.
> Let's take a walk, we four.
>
> I think the dogs would like it, too.
> They'd love to chase some sticks
> And gambol on the dewy hills.
> Let's take a walk, we six.
>
> Oh, God is in His Heaven,
> The day will turn out great.
> I'd best invite the neighbors.
> We'll take a walk, we eight.
>
> And then I'll call my OC friends.
> Before, I hadn't any,
> But now I do not walk alone.
> I take a walk with many!

*   *   *

Paul's gift illustrates what is difficult to learn and impossible to teach: humor. All therapists recognize it as a tool par excellence, yet its grasp exceeds our reach. To the "gifts of the spirit" Paul lists in his Letter to the Galatians, some evangelicals have added "the gift of hilarity." Who cannot help but celebrate that?

Frequently a measure of compensation is found in inequalities. For example, the blind have other senses that enhance, or a missing limb can result in another being strengthened. In all the suffering of this world, the one gift we would all cherish is the compensation that Paul has cultivated: the gift of laughter. For that, let us thank and beseech the Giver of all true gifts.

WHAT WE CAN LEARN FROM OCD

We undoubtedly agree on what we already know: being religious, as any reader of the book of Job will assure you, does not consequently give a person a "bye" with OCD. Genetic factors play a role, as strep infections in early childhood may do, or lesions to the brain. Evolutionary factors, such as mammalian patterns of repetition, are a given with which many persons have to deal as a part of their suffering. Religion, as we have read in these stories, can provide motivation and staying power.

We had one of our most interesting group sessions on an evening when the group came prepared to answer the question, "What have you learned from your OCD?" The question still lingers and answers still trickle out. Let me share two with you, as both of these persons are profoundly religious. "Anne": "I have learned to value my feelings." "Paul": "I have learned to appreciate my wife."

One thing I think I can say on behalf of us all is that we have learned the religious irrelevancy of medication. Religion has its best chance to flower in a sound mind in a sound body. If it requires a medication to create that condition, let it be regarded as a gift of God. If it appears to be the only way to break through a biological barrier to that soundness, let it be regarded as an agency of God.

As we reflect upon these case stories, we recognize that in any group of seven individual studies of OCD it will undoubtedly be illustrated that religious teachings have been a mixed blessing. It has sometimes provided torment—and then strength for the tormented. What needs to be learned is to separate the sheep from the goats of religion. We need to identify both the teachings in the various traditions that are truly helpful and those teachings—however well-meant and once relevant—that have outlived their usefulness and need to now serve their time in the landfill of church history.

In the matter of learning from OCD, I cannot predict what anyone else may learn because learning is, by its nature, a personal experience. What I suspect is that the process will be similar to mine: it starts by confirming much that is known, raises more questions than produces answers, and ends by meddling in a belief system where curiosity was never invited.

Some learning is obvious. In these stories, we can see that religion does not cause OCD any more than OCD causes religion; just because you learn Hebrew does not cause you to think you are Jesus. OCD often makes an appearance in characteristics of a personality developmental stage prior to the stage where religious factors make their appearance. Religion can, however (if a vulnerability exists predisposing a person toward OCD), provide an environmental framework through which OCD may be expressed. We have a term—codependency—for those who inadvertently reinforce OCD by caving in to its demands. Perhaps we ought to coin a term for any practices of organized religion that foster it.

What *I* personally did, first of all, was to relearn two principles. The first is perhaps one of the Church's oldest maxims: *grace does not do away with nature.* Prayer does not grow an amputated leg; where no cure exists, there is no cure. It also sets a context: no cure does not mean no healing; it is to the depth and height and breadth of religious understanding that we rightly turn for being healed and whole.

The second principle is *feelings do not make it so.* Religious feelings of great intensity characterize OCD; just feeling it does not alter pathological content. We need a broader context in which to put our religious passion. Considering the pathology into which religious intensity can lead any of us—scrupulosity, for instance, can have the qualities of a virus and develop into a social contagion—it centers on taking the consensus of the universal Church most seriously as a corrective. As we are led into further spiritual understanding, we modify carefully what has been generally accepted in most times, in most places, by *all* the Household of the Faithful. Just as in a group, one member may become anxious and begin talking obsessively. It is most helpful to have the corrective opinion of the group, so any faith group needs the corrective, at times, of the larger ecumenical perspective.

In answering for myself the question that I posed to the group, the foremost answer only came in the course of writing this book. I have been astonished at how much OCD and religious feelings are intertwined. At one point, one of the readers even asked if religion is actually obsessive-compulsive behavior. It is not, but the very question illustrates how closely the two move in tandem. It seems to me that this issue may be classified on three levels for purposes of discussion: the subreligious, quasi-religious, and implicitly religious.

Hoarding: Subreligious OCD

I had previously recognized hoarding as an anal-retentive dynamic, as Freud would put it. The person captured by the hoarding dynamic will be able to recognize that it is characterized in the same way as a two-year-old. There will be preverbal, hostile, and passive-aggressive elements to it. It is, however, not easy to learn to laugh at oneself when recognizing that both the child in "the terrible twos" and hoarding have that same characteristic trait of saying, "No!" With the the two-year-old, resisting the adult is an art form—as illustrated by the family trying to change the needs of the hoarder. Intense feelings can surface when pushed too hard, but are usually limited to crying, and if rage erupts, it is indicative of regression into a tantrum. What I had not appreciated was that hoarding creates feelings of safety, of sanctuary.

Hoarding represents an ultimate concern, therefore it is inherently religious. The emotional age however, out of which it arises, causes it to be inadequately verbalized, so that the hoarder has a similar difficulty to a two-year-old in expressing a range and depth of feelings. It is subreligious, but there are *religious sensations.* The sensation of the creation of sanctuary will be outside of discussion, a gathering and retaining against insecurity that is beyond being analyzed by the hoarder. Emotional identification will be created in a place where I am sage and I can preserve Me. It is an identification *with.* Another person attempting to transfer that private hoard to a public landfill is felt as if it were transferring a personal identification. It is as if Dante and John Milton were to come to earth to collaborate on a new saga of an angel thrust from paradise. As I have thought more deeply, I am not astonished to find that interfering with hoarding is felt as a *transgression.*

Superstition: *Quasi-Religious OCD*

Superstition is almost omnipresent in OCD. In fact, Reann Dumont's *The Sky Is Falling* is organized around the concept of superstition.[7] On one hand, superstitions will not be expressed concretely, any more than explicit religious ideas, when OCD is experienced on a two-year-old child's developmental level. On the other hand, superstitions will be expressed on the three- and four-year-old child's level, as will some recognizable religious thought.

It should have come to me as no surprise how, in the era of early humans, magical thinking arose long before the higher religions evolved. Anyone involved with OCD can readily identify such magical thinking; what is not often appreciated is that there was, and often is, an overlapping of magical thinking around sensations/feelings/thoughts and the beginning of identifiable practices of the higher religions. Consequently, it is understandable that some aspects of superstition should find expression in contemporary religious practices.

In working with OCD, I must now admit to myself that I have suppressed my beliefs about magical thinking in religion: magical thinkers have their beliefs; I have mine. I now am aware this was a spurious acceptance, a permissiveness I would have questioned in a parent, but failed to do so in some pastor's parishioner who was a referral. That is the ethical quandary with such referrals for counseling. How does one do justice to the counselee when the referral source is a codependent in OCD-related superstitions?

I question my tolerance of magical thinking when I come face to face with a person such as "Anne." Vulnerable to anxiety, and in a time of high stress, she found a prayer card in a hospital. On it she read that if she prayed for something nine times it would come true. It led down a pathway ending in a pit of depression and a hospitalization. In the name of religious tolerance, I have walked around magical thinking that is destructive to people. It saved conflict, but at the price of their eventual disillusionment.

A core quandary among those of us characterizing ourselves as "religious" is how to accept persons of different religious beliefs who appear to us to have streaks of superstition. How do we accept the person without being permissive of pathology? I suspect as I flinch about my lack of courage, a great many pastors and church leaders will join with me in that.

Implicitly Religious: OCD As Scrupulosity

Blasphemy and scrupulosity are both highly verbal and both originate in the upper range of the stage of early childhood. Scrupulosity is not necessarily confined to the religious person, consequently taking an explicitly religious expression; however, because of its focus on anxiety about guilt, it can be said to be implicitly religious.

In seminary, in New Testament classes, we dealt with the Gospels as a collection of separate pieces of oral tradition, in which the teachings of Jesus were collected and later put into written form. For a person interested in mental health, some of the sayings attributed to Jesus are very hard to swallow: if you think about something sinful—such as lusting—that is just as bad as having done it; be perfect as God is perfect; if two or three of you agree on asking something in Jesus' name, it will be done; and that infamous one to those working with psychotics, that elusive but torturing sensation of having committed some "unforgivable sin." Being unfamiliar with OCD, I simply regarded those kinds of stories as characteristic of the first three Gospels; neither I nor the teacher recognized they were clustered in Matthew.

Initially, the way I used to deal with those texts was to take the perspective that they were examples of oriental hyperbole, much as many educated persons probably have done. Next came a psychological construct: they were misinterpreted by persons who thought in concrete terms. In actuality they were examples of mature abstract thought and were of benefit when intellectually interpreted and for meditation. Then for years I just looked the other way, scanning some passages without taking notice of them. Next I went through a phase when I would just "bite the bullet" and regard them as "OCD-friendly" and out of character with what Jesus had to say.

These stories seemed to reflect perfectionism and even superstitious thinking. They seemed to be separate stories preserved out of context or perhaps elaborated, and among the collectibles some followers wanted to preserve because of the social setting in which they ministered. The result was that a teaching preserved in one

Gospel might be omitted from another. A story in one tradition or in a part of the early Church was unknown elsewhere, having been evaluated as of lesser relevance to the persons to whom that Gospel was addressed. Obviously all stories and teachings of Jesus were not regarded as having equal value by the individual compilers of the four Gospels, neither by them—nor us.

At the same time I had been identifying a half dozen or less passages that seem remarkably "OCD-friendly," I had read a hundred passages—like you—for each one of those half dozen, in which I was variously enjoined to love my neighbor as myself. As Mark Twain commented, it is not what he did not understand about the Bible that bothered him, but what he did.

Today, having studied both scrupulosity and Matthew, I recognize that, until I learned about OCD and scrupulosity, I never understood Matthew. I have suddenly come to understand a great deal more about the circumstances in which Jesus found himself and how events occurred: and I am grateful that the study of OCD has opened up to me new treasures and understandings of the Good News—and consequently a new insight into the events of my own time.

Some Directions for the Churches
As We Learn More About OCD

"The just shall live by faith alone" is great theology; it is inadequate OCD treatment. Analysis, such as the distinctions concerning the identification of mortal sin, is more helpful; this is true not only for Catholics but for Protestants and presumably other faith groups. "Faith alone" is context; religious analysis is a necessary process as part of treatment.

We need to learn from one another—on tiptoe and finger to lips, if not in church councils—for the sake of suffering parishioners. A basic course in pastoral counseling in a seminary without St. Ignatius' teachings about working with the scrupulous is a course with at least one day without God's sunshine. Without a grasp of his "do the opposite," no pastor is prepared to cooperate with exposure/response treatment. A theological understanding of "sin" is flawed, if not defective, without reference to a "defective conscience."

To learn will take unlearning: the brutal persecution of Catholics in England in the late Middle Ages probably has prevented much reading of the spirituality of John Bunyan in that faith group. What we Christians probably are going to have to do with some of our traditions, in light of religious obsessions and compulsions, may have already been faced and accomplished in other groups—perhaps Reformed Judaism? Much can be learned from them in dealing responsibly with tradition.

Some Directions for Proceeding Clinically

Several "wedge issues" are built into the dynamics of having both OCD and religious faith. The research data indicate that Orthodox Jews with OCD in Jerusalem can differentiate between compulsive and authentic religious practices; probably anyone from any faith group can, too. Knowing the difference between the authentic and the inauthentic is a wedge to be hammered home.

Superstition is such a wedge issue. If a person is tapping in patterns of seven to keep a husband from a car wreck, such questions as, Who is in control? Do you control destiny or God? Can you? Are you God? come into play.

How much control is realistic? Almost always not only frustration but anger, upon which the superstition floats, can be exploited to assist in breaking apart the belief and the anxiety.

Another issue is perfection. Obsessive-compulsive disorder, per se, is not amenable to insight, but perfectionism is often readily acknowledged and verbalized. "No one is perfect but God" is generally accepted as a given and a basis for challenging perfectionism. Since a little gentle teasing is all to the good, you might add that the only perfect person for whom that claim is made was killed because of it, so please be cautious about volunteering.

The fourth issue is the contrast of an implicit religious sensation with an explicit religious thought. Hoarding has a feeling of "sanctuary"; it rests on unconscious religious sensations having to do with security beyond home, comfort, and reaching for an ultimate satisfaction. When someone begins to clean, the complaint is, "I can't find anything"; the religious feeling, however, is that of "transgression." This can be countered with a consciously religious proposition such as:

> Your home is God's garden, and your hoarding is a weed in that garden.

Since OCD often deserves a personalized nickname, some people respond to hoarding as a *weed*. Although emotion-laden imaging has disadvantages as treatment, it is vital for motivation and maintenance.

You will note that the clinical direction of what has been written moves toward a "search and destroy" mission to clear the forebrain, with the very real advantage that religious experience leads deeper into the midbrain. This expresses the notion to be explored in the next chapter—the functions of the two hemispheres. This may be briefly described as the religious inadequacy of "intellect without faith" or "faith without intellect." Clinically, one must admire John Wesley's dictum: "Let us unite those two so long divided, Knowledge and Vital Piety."

The Large Mission Before Us

You read "Thirty-Five Years in the Dark" and sadly realize how long it has taken for OCD to be recognized. The average is seventeen years for an accurate diagnosis of OCD to be made. We can comprehend that ten years ago there was little general understanding of OCD, but such a lack will be inexcusable ten years from now. What we usually understand is that much of the continuing education of medical practitioners is carried on by drug company representatives. Continuing education of mental health counselors is even more happenstance, in that it largely depends on which seminars happen to be offered. The level of continuing education by pastors is often a matter of conjecture. All will agree that much of what they learn is from their own patients, clients, and parishioners—and this is an opportunity for those with OCD. If there is to be any basic teaching about OCD in the next ten years, it will be by patients willing to talk and professionals who listen.

SUMMARY

Of all the religious sculptures in the Christian portions of the world, the statue of the Blessed Virgin is undoubtedly the most evident. Not far behind, in the Middle Ages, was the knightly figure of St. George. St. George, mounted on his trained warhorse, is slaying the primordial dragon. With that metaphorical image—and proverbial folk wisdom—of the saintly person utilizing his disciplined body to conquer the primitive, undisciplined impulses of the flesh, we turn next to the development of the brain, its significance for personality development, and the implications of this for OCD.

Chapter 6

Homo Sapiens Sapiens:
We Have Found the Enemy,
and It Is Us

Brain science alone does not—and cannot—capture the significance of human life. No physiological process adequately
accounts for human purposing. Cognitive science alone does
not—and cannot—capture the significance of human life.
Cognitive science alone does not—and cannot—evaluate the
values with which we engage life. No mental representation
adequately accounts for human presence. Nor do belief patterns alone create the conditions which make for life. No cos-
mic consciousness adequately accounts for human behavior.
But together, brain activity and belief patterns, as mediated in
cognitive processes, provide a convergence of the crucial features with which we can engage faith and action.[1]

> James Ashbrook, PhD, *Brain and Belief,*
> pioneering pastoral counselor in neurobiology

What will be proposed is this:

one brain
two memory systems
a behavioral one bordering on the instinctual
one with a vocabulary capable of passing SAT tests
when working harmoniously, creating "common sense"
separately, we have a "party animal" versus the dedicated intellectual
at the extremes, impulsive bestial urges versus a rationalizer playing
Trivial Pursuit

It has been a long time since ancestorially we shared a great deal in common with frogs, yet every beginning biology laboratory class slices them up to help understand our nervous system. None of our evolutionary prototypes have looked like mice for a while either, yet in the laboratory they help develop our medications and do stand-ins for brain probes. The brains of mammals were well organized a very long time ago and their neurons then, and our neurons now, are the same. Our brains are mainly different in how those neurons are proportioned. It is no surprise when we find linkage in our behavior to what has gone before us.

The most prevalent forms of OCD symptoms would be oldest and most useful for survival: checking and contamination fears. What we term OCD would have similarities all over the world. Sex and violence as obsessions would be closely associated in the developing brain. There would be a need for control, to set things in order. Guilt feelings would appear at some point; there would be a transition of symptoms in the directions of perfecting, such as symmetry and straightening. There would be a transition of symptoms from such things as fear of violence to a fear of committing violence, from fear of being contaminated to fear of contaminating. Superstition, as a need to control, emerges first and later religious concerns emerge, gradually evolving into moral and legalistic applications in the quest for perfection. Such a quest would be self-defeating—when anxiety drove this to an extreme—by demanding an irrational outlay of time and energy in personal, interpersonal, and vocational terms.

From the perspective of evolution, we can see why socioeconomic status has no characteristic relevance in this regard. Obsessive-compulsive disorder was a characteristic of our specie prior to such factors as social standing or economic worth among humans. It helps explain why some forms of "mental illness" are characterized by emergence later in life or earlier in life: they simply reflect a greater span of life expectancy in the course of our ancestral history.

What this does also explains why so many persons, sometimes estimated at 80 percent of the population who do not have a clinically significant level of OCD, exhibit some characteristics of it, such as those which are useful. It is the common human heritage of us all: we are all descendants of those survivors who successfully practiced those behaviors. We all are inheritors of traumatic, biologically altering events; some persons have more, by reason of random selection combinations. All of us have some tendency to block out events as one coping skill to deal with overwhelming emotions, but all of us are vulnerable to stress for we have evolved from an environment in which threat was omnipresent: plague, famine, fire, and sword. We will now turn to the evolution of the human brain to see the implications of this.

Since it will be obvious that my knowledge of neurology runs more into footnotes than authorship, the chapter will be developed on the "KISS" system which my computer person favors: Keep It Simple, Stupid. We will explore the reptilian brain—the old brain, as in frog; the mammalian brain—the midbrain, as in canine; and the new brain—as in the forebrain area which we are now utilizing. The way it evolved all three should harmonize well: How do you feel? How do you feel about it? What do you think about it? All together now: What are you going to do about it? But that is not always the way it works out . . .

THE OLD BRAIN

As in all vertebrates, at the top of the spinal column is the brain stem. To the rear is the hindbrain where, to be crude about it, the executioner likes to put his pistols and, to be more sophisticated, is the source of those nursing notes taken of your "vital signs." It would be helpful if every public library had a video section that included the PBS series on the brain. For those with a reason to be interested in seeing a panic attack taking place it makes for fascinating viewing.

The panic attack begins in the new brain—the forehead area—as thought, and resembles twinkling white lights on a Christmas tree. As the panic attack develops, the twinkling drifts farther and farther toward the rear of the brain stem. By the time it gets there, in the full-blown panic attack, the color has changed from white to blue and the twinkling becomes as chaotic as a lightning storm . . . as have your "vital signs": rapid pulse, sweating, pounding heart, heavy breathing. When the panic hits the hindbrain, little wonder the scare is "Am I having a heart attack? Am I dying?" The old brain has the capacity to mobilize the body to an emergency—it just is not good at identifying what an emergency is. It can temporarily prevent the logical part of the brain from doing its business by absorbing all the energy in the brain's electrical grid. Panic attacks and OCD, of course, have a lot in common and sometimes overlap, but they are distinguishable.

In the attempt to control panic attacks relaxation techniques were developed that targeted the hindbrain, such as deep breathing, respiration, and heartbeat. It has been a matter of importance to determine if the stretching and breathing of Yoga or the "ohm" of the Buddhist monk could also positively affect OCD. Unfortunately, as of this date, these positive results are limited. The problem probably is too much bony spine between the target sites: the relaxation techniques work in the area of the hindbrain; on the other side of the spinal column lies the area initiating OCD.

On the forebrain side of the spine is the basal ganglia area that includes the amygdala, an almond-shaped area sometimes referred to as "the factory of the emotions."[2] This is the area for emerging sensations and instinctive responses concerned with survival and has existed as long as there have been vertebrates; it is also the area of agitation in OCD attacks. The amygdala is responsive to sensory challenges, such as, "Will it hurt me?" "Should I fear it?" "Do I hate it?" *If all the alarm bells sound in the reptilian part of the brain, it is apt to launch the new brain into catastrophizing even if it is a false alarm.* An implication of this is that, when imagination runs wild, the control system is collapsing.

In all these forms, there is a "state specific" in which all the totality of the body is coordinated—"entrained"—in order to serve the purpose of the dominant sensation or feeling. In an emergency—or mistaken emergency—the "factory of emotions" becomes a power train directly interacting with the midbrain and new brain, flooding glucose over all of it. It simultaneously throws an alarm through the spinal column to the emergency crew below to activate cortisol and insulin. When the amygdala sounds "battle stations," the whole team moves fast: a very handy response system if those paleontology reports of the size of wolves "back when" are correct.

If the urge is to fight, the hands swell so they grip a weapon better. If the urge is flight, blood flows into the large muscles of the legs. If the urge is to stillness, it must be like a submarine: "run silent, run deep," "all slow." Perhaps there is a "think fast" mechanism in the forebrain, too; apparently it gets an extra blood supply. When OCD strikes, sufferers may notice their forehead has become warmer.

The raphe nuclei, which manufacture the neurotransmitter serotonin that is targeted in OCD medications, are adjacent to the amygdala. If something dramatic happened in the amygdala, it will affect the raphe nuclei. Given the linkage provided by serotonin between the nerve endings of the brain, it will consequently alter the communication system all over the brain. For instance, among chimpanzees the alpha male has a high threshold of responsiveness to group interactions—and has a high serotonin level. If the dominant male is confined in a room with a one-way mirror his serotonin level drops.[3] He can see the group, but they cannot see him and make no response to him. We then have one very depressed ape.

Since we are dealing with a closed energy system, it might remind us of the starship *Enterprise* under attack. Captain Kirk orders the force-field shields up and then orders Scotty in engineering to shut down all systems not needed in an emergency so energy can be transferred to the shields. You might suspect in a dramatic situation that, if the manufacturing site shut down, all the receptacles between the brain endings would shut down as well, in order to conserve what serotonin was left in the "pipelines." Any engineer, as well as physician, would venture an opinion that it might take some effort to get the system up and working again if there were too frequent emergencies—real or mistaken.

THE MIDBRAIN

The brain stem area slowly grew into the mammalian brain. In one evolutionary eon, the skull was not only enlarging, but a bony vertical crest developed from back to front; this was long before the bony ridge of the Neanderthal's brow on the horizontal. At one point a group of prehumans even had a brain heavier than ours. Perhaps a simile for the enlargement of the brain and the age of the mammals would be the rings on a tree. Now comes what is new and important for understanding OCD.

There appear to be *two* memory systems in the brain.[4] It would certainly explain why someone with OCD might jump to the conclusion that he or she was crazy, with bizarre interjected thoughts or an unacceptable waking dream/fantasy, such as committing an out-of-character act of violence, popping in without warning or invitation. It would explain why some highly intellectual, religious persons have even thought these interjections must be the work of the devil; they are so contradictory to the person's desire and character. This may even suggest a reason why a teenager will insist, beyond all parental reasoning, that he or she can study better with that loud music playing; it drowns interjecting thoughts!

One system is that of which we are aware: our individual remembrances and experiences. Even the forebrain can be subdivided into two systems, since there is no "line of demarcation" as the brain evolved. There is an *intellectual* knowing—I remember the multiplication tables—and there is an *emotional* knowing: what I have experienced. You can read about going to Rome on a vacation; you can stand in the Forum and *look:* this is where Caesar was murdered. It is this experiential knowing that slides back from the knowable into the unfathomable.

The physical basis of that difference is in the limbic system, a ring on the outside of the brain. On the forehead side of the brain, you have the cognitive "knowing." The farther back you move into the midbrain, the more you move from an existential "knowing" into a "gut" feeling blending in with visceral sensations.

All the basis for our knowing is, of course, sensations. We sense, then we think. The limbic ring passes the information back and forth; get a lesion on it and the person can become wildly impulsive—and now we realize, this can also initiate OCD, thrusting the person into a deeper part of the brain where repetitive patterns reside.

On the inside of the limbic ring, you have the receptors of the five senses. And there is the "sixth sense": a way of knowing what you could not know. With it the combat veteran has an impulse to move from this shell hole to another; paying no attention to that intuitive sense may result in a woman's frantic statement made at a rape crisis center. Included in that deeper part are areas called the hippocampus, hypothalamus, and thalamus. This is new learning—hippocampus: memory, especially short-term memory; hypothalamus: memory, temperature control, sexual drive, hunger, and thirst; thalamus: awareness of pain and the mediation of some processes of memory, an association with the senses other than smell.[5] *This is the area of the second memory system and it is of a different nature, of course, than the one associated with consciousness,* that is, "emotional memory" versus "working memory" as they are differentiated in *emotional intelligence.*

It makes a lot of sense that there would be such a primordial system, but to the degree to which there is a continuity we would largely fail to distinguish them. The two ways of registering trauma in the mammalian brain and in the new brain would exist on a biological continuum, but under ordinary circumstances a boundary would also exist between them. In the PTSD the boundary has given away under the pressure of stress or due to a startle repsonse and a flashback occurs. A similar process also occurs in the mammalian brain, resulting in an OCD episode. After twenty years, when Ulysses returned home from Troy, his hound lifted his head from the floor and licked the old disguised beggar's hand. His wife, too, recognized him in time; each remembered, but based on a different set of sensory input.

Until now, we did not sufficiently recognize that they were different systems—and that we humans had both. Both systems rely on sensory input, but the more primitive system stores the memory as imagery while the newer system relies more on language encoded in the brain. Midway between the two and overlapping is a blending: we see it in pictographs on cave walls, hieroglyphics in tombs, calligraphy in writing, rest room signs in airports. We still use the mammalian system for security purposes: friend or foe recognition for military pilots is based on silhouettes. Conscious awareness is too slow. You are dead.

What is being hypothesized is that with a startle response, a "spike" occurs that probably can be graphed as a brain wave and which, in the case of those with OCD, ignites obsessions and is consequently labeled as "bizarre." The stimulus evoking the startle is matched to the images recorded in the mammalian brain—somewhat like the way the FBI might do with fingerprints. In the average person, that 80 percent group with a subclinical obsessive-compulsive level of responses, the "bizarre" spike seems to be simply interpreted as just a "weird" thought or impulse and is immediately shrugged off or dismissed after a preliminary consideration. With those whose memory banks match up in a pattern—consequently vulnerable to extreme anxiety—the spike is not so readily dismissed and obsessing begins like a fishbone caught in the throat.

It probably is similar to the silhouette system the animals use; a mouse knows the shape of an owl. It is not instinct: if a robin is raised without a mother for the first six weeks of its life, it will not know the shape of a hawk. Once learned, however, it persists. In the mammalian portion of the brain, the only seemingly instinctual fear may be of snakes, but yet, as individuals, there are fears that do not seem learned. When your "blood runs cold" at some sound, when some sight causes your "hair to stand up on the back of your neck," *something remembers.*

Everyone has had such experiences. I can be reading quietly with Frances, our yellow Labrador, half asleep on the floor. Suddenly, she will be up, tail stiff and ears flared. Nothing is there—no sound, no movement. Yet there *was* something. Security is involved. It is the *startle response*. It is that which puts you in motion in an emergency before you know you are moving. When it is either the quick or the dead option, it is just there. It is not planned; it is in DNA, a prepared program of strategies for survival.

The advantage of this system can be seen on any Sunday afternoon in the fall. When you see a great running back, "a natural," the old pro announcer will remark that the moves cannot be trained. Somehow, the reaction time is just shorter than other players' and he seems to know where everyone else is on the field. It is a process similar to an emotional hijacking; when the optic nerves signal an emergency, the message gets halfway toward the hindbrain and then short-cuts to the amygdala. It is this shortcut that is involved in the startle response. The mammalian warning system has matched up a pattern. The alarm signal goes off and there is no need to think, the magical halfback just moves; similarly, the chemicals magically appear and the life-or-death response rolls, too. The problem is, "What if you have OCD?"

What initiated this prepared program for strategies of survival was trauma, that is, learning by surviving. We know that sufficiently intense trauma produces a chemical response so that the image of the trauma is imprinted on the brain. This is the flashback of PTSD.

Post-traumatic stress disorder exists in the newer sections of the brain that have access to consciousness; however, the trauma imprinted on the DNA is through the unconscious.

The two ways of registering trauma would be similar with both on a continuum, distinguishable yet similar in the two memory systems. At one end would be a purely unconscious memory, but still a memory. At the other end would be an episodic, conscious remembrance. A person is going along, minding his or her own business and suddenly, *the feeling*. It may be from either system.

The response that is registered can be rage. It can also be that certain something "across a crowded room," when it may not be convenient to have eyes lock and "smoke gets in your eyes," but nevertheless it happens. It is associative, a triggering of memory—and it need not be the stimulus of a conscious memory, but an emotional one from below consciousness. Both can be readily mistaken for reality. When those "second thoughts" begin and someone thinks, "I don't know whatever came over me!" that is it—the primitive memory system versus the more newly developed portion of the brain. If the memory has been stored in "the working memory" of the individual, it can usually be analyzed through association. If it is in the more primitive "emotional memory," there is no recoverable association and logic fails, as everyone with OCD knows.

That more extreme anxiety comes with a threat to life: my life, his or her life, hellfire. The alarm system picks up the startle response and relays it with the force of a ship's horn signaling to grab a life jacket and head for the lifeboat station. What we know of OCD, however, is that it is a false alert; the alarm may have been set off by a sound—perhaps a "thud"—and the midbrain's system matched with something such as a head being bashed in. The prepared program for security calls for instant checking; when it is referred to the newest part of the brain, the question is, "Check what?"

There is a possibility of a false positive with either memory; the radar and sonar of our sensory sweeps pick up something and misread it. Any of us can recall embarrassing incidents in which feelings have been transferred to someone, and how mistaken that first impression turned out to be. This undoubtedly has happened as long as there have been senses. In the interests of survival, such misreadings are simply tolerated—the snapping of a twig was just that, not the approach of a predator. Misreadings are, however, most inconvenient if you have a blood relative with OCD, the "royalty of impractical jokers."

This prepared learning is based on the reality that the senses exist for arousal—pain, pleasure, food, sex, and defense. Since the brain is a continuum, there are updated versions of this. Jung's archetypes (such as the cross) are one example of prehistory flowing to contemporary experience, or in a repetition compulsion, in which there is a recycling of a past experience in such a way that a present event is experienced as if it were that past event. Obsessing begins with stored sensations rather than thought. Double-check. Be certain. Caution/fear/paralysis/panic/death/hell. The DNA historic route has many options for intruding on the here and now. It sets the stage for an emotional hijacking.

When the emergency alarm is sounded, whether real or a misreading, a "stand down" will need to be sounded eventually. It may be by surviving, if the emergency was real. We may shake for a while, but we eventually "settle down" again. It may be because of a false alarm, a startle response setting in motion the whole biological system preprogrammed for survival. In this case, if the false alarm is set off from the primitive memory, the working memory with its logic will fail to control the emergency system, even if it recognizes that a false alarm or reality is being misinterpreted. The primitive memory will have accessed the whole power to maximize survival, so that it seems impossible to "settle down," i.e., cease obsessing.

Relief will then be sought through whatever preferred sense the person has for mapping his or her world, such as sight or touch . . . behavioral repetition to quiet the body. If that preference is by "the ear gate," verbal reassurance will be sought, the problem being reassurance is sought verbally and received verbally. The reassurance is from the newest part of the brain of the person attempting to be of help to the newest part of the brain of the one seeking help. Unfortunately, this new brain was yet to be evolved when a fully developed startle response was a necessary arousal-for-survival.

Many parents and wives may not be able to lecture upon the truth of this but can illustrate it in great detail. Reassurance does not satisfy the flashing warning light for "kill or be killed," "run like hell," or "dive for cover!" It also does not connect with the finest Scripture passage quoted by the pastor or most astute Freudian insight by the counselor. The glucose continues its high metabolizing ways, but so does the issue of maximizing the power of that newest part of the brain; this, too, is as old as Socrates' teaching, "The unexamined life is not worth living."

THE NEW BRAIN

When the Good Lord had finished working on the hypothalamus project—development of a center for body temperature, hunger, thirst, sex drive, and (some experts add) aggression—He must have felt uneasy. It argues theologically for the inclusion of the feminine as well as the masculine nature of the Godhead. She must have realized that there were design problems in associating those last two because the next creative act was to start developing an area with a capacity for logic.

However it was, in the development of the specie differentiation began to occur. Males made tools, hunted and fished, guarded and raided, consequently were muscle orientated, tended to silence, less emotionally expressive, more isolated. Women gathered and plucked, cooked and clothed, socialized, and cooperated in child care. Brains even began to differentiate along gender lines. The effect of that is shown in the way boys learn and need to be taught, which is only now beginning to be considered and to be reflected in treatment implications.[6]

Ideally, the evolving of the brain should have made a smoothly working checks and balance system. The mammalian brain provides a checking for security and access to an underlying power to implementing security needs, double-checked for reality by the new brain and a coordination of the two in feelings leading to intuitive judgments and "common sense."[7] In practice, in contrast to the ideal, without that coordination of the two systems you have—not "reason as the crown of the human"—but the infamous PhD, where it is "piled higher and deeper" in the process of "knowing more and more about less and less." The intuitive powers of the mammalian brain keep the new brain in touch with reality rather than drifting off into speculation. The new brain provides a damper switch on the impulses of the mammalian brain. Without that, you have loud parental explosions, such as, "Boy, don't you ever think first?!"

This ability to think first is complicated by the division of the new brain into the left and right hemispheres. The left hemisphere—which relates to developing of the broca area on the left side of the skull when words before language were formed—is the physical basis upon which the jokes at the Lions Club are made about "the personality of an engineer." The right hemisphere is the physical basis for the jokes about the personality of a "blonde" made by the "boys" in the locker room (and the same basis upon which the "girls" in the coffee klatch discuss the "jocks" in the locker room).

Both right and left are relative, of course; left brain for the right-handed will be analytical, philosophical; left brain for the left-handed reverses it. A demonstration of this reality is that no one wants a stroke for the right-hander, which brings a speech impediment. This means a clot on the left side of the brain. Limbs not functioning on the left side would indicate a clot on the right.

What this means in the functioning of the brain is what Dr. James Ashbrook used to refer to in his lectures at the Garrett Evangelical Seminary as "the rational left and the relational right" in regard to religion, with the dominant right side more focused on surviving (as in heaven) and on the left with saving (as in universal redemption). Often this biological difference is referred to as "Mary" and "Martha" types of religion: thoughtful versus muscular Christianity. Most of us have a dominant hemisphere, just as we choose to swing a golf club one way or another. One flows, the other dissects. The dominant hemisphere is our preferred way of mapping our world; "psyche it out" or "think it through." Fortunate is the batter who switch hits depending on the pitcher. Fortunate indeed to be a "switch thinker" depending on circumstances, and to some degree, *it can be taught by a good coach or a good therapist.*

This may be easier for women than men. Women use more of the brain than men do, though this has nothing to do with "intelligence"; between the hemispheres is a connecting strip and it is wider in females than males.[8] Since it has been widely noted that women who are intensely distressed about some "mental condition" will seek treatment while men will repress that condition and finally be hospitalized, this may reflect the use of more of the female brain so there is less denial and more consideration of options and resources. It may also mean that, while OCD occurs equally in adulthood with respect to gender, males may be less flexible than females and so need a different approach in beginning treatment.

We might suspect the right brain-dominant folk would preach "morality," the left brained preferring to lecture on "ethics," neither quite grasping the other's point. In religion, mysticism will flower in the right hemisphere, theological discussion in the left. The left is also more global, but it is always wise to avoid a misplaced concreteness in these generalizations as the brain's hard wiring will criss and cross.

What is important to the understanding of OCD in relationship to the functioning of the hemispheres of the brain also helps us in the understanding of our individual and social preferences and styles in religion. It opens at the same time the possibility of some forms of pathology that have the appearance of being religious in nature. It should be remembered that, on average, OCD appears earlier in males and that in childhood males are more apt to demonstrate right brain behaviors. In expression of religious pathology, it seems the left brain is affected. Blasphemy and compulsive praying are certainly highly verbal; scrupulosity is also verbal and highly overanalytical. The situation appears to be that those who are aware of a pathological expression of religion will have a dominant left hemisphere, but may have religion as a "personal experience" as a therapeutic resource. Those with a dominant right brain will have a more vital sense of personal religious experience. If OCD is a factor, however, they will not likely be conscious of any religious pathology. It may either lack obvious religious expression (as in hoarding), be expressed in an inappropriate boundary setting (as in aggressive witnessing, "fraternal scrupulosity"), or else be so primitive (and in some instances out of touch with reality, as in schizophrenia) as to merit psychiatric attention. In the right brain, there will be "feel good" religious expressions, though lacking in ethical analysis. Both will suffer equally from the defect of perfectionism, both equally in touch with tormenting anxiety.

Let it be noted that religion often has a self-correctiveness; it is often noted historically that what begins as a sect or movement gradually evolves into a more static dynamic and has the structure of an organized religion. In the course of this the "insiders" tend eventually to shift toward broader values, an evolution in emphasis from the subjective toward the objective, right hemisphere to left hemisphere. This is not all gain, as John Wesley observed. In this shift, religious feelings may lose their vital powers. The issue therapeutically, as well as religiously, is how to have *balance*.

Turning now to the broader context of the spectrum of OCD disorders, the differences may well be found in the distinctions of the hemisphere. In hoarding, there is underanalysis: everything is of significance and nothing is of significance. In hypochondriasis, everything is overanalyzed, with suspicious sensations researched to the maximum. When there are anomalies, such as in trichotillomania, in which the female gender tends to predominate, the age of appearance is earlier for that gender than ordinarily for OCD. In trichotillomania, sufferers appear also more emotionally volatile; we may be seeing an uncharacteristic dominance of a hemisphere for that gender at that early age—the right hemisphere for females.

The implication of the differentiation of the hemispheres is significant. Consider the wisdom of the Church about scrupulosity: "do the opposite." Since the dominant hemisphere in persons with OCD appears to be the afflicted one, it suggests that an extension of that wisdom could be "use the opposite." The traditional wisdom of the Church is reflected in the practice that when the "rational" left hemisphere is caught up in scrupulosity, refer to the "relational" right by bringing allies to lend a more sturdy conscience and role model. Undoubtedly, this insightful practice can be further extended.

Considered as a whole, in addition to reason and up-scaling feelings, the advantage of the new brain is to be able to have an imagination and that can result in living better and better still. Inventions are created and poetry written; empathy arises in late childhood along with the capacity for abstract thought to replace the simple "feeling for" of early childhood's sympathy. There are trade-offs, of course. With an internalized conscience not only authentic guilt feelings arise, but so too can the inauthentic ones, such as we associate with OCD. With the development period in childhood in which the child wants to ask the big questions such as, "What is God like?," they also want to know where babies come from, and have an early recognition of death. Usually the death of a pet is more meaningful than the death of an adult—such as a grandparent—but death it is and death must be acknowledged.

In order to dampen anxiety, worry is substituted. It begins to be hung around the person's neck like an amulet to ward off the evil spirits of more primitive emotions. It comes with a promise that if forethought is exercised, harm may be avoided. Worry stays to affect that peculiar characteristic of those with obsessive-compulsive tendencies toward a lifestyle of being off balance because mentally the next step is already in the air before the last step has been completed. It has the appearance that the person is fleeing from the past into the future.

To have worry indicates the primordial memory system has sufficient potentially explosive anxiety. The person is unconsciously motivated to distance himself or herself as far as possible from what is apt to go off unexpectedly—obsessing, panic, or perhaps depression. It may even give some pleasure to worry because it carries the illusion that the person is doing something constructive—even when living a depressed lifestyle or simply recycling in a self-perpetuating loop of frustrations. In the age-old discussion of heredity and environment, the escape from the negative aspects of one's DNA would seem to be toward creating an environment sufficiently therapeutic to alleviate extraordinary anxiety.

ADDING IT ALL UP

It is fascinating to watch a human fetus develop in one of the PBS television documentaries. Referring again to Piero and Alberto Angela, who wrote in *The Extraordinary Story of Human Origins:*

> During the nine months of pregnancy, the fetus seems to go through the various stages of evolution from the fetus in an early developmental stage having something like gills, to a reptilian-like spinal column and brain ending, to a later mammalian-like form and finally to the recognizable form of the human being.[9]

An interesting question is whether, as the brain increases dramatically in size in the months following passage through the birth canal, it continues to exhibit the history of our kind. Since life is characterized as being on a continuum, it is logical to expect that in some way the birth experience is simply a marker in the human unfolding and our brain continues to resemble the evolutionary process of our ancestry. If the brain increases by a third after birth (and the connecting tissues are very much in process of developing during that period) it is reasonable to speculate that, if there is a recapitulation of human evolution, after birth we are seeing a third of our history in those first months. Since the connecting tissue, or synapses, are continuing to be formed throughout childhood, it seems reasonable to expect that in some fashion this, too, represents human development . . . human development as long as humans have the insight and continue to recognize connections.

It is clear that the human brain is a product of process and still in process. *The human brain is changeable;* Dr. Jeffrey Schwartz concluded this in the research that led to *Brain Lock.* In effect, he shifted the time span from evolutionary eons to a measurable treatment period. How this takes place is not only a treatment issue, but is beautifully described in a special report on infant development in the February 3, 1997 issue of *Time* magazine. It is "must reading" for today's parents and policymakers and for those working with OCD:

> At birth a baby's brain contains 100 billion neurons, roughly as many nerve cells as there are stars in the Milky Way. Also in place are a trillion glial cells, named after the Greek word for glue, which form a kind of honeycomb that protects and nourishes the neurons. But while the brain contains virtually all the nerve cells it will ever have, the pattern of wiring between them has yet to stabilize.

The pattern of "wiring" develops remarkably quickly in the infant's early months, but it probably never completely loses its ability to change as long we live.

What is important in this for OCD, however, is the relative lack of connectors in the brains of those with OCD. There is a lot of gray matter and a tendency toward "intelligence," as has been noted, but there is a relative lack of white matter, the connectors.[10] Without sufficient amounts of "connectors," what might be the implication is a vulnerability to regression. When stresses accumulate, the tendency to retreat to a simpler time, often as a positive way of coping for persons, but perhaps it is also a time when connections between events were not ready to be made.

There are several helpful implications here. One is that parents who fear their child may be genetically vulnerable to OCD potentially have a tool through ordinary techniques of infant brain stimulation to help develop a greater amount of brain connecting tissue. It begins with learning cause and effect with a colorful mobile to be set in motion with a touch. It continues with a visit to the educational section of a toy store and reading what is appropriate to an age level. It means a relatively quiet mother being more adequately vocal with her baby: talk, Mother, talk! Instinctively a mother will have the right tone and words for the distinct "dialect" of baby talk! Read that book to him and her, Daddy: all fifty, going on seventy-five times!

Second, the implication for treatment is that the lack of connectors might explain why an intelligent person with OCD may be superstitious—a sense of inadequate relatedness, so a sensation of terror might attach itself to something totally unrelated—If I do not straighten all my shoes my (aunt's/mom's/grandma's cat: underline one) will die. It should be noted that the outbreak of OCD never means the loss of intelligence, rather the lack of connectedness becomes evident—and offers an avenue for treatment.

Third, the "cognitive" aspect of cognitive behavioral treatment meets the therapeutic requirement of developing more adequately the connectors to establish a healthy sense of how things relate as they have not been doing that adequately. The strength of this aspect of treatment is reality testing, which is nothing more, or less, than an adequate grasp of relationships.

It seems reasonable to assume that the purpose of the brain is to carry out an organizing function: mapping one's environment and coordinating a response. Both the emotions and intellect processing information ought to be conformable to the brain's sensory receptors receiving data. In OCD, this does not hold true: I *feel* the lock is unlocked; I *know* the lock is locked.

There are several things to be noted about this level of awareness below consciousness that will be important for therapy: (1) it is a neurobiological activity, not a neurotic or a psychiatric condition; (2) it has its own alarm system and it will resemble more that of a mammal than the logical, modern "human"; (3) if this was strictly a mammalian event, without reference to biological events related to "human" development of the creature, the startle response would have occurred, a sudden surge of emergency response initiated and, almost as quickly, subsided; (4) the "human" aspect is a prolongation of the startle response, first in thought and usually in behavior; (5) in its intensity its activation is overriding; (6) if there are any words leaping to mind, they are limited; (7) the ability to think also will be limited in scope; (8) it will have its own value system; and (9) there will be no concept of time. The whole system is so interlocking—and at such a primitive level—it is no wonder a medication resetting the seratonin balance affects both anxiety and depression at the exalted level of consciousness.

We might regard the brain on the "macro" level as rather like our planet, Earth. It has geological "plates" that shift about and consequently there are "fault lines"—boundaries that are sometimes adequate, sometimes less so, especially under severe stress—just as the three generalizations about the evolution of the brain indicate. On the "micro" level, we have the trauma banked in DNA in the primordial memory system. The fault lines along which the earthquakes and volcanoes make their appearance correspond to the disconnectedness and resulting pressures when the two memory systems collide.

One interesting theory now discussed in some psychological circles concerns the function of dreaming, in which it may operate as the digestive system of the brain/mind. In its sleeping state, the brain accesses both memory systems in dreaming. The combining of the two produces the distortion of the dream. The dream resembles the slippage of the earth's plates reducing the buildup of stress, nature's relief system for the prevention of an emotional earthquake. Deprived of sleep—*deprived of dreaming*—and a vulnerability to an OCD attack readies.

This function of the dream has a bearing on the notion that the state in which OCD occurs is separable from the rest of the personality. Little evidence exists that the dreaming of those with OCD is significantly different from those with that clinical level of repetitiousness. This lack of significant differences in dreaming indicates OCD is a waking phenomenon; although there may be terror dreams these also occur with persons not having OCD. Only when conscious does the primordial system go fully into operation.

The startle response associated with post-traumatic stress disorder may cause the wife of a combat veteran to stand back from the bed when she says, "Time to get up, Honey" rather than shake him, but this is based on the history of an individual. A youngster still in school may begin obsessing and then go into rituals almost after waking, but there is waking. To the contrary, no one seems to stagger out of bed and immediately begin a ritual of hand washing without first obsessing. A person with OCD may brush his or her teeth in an exaggerated fashion, but that ritual is not in response to the startle response to the alarm clock; if the alarm clock sets off multiple showering, it will generally occur when anticipation of stressful events becomes obsessing.

Both the incident of PTSD and that of an OCD episode seem initiated by a startle response; the former will begin to decrease with full awareness; the latter slides from awareness into a trance-like state begun with obsessing and continuing in awareness until swallowed by a trancelike state. With the PTSD incident, we are seeing only one memory system involved; in the OCD episode, two.

What a tragedy we witness for the individual when an event occurs and the consequence is PTSD. It is similar in nature to the tragedy we see in OCD. In the former we see an unfortunate event reenacted in the life of an individual, in the latter we see a "lottery" of passing on and combining DNA with the biological emergence of OCD in the individual. It is easy to celebrate that random selection when a combination results in a creative advance, such as in a Bach or Brahms. It is often heartrending when an opposite occurs.

Extremes do occur. The majority of an OCD support group may be debating the excesses of guilt over minutiae, perhaps occasioned by repeated reinforcement of generations of ethically sensitive ancestors. In the same group may be someone struggling valiantly with kleptomania, perhaps like some biological "sport" when a new variation of some vegetable appears. In the neighborhood some burglar may be pilfering a home, taking the bright and shiny and leaving—his mess—with all the thinking process of a pack rat.

Quality controls are yet to be developed as we begin to understand how to participate in evolution.

What must be made clear is the nature of time. Time is *not* "an ever-flowing stream." All we have is a "now," a "concrete occasion" as Alfred North Whitehead would say. The past is housed in the present, and the future is just as instantaneously emerging from it. When we speak of the past being housed in the present, it is not some such notion as contained in *The Search for Bridey Murphy*.[11] In that literary work a generation or so back, hypnosis was used to effect past-life regression. Whatever the reality of past-life regression, in which a person's past identity and experiences may be recaptured through hypnosis, this is not what is intended here (although it might be a next generation research issue). The reality suggested here is that through DNA, along with instructions as to how to develop a kidney, a little toe, appendix, or neocortex, emotional experiences of sufficient chemical intensity are being passed along as an inheritance to a present human life-form. The suggestion here is that we are looking at a process similar to PTSD: flashbacks, only of an emotional and unconscious nature, instead of visual, conscious ones.

To an outsider, OCD resembles the goldfish bowl in a Chinese restaurant with curved glass so the water magnifies the goldfish into giant carp. The fears are so blown out of proportion, the superstitions so exaggerated that outsiders have been inclined to regard the person with OCD as "crazy" and the insider wonders as well. The fears are real, however, as real as the trauma that imprinted those fears on the DNA that preserved them. The feelings of terror are real also, as real as the amygdala responding to the alarm signal set off to preserve life. In an authentic emergency, the emergency system can literally be a "lifesaver." If the emergency system is not on target, what was evolved as lifesaving is perverted into terrorizing.

There are always trade-offs in the random combination of DNA; some individuals have an exaggerated potentiality for music, some to compose or perform—others to obsess with tunes from which they cannot free themselves. Others have just a randomly occurring potentiality for gallstones or an illogical terror of fire—or to write charming children's books. Almost always, there are combinations of the pluses and the minuses—and we all have to cope with something. Rare, indeed, is the person with no gifts with which to benefit those here and to come.

What then is to be said of such a combination of the positive and negative, advantage and disadvantage? Perhaps this could be shown in what Swiss psychiatrist Carl Jung, would doubtless have seen as an archetype: we Christians link the cross and the crown together in stained glass in our church windows.

Chapter 7

Theory Made Practical

As Jesus was walking along, he saw a man who had been born blind. His disciples asked him, "Teacher, whose sin caused him to be born blind? Was it his own or his parents' sin?" Jesus answered, "His blindness has nothing to do with his sins or his parents' sins. He is blind so that God's power might be seen at work in him."

John 9:1-3

What is visible to the outsider, let us say a parent, is the compulsion. She hears the door open, close, open, close: then comes the response, "Quit that, and I mean now." Open, close, open, close: "You hear me? Now!" The suppression-of-symptom scene may also be played with father and daughter at the light switch. What follows is like summer fun in the swimming pool; three or four of us would try to hold an inner tube down. Eventually it squirted up. That was fun. The suppression of OCD ritual is not fun; it squirts sideways in anger and generally results only in a shift in symptoms. Energy cannot be destroyed, just transformed. The amygdala has plenty of energy when life appears to be threatened. A parent may enforce a change of subject, from hand washing or flipping switches perhaps, but the primordial memory bank usually has plenty traumas as alternatives. If hand washing will not do, try cleaning; if checking of locks is punished there are other less visible things to check or straighten. If worse comes to worst, the check/check/check a child does, if violently suppressed, is likely to become a health concern after every snort, sneeze, and sweat. After all, no parent can get mad about that. The treatment problem is how to let the air out of the inner tube—not the compulsion, but the obsession.

Enter the attribution theory. A host of options exists for the obsessive-compulsive disorder. Mom may attribute it to the kid trying to drive her nuts; Dad may attribute the problem to lack of willpower; the evangelist on the radio may take a crack at assigning the whole problem to the work of the devil. Personally, it would be hard to better the teaching of Jesus we have just cited; it is, however, the larger context into which to set the issue, and that is reserved for the final chapter. Before we get to that, we need to acknowledge the current attribution: OCD is a neurobiological condition. To do justice to that we need to deal with two related areas. The first is to continue the theme of human evolution, which we will do in terms of "diagnoses"; the second we will deal with as aspects of the evolving human in terms of personality development.

DIFFERENTIAL DIAGNOSIS

As an example of one of the diagnostic differentiations needed to be made is between the obsessive-compulsive disorder and the obsessive-compulsive personality disorder (OCPD). Obsessive-compulsive disorder is characterized by symptoms, while the OCPD is characterized by traits. If a therapist is going to treat two counselees, there may be a difference. The one with OCD may compulsively wash his hands, for example, and consequently distress his wife; the other with the obsessive-compulsive personality likely gets a different marital response: "Stubborn. You cannot believe how stubborn that man is!"

> In fact, the two conditions may not even be related . . . Apart from their idiosyncratic obsessions and rituals, people with the disorder are not *necessarily* preoccupied with rules and schedules, excessively conscientious, orderly, morally rigid, fussy about details, indecisive, or perfectionistic.[1] (Italics mine)

The "personality" is apt to resemble the jokes at Rotary Club that an accountant tells about his profession when he is asked to give a talk; not many "washers" accept speaking engagements and none of them have "knee-slappers" to warm up the audience. Obsessive-compulsive disorder "eats" time in large quantities; with OCPD you would want to get that person to hold the stopwatch to measure the length of the other's rituals—find the perfect bureaucrat and you have found the perfect diagnostic illustration.

The person with the personality disorder never met an overtime challenge he or she did not like, while the individual with OCD may have never met a vacation he or she could take. Both are apt to be highly responsible to the point of being overly so; both can be authentically religious. The sufferer with scrupulosity and the person with the personality disorder may both be perfectionists, both morally rigid and seemingly ready to fizz about trivia. But the sufferers from OCD's scrupulosity will likely drive some friend "up the wall" with the need for reassurance. The boss with OCPD will have the secretaries in the pool hiding in the bathroom, when they hear the shuffling of papers as he or she comes down the hall.

When the two disorders are sufficiently severe they are likely to be treated with the same medications, but an evolutionary approach makes clear the distinction: OCD is far older and usually expresses security concerns; OCPD is more of a response to social demands—a time when governments needed bureaucrats and merchants needed accountants. The two overlapped, in that both display the feeling that perfectionism offers. When security disorders are viewed from the perspective of personality development, they may exhibit the anal characteristics of early childhood. Both may come into therapy complaining of marital problems; with OCD, that has to be treated first and perhaps later getting into marriage counseling, if that proves necessary. With OCPD, working on the marriage may very well effect positive changes in work habits and relationships.

Either one, though, could be severe enough to warrant medication—and it would be very likely the same medication, so there is some relationship, probably a historical one, reflecting a time when societies had evolved to where the qualities of the personality disorder were a societal asset. Both exhibit how, over time, a functional asset can become dysfunctional.

RETHINKING DIAGNOSIS

The last two editions of the *Diagnostic and Statistical Manual of Mental Disorders* contain a decision tree to facilitate diagnosis.

This is a Yes or No, follow the lines, eliminate this or that alternate possibility, finally arriving at a diagnosis. Looking at it one way, the "tree" does exhibit some evolutionary characteristics; it moves from the biological/medical conditions to the highly culturally determined ones, such as marital or vocational conflict. Examined more closely, however, the "tree" is a jumble. The medical conditions include the genetic and the accidental, such as an accidental blow to the head of a young person that results in rages. This is classified along with vascular dementia, the hardening of the arteries among the elderly leading to a mental illness. It is with justification there is some questioning concerning classifying OCD as an anxiety disorder.[2] This leads to exploring diagnosis from an evolutionary perspective.

Looking at it this way, a "decision tree" looks not so much like a spreading oak as it does a much more vertical, tightly branched evergreen rising from the hereditary to the environment.

Mental Factors Contributing to a Diagnosis

> culturally defined mental conflicts
> adjustment disorders
> psychological issues
> personality disorders
> anxiety disorders . . . mood disorders
> O
> neurobiological disorders
> posttraumatic shock
> C
> dissociative disorders
> D
> spectrum disorders
> psychotic disorders
> impulse control disorders
> autism

Biological Factors Contributing to a Diagnosis

If we view "mental illness" from this perspective—that is, the effect of survival needs and consequent adaptations—we see diagnosis moving from a more physical mode to a more culturally defined one. It moves from the more or less purely physiological and individual mode toward a societal interaction, from earlier forms of human existence to more culturally refined—and defined—existence. Mental illness is thus seen at least partially defined by the environment in which it exists, but is biologically rooted. It will then eventually find a contemporary, culturally "flavored" expression.

What is important in this for OCD is that there is often a more than adequate supply of gray matter in the brains of those with this disorder, which would explain a tendency to test higher in IQ than the general population. There is, however, a relative lack of white matter, the connectors. Thus, we are looking not so much at an "illness" or "disease," as a dysfunction or a malfunction reflecting a biological lag time in which some individual's organism has failed to meet adaptational needs to a changing environment. Diagnosis pinpoints the evolutionary lag time of an individual.

In setting autism at the base of the diagnostic model, this reflects the report of the person with autism, in Chapter 1, in which the individual shared her regression to a mammalian perspective and interpretation of stimuli. We also need to recognize that autism probably exists in several forms, characteristic of the neurobiological disorders. In one form, the person regresses from being verbal and moves toward the nonlingual; in another, the infant never becomes lingual, but both can be diagnosed as one mental condition. This suggests, from an evolutionary viewpoint, that autism represents a period of human development when a capacity was forming around verbal abilities, perhaps waiting for the development of the larynx. Since autism often is seen interrelated with repetitive behaviors, it also suggests that obsessive-compulsive behaviors have a continuity as old as autism and may explain why, in a small percentage of cases, that compulsions exist without obsessions. This would also be true of obsessions without compulsions at the other extreme of the OCD continuum, both of being and of time.

If we look at the more severely disadvantaged humans, such as those with autism—in which there is reason to believe the person thinks in pictures rather than words—we would expect to see links to another severe condition. It would be no surprise that in a psychosis, a visual image—a delusion, a hallucination—would appear as real: and given sufficient regression in earth time, such an interjection might not be so far off from the reality in some eon.

In psychosis, we would expect to see symptoms expressive of developmental stages on either side, such as the association of reason with delusions of persecution on the upscale side, and on a more primitive side, there would be strange physical sensations. On the more evolved side, there would be fears of an unforgivable sin, much as in scrupulosity. On a downscale side would be a condition such as speaking in a "word salad." In all cases, we are walking among the burden bearers of the evolution in which we all have participated, some more fortunately than others, and those more unfortunate deserve a special honor for they exhibit our burdened past.

In regard to psychosis, to set this as it is on the scale reflects that schizophrenia is a relatively advanced condition from an evolutionary perspective. The affective (emotional) form of schizophrenia would be the more primitive, of course, since schizophrenia in its form of a "thought" disorder requires a more highly evolved brain in which "thought" takes place. Obsessive-compulsive disorder, in its continuum, is even older than psychosis because checking and contamination fears existed earlier than "feeling" or "thought." These older behaviors, however, were not a "disorder" in that they were highly functional. Certainly they are far older than impulse-control disorders, as these depend upon some form of social development, but, again, there is little to relate to a diagnosis of OCD, other than the presence of a continuum of behavior from functional to dysfunctional over an eon of environmental change.

With the "retarded" we are now back to a most primitive stage of development in which we can often see compulsive behaviors, such as rocking or head banging. What this suggests is that, viewed on an evolutionary scale, these are not aspects of mental illness or even of dysfunction, but rather these are burden bearers frozen in developmental time who are deservedly "special" to us.

When we look at diagnosis from this perspective, it is clear the search for "the missing link" is not to be found in the uncovering of some skull embedded in earth. It is the living organic human brain, with its strange bodily sensations of grunts and grimaces that is the link between the mammalian and the distinctively human. It is perhaps God's little joke that a mind has been searching for a brain and could not find it. The proof? Yourself. If you have kept up on nutrition, you undoubtedly have become less carnivorous and more herbivorous in diet for the sake of your health by eating plenty of fruit, relying more on grains, and decreasing your consumption of meats. Evolution is displaying itself as we understand what our bodies utilize best.

When we are considering Tourette's syndrome, as a spectrum disorder, we have on the downscale side of an evolving continuum an association with grunts, as if vocal chords were undeveloped, and tics, as if the body had been put together by a committee. On the upscale side would be "shit mouth" words—very basic anal words or in the more sophisticated, blasphemous—their expression often unknown to the utterer. Such a situation is not unusual when the young child comes home from neighborhood play with words that leave the mother aghast and the child has no idea of their meaning.

At almost any phase relevant to diagnosis, evolutionary theory would suggest there would be a differentiating factor as to fight/flight/stillness as tactics for survival. A bipolar quality would not only be in some, but actually all three tactics in some categories. You would expect to find in OCD anger, avoidance, and slowness; in depression would be manic and/or agitated, withdrawing and sullenness, and lethargy, dependency, or even ideation of death. In attention deficit disorder, you would expect to find manifested as hyperactivity, in a somnolence form, and as a potentiality for withdrawing from socialization activities.

From the perspective of evolution, it becomes clear why some medications positively affect seemingly contradictory conditions. Thus in OCD, medications of the serotonin reuptake inhibitor family are used for both anxiety and depression. Little wonder: conditions of OCD antedate the differentiation of anxiety and depression on the evolutionary scale. Dropping down on the evolutionary scale, we find those suffering from Tourette's syndrome responding to major tranquilizers, just as those with psychosis. The same continues to be true of bipolar disorder: lithium will treat the extremes of the manic (fight) or depressive (flight) because it addresses a condition antedating that differentiation.

Examining depression, with its expressions of agitation (fight) or lethargy/withdrawal (flight), or its extreme of suicidal ideation (playing dead), the antidepressant medication family is apt to address all expressions because it addresses conditions antedating the differentiation from which the condition evolved. A similar situation exists in the attention deficit disorders: Ritalin addresses all. Such a way of thinking explains why there is so much comorbidity associated with OCD: it is because the trunk and the expressions of it are in the more biologically rooted illnesses, such as psychosis; it branches into anxiety and depression, and then on to neurological individuation and, ultimately, primarily culturally influenced ones.

When we look at the "decision tree" of mental illness from an evolutionary perspective, we are simply looking at the human condition expressing itself in terms of dysfunctions from the prehistorical to the historical. That condition arises out of physiological conditions and obviously never totally departs from them, even when situational and environmental determinants change. It never totally loses its characteristics of fight/flight/slowness.

Several conclusions can be advanced:

1. Now we can question the appropriateness of using OCD as a category of anxiety, as well as confirming OCD as a neurobiological disorder. "Anxiety" should be reserved for "angst," as a unique quality of the human experience, in which we regard the threat of "non-being," as theologian Paul Tillich would phrase it. In any of the forms OCD takes, and in the vast continuum all of us experience, a fear is a fear is a fear.
2. Obsessive-compulsive disorder may be regarded as a psychiatric condition only in one regard: when it exists with such an intensity that it is identifiable with a more primitive mental/physiological condition approaching the psychotic (or the extremity of depression) as to be rendered totally dysfunctional or intentionally suicidal.
3. The extreme range of OCD symptoms simply reflects that OCD evolved over a long range of time. The oldest of the survival mechanisms is probably the "pure" compulsion. Checking is probably the oldest of the obsession and compulsion combina-

tion. The latest of these expressions are the most cognitive, "pure" obsessions.

4. Causation for OCD arises from two sources. First, the gap in evolutionary time between when obsessions and compulsions were functional and later became dysfunctional and, second, in conditions of posttraumatic shock, which have become part of a genetic inheritance.

5. Vulnerability to OCD arises from multiple causes, such as strep infections or brain lesions, which occasion a regression to one of the conditions we categorize as OCD.

6. An evolutionary perspective can also give us a greater appreciation of other forms of what we regard as mental illness and its transformation. In the case of "depression," it can be perceived as simply the human emotional circumstances throughout history, recorded and unrecorded: it was "plugging" along, just surviving. In its most primitive conditions, it is simply a "dogged" will to live. In its most extreme, reflecting conditions of slavery or captivity, the decision of suicide was that of dying with dignity, by choice. In what we regard as "manic-depressive," the manic was *very* useful: it was the fighting frenzy that won. What is truly miraculous is that it became, not the frenzy of the "berserker," but of many artists, such as when Handel wrote the *Messiah* in London in just three days.

7. As OCD evolved over a long range of time and consequently has a purely physical expression at one extreme and a more purely mental expression at the other, we get a diagnostic and consequent treatment advantage in dealing with depression. Depression is, of course, almost omnipresent with OCD. The question is *before or after*. If depression comes prior to the explicit appearance of OCD symptoms, then the depression has a hereditary origin (or one so severe as to be physically imprinting, such as losing a parent in infancy). If the depression appears after OCD, then we are dealing with a consequence of OCD, more personally and socially, rather than biologically. Determining this affects the consideration of medication and a psychotherapeutic approach: the later the depression, the slower to medicate.

8. With this perspective, we can be less judgmental and take more socially therapeutic actions in regard to a primitive con-

dition such as kleptomania. It simply becomes an acknowledgment that we emerged from a time when one took what was needed to live without any thought about the effect on other life-forms. With impulse control problems, a similar need exists for less judgmentalism and more relevant treatment. The treatment issue may incorporate punishment, as appropriate to the individual's developmental level, but "rehabilitation" is an inept way of perceiving the problem, rather than targeting growth toward a higher developmental stage of personality. *Growth*, not regression/rehabilitation, is the means to the end.

SYMPTOM SELECTION

Genetic tracks are easily observed in support groups, but symptoms do not always "breed true"—the mother may count but the daughter may clean. Mendel, in his monastery garden, would have difficulty as a bean counter doing an OCD research project. Some accounting of emerging symptoms therefore needs to be made.

Some selection of symptoms run in the survival mode: fight or flight—to which we add stillness, and like the submarine individual "run silent, run deep," and "all slow" if the hunt closes in on them; The ultimate expression is in the catatonic form of schizophrenia, the lesser form is found in agoraphobia or in the somnolence of some persons with attention deficit disorder.

Some symptoms may express family traits to some degree: mother may clean and teach daughter to clean, but likely the daughter's OCD will also erupt in other ways, as well. A mother who hoards may have a daughter who reacts with cleaning. Being fight prone or fight phobic will affect the person's traits and influence—but not prescribe—the person's OCD symptoms.

Some symptoms reflect socioeconomic conditions, as the continuum of hoarding expresses. A person of limited means may find his neurological compulsion to hoard taking the form of exploring what other people discard in the trash and which he will take home as valuable. A middle-class man may well find it impossible to throw away the mail while a woman may shop and bring home what amounts to piles of unaffordable yet inexpensive costume jewelry; a professional may be unable to discard any of hundreds of journals.

Middle-class persons with any amount of disposable income may become collectors—such as with "Barbie Dolls" or "Beanie Babies"— and "disposable income" to the point that collecting disposes even one's credit rating.

The upper, upper-class will find an expression suitable to their position, as probably did the art-loving popes who collected the Vatican into bankruptcy. Having a computer with practically unlimited memory now expresses the ultimate in the person saving what will not save the person.

It has all the qualities of a religious frenzy. "Manic" is not a bad word for it either. In fact, the most creative shopper I ever worked with managed that manic phase of her life by shopping with a buddy of similar persuasion. The one store they would hit was a rock collectors' shop, and they learned to appease their need to collect with a big bag of pretty pebbles and a roar of laughter at the silliness of it all. Diagnostically, a determination of this condition is simple: in a proverbial story, an Arab in his tent one cold night felt sorry for his freezing camel outside. He charitably let the camel put a nose, and then a head, inside. Gradually the Arab found himself on the outside and the camel occupied the tent.

Life is a feedback loop from past to present. The anxious surveillance as a child in a severely dysfunctionally family can become checking if the coffee pot is off. In an individual's history, a home that was burned in childhood can become expressed in a need to hoard. So, perhaps the ancient trauma of prairie fire may become anxiety about fire and an obsession as to whether the computer has been left on. The social need to preserve one's culture or to impose order can be transformed into regulations, then into tradition and so into scruples, using the familiar pressure tactics of teaching and preaching to generate fear arousal. More than hat size can be tattooed on one's DNA.

Scruples, fed by "holier-than-thou" preaching and guilt arousal are so deep, they can take the form of compulsive witnessing—a projection called "collegial" scrupulosity. As one might expect, "saved by faith alone," or Christian charitableness, stands little chance against "hellfire-and-brimstone" sensations; so Section B of the revivalist's sermon is more powerful than Section A. That, too, needs to be learned from OCD; religion, when driven by anxiety into obsessions, can become expressed not only in avoidances, but also in aggressiveness.

Now, let's look at the fear of contamination from a perspective of social history, rather than that of the individual. In the bell tower of the Rathaus (city hall) in Munich, dancing figures appear to celebrate the hour; they represent the survivors of the Black Plague. So deep has this been burned into our collective unconscious that the first, simplest prayer of childhood comes to us from those plague experiences. After supper and before retiring to bed the family said "good-byes," rather than "good nights":

> Now I lay me down to sleep
> I pray the Lord my soul to keep.
> If I should die before I wake,
> I pray the Lord my soul to take.

Do we wonder that contamination fears often reflect, not "you contaminate me," but the fear that "I contaminate you"? Take but just a moment to reflect on the post-traumatic stress disorder: what survivor guilt may appear—as well as relief to have survived—to take a "U" turn when stress next deepens? Add to these the chemical imprinting of more contemporary contagions, such as tuberculosis; this fearfulness is played upon in *La Bohème* as Mimi dies and was evident in the reckless gun fighting of Doc Holliday in the Old West. What would be astonishing is if, with the AIDS epidemic, we do *not* see more implosions of contamination fears.

Looking at the sweep of the prehistorical to the historical, what a marvel, then, that we are privileged to witness an OCD support group's agonizing over guilt! In a world out of which we came it was eat or be eaten, kill or be killed; now we turn aside from our morning papers, which report genocide, rape, and plunder, and attend an evening OCD support group to listen to what purports to be the ridiculous minutiae of ethical issues in some sufferers of scrupulosity. Out of tragedy, are we witnessing a triumphal process, perhaps at midpoint? We see the agony with the genes and recorded history of five generations or five hundred . . . or fifty thousand. Are we not seeing a partial triumph in consciousness over interjected "bizarre" thoughts and irresponsible impulses? Are we not participating in the process of perfecting a conscience? In the struggle to differentiate between false and real guilt, in the "defective conscience" of scrupulosity, we are witnessing the transitional process of the human brain. It is a movement from the loss of one goodness of fit in bygone eras to a new goodness of fit in a world still in the process of creation.

PROGRESSION AND REGRESSION

Arriving home from another support group session, it might seem to our tourist from Jupiter that she was seeing a multilayered, classic wedding cake, with the little formal figures on top. Let the mind drift downward to the foundation layer, imagining that the bottom layer represents that little extended family group of upright figures on the African savanna. It is a little group of Not Stills, Not Yet: not apes of the forest, not yet the clan to come.

If you were a Jane Goodall and could make friends with them—this midnight minus a few ticktocks on the human time clock—you could make benchmark observations. They are fearful, timid, cautious, and interdependent; they have limited self-awareness, locked into immediacy and dependency; only the children frolic while adults exist with unrelieved alertness. You could not say they "think" or "feel," but the rudiments are there for caring and anger, as well as for using tools. You could not impose a word such as "pragmatic." After all, what is the alternative? You could not impose a word such as "mood," for a best-case scenario is a juicy root and the worst, a poisonous snake.

Letting your mind drift in time, and in fantasy, up the layers of the cake, words would form to characterize what evolves. Words such as "dependent," "introspective," "inhibited," and "depressant." If I may free-associate, what comes to mind is a term from a report on a psychic reading: the person had an "old soul." It suggests that some persons in the genetic lottery of the ages would be more directly descended from such a group in the expansion from ten thousand Not Yets/Will Be to a billion. All would have some such characteristics, some more, some less. In any increase, such as to six billion, there would be some who seem almost "newly minted," but given enough stress they, too, could regress.

Permit a fantasy about the figures at the top of the cake: so stereotypical, inflexible, "goody-goody," and, well, *wooden*. How different persons become with group participation! It sheds a different light on treatment. One could empathize with old Geppetto the woodcarver in his workshop, carving and painting his puppet, Pinocchio. Have you ever been in a support group where, afterward, someone said, "Man alive, *that* was a good session?" Yes, you almost see the dancing of the sparkles in the workshop. In the Pinocchio myth, one thing the wood/human puppet had to learn was to resist temptation and never fall away from the true and real. Otherwise his nose—guess what?—would repetitiously grow.

But where does one find the courage to change? Where would those timid creatures of so many years ago find the courage to migrate? You would find a few adventurers, of course; the careless ones seldom reported back. On the trek across the world, you would expect to find a few bold, a few old, but not many combinations of the two. What motivated the movement? What we already know: escaping natural calamity, overpopulation brought on by an increasing food supply, and primogeniture. That is, the oldest, biggest, strongest, and meanest kept all: "Little brothers, if you don't like serving me, you know what you can do about it." They did, and some females, too.

Observe persons coming into a group or into individual treatment. They are, for the most part, introverted, downcast, and inhibited. From knowing OCD, you understand how these qualities could be genetically ground into them, as well as individually socially learned. Here in this nation of immigrants, however, it would be difficult to believe the courage that got them here is not also genetically stored in those same genes. It is simply a question of accessing the creativity that is the very nature of the genetic process.

BAGGING THE GAME: IMPLICATIONS OF EVOLUTIONARY THINKING

It should be noted that obsessions and compulsions are combined about 80 percent of the time, leaving only small percentages as purely behavioral or purely mental—which actually may be a mental ritual. Understanding the development of personality in childhood is helpful at this point. Quite early, perhaps at age one, repetitious behavior can exist—rocking, head banging—but cognitive processes are limited. Moving into the next period, ages four and five, the child is into a cognitive area. Now repetition may be mental, there may be an imaginary playmate, or, in an extreme case such as abuse, the child may fantasize about being the wall of the room. Repetition now serves a defensive purpose against anxiety. To deal with these conditions, exposure/responsive prevention has worked well with the physical rituals and less well, up until now, with the mental ones.

The defensive condition we see in such cases, and in OCD in general, is an alerted state of consciousness, a trance state. In the case of a combination of obsession and behavioral rituals, we have a natural process of resolving the obsession through the ritual—the more rapid exhaustion of glucose through activity. In the pure obsession, there is no mechanism for the rapid exhaustion of glucose, therefore the pure obsession tends to persist for a longer time. The problem in treating the pure obsession may rest there: we have had little success at affecting the rate of metabolizing glucose; we have photographed it; we just have not been able to sufficiently alter it. Exercise affects it, but also plays a role in recycling the problem.

There has to be a predisposition toward extreme anxiety for OCD and the spectrum disorders to occur for, among other things, a glucose "rush" to take place. The DNA has to convey sufficient trauma so that a startle response is "hair triggered." Some trauma must be in all of us, but some combinations over the thousands—even millions—of years will present random combinations that reinforce one another, so some are more vulnerable than others. Some combinations can be identified in "heredity," such as "my mother—or father—was a cleaner."

Some vulnerability to regression will occur in the form of a strep infection, brain lesion, or having the wrong ancestor a couple of generations ago when a peculiar form of measles was going around. We will be finding others, of course, but this is the proposed hypothesis: the vulnerable to severe anxiety, when exposed to sufficient stress or trauma, will regress (or be locked into) the personality characteristics of early childhood (ages one-and-a-half through five). *These personality characteristics can be characterized as "the child of OCD."*

To effectively treat OCD when it erupts early in childhood is quite a trick. Usually, when it comes early, it brings with it as many symptoms as fingers on both hands—and those doubled up into a fist with intensity. The implication is that when OCD erupts in the adult, using the completion of puberty as a boundary, we are dealing with a regression, a more "mature" personality regressing into a lesser one. When OCD has its outbreak in childhood such as caused by a strep infection, that is, in a more immature state of personality development, there is no regression. With the more mature adult, when the body's glucose is exhausted, relief is experienced as the individual returns to his or her normal mental and physical state. The child has nothing to which to return, so the problems of OCD are simply reinforced.

The OCD of childhood and adulthood is not different, as the OCD experience of the adult and the chronological age of the child overlap. For the child, there are no clear boundaries along which regression can occur and then reverse course. The "child of OCD" for an adult may be age three, but for the *actual* child with OCD, that child *is* three; no regression is possible. A "double dipping" happens; it is a reinforcement of what is and a multiplicity of what exists. The early eruption also suggests a variety of symptoms are available to find expression. In the child's brain, few defenses have been established by passing through more than one developmental stage above where OCD is to be found.

So it is that we may find a child with an anxiety about wearing clothes. We can speculate that this represents a time when clothing was "unnatural" at some primordial phase of our evolution; such speculation may be accurate, but the question is how to make it relevant. It is fortunate, indeed, for the adult sufferer when that symptom has been modified into just having to change clothes a few times before it finally feels "just right." For the young child it becomes part of treatment planning to raise the symptoms to the level of changing clothes and becoming habituated to wearing some clothes that feel "just right."

PERSONALITY, OCD, AND SYMPTOM CREEP

In *Tormenting Thoughts and Secret Rituals,* Dr. Ian Osborn quotes a theory of personality development that he associates with OCD:

> high in harm avoidance, timid, inhibited, apprehensive, tense, shy, easily fatigued, and pessimistic about the future . . . low in novelty seeking, reflective, loyal, stoic, slow-tempered, and orderly . . . good scouts . . . high in reward dependence, sympathetic, eager to help, and sentimental . . . people pleasers.[3]

Part of the difference OCD makes can be described in psychological terms. An extrovert will find it easier to maintain contact with immediate sensory data; an introvert may find it more natural to respond to an internal process. It is not that the introvert is more likely to misinterpret sensory data; it is that physiologically the introvert is less likely to be able to resist having the body entrained by what is, in actuality, a false alarm. The brain's internal boundaries of the extrovert almost by definition tend to be firmer; in the introvert they are almost by definition more flexible through frequently used electrochemical processes of self-exploration.

These characteristics can be seen from other perspectives, however. Erik Erikson describes the developmental tasks to be resolved for the child ages one-and-a-half to three as "autonomy versus shame and doubt," and "initiative versus guilt" from ages three through five.

Now consider how Dr. James Fowler describes the child in that period:

> Imagination, not yet disciplined by consistent logical operations . . . attempts to form images that can hold the mixture of feelings and impressions evoked by the child's encounter with newness of both everyday reality and the penumbra of mystery that surrounds and pervades it. Death emerges as a source of danger and mystery. Experiences of power and powerlessness orient children to a frequently deep existential concern about questions of security, safety, and the power of those upon whom they rely for protection. Owing to a naive egocentrism,

children do not consistently differentiate their perspectives from those of others. Because of this lack of perspective taking, and in virtue of an as yet unreliable understanding of cause-and-effect relations, children construct and reconstruct events in episodic fashion. While appreciative of stories and capable of becoming deeply engrossed in them, they are seldom able to reconstruct very adequately the narrative pattern and detail of a story. . . . There is an appreciation for stories that represent the powers of good and evil in unambiguous fashion. These make it possible for children to symbolize the threatening urges and impulses that both fascinate and terrify them. . . . There is in this stage the possibility of aligning powerful religious symbols and images with profound feelings of terror and guilt. . . . Such possibilities give this stage the potential for forming deep-going and long-lasting emotional and imaginable orientations in faith—both for good and ill.[4]

It is clear that many of the general characteristics of the child at this age parallel those of OCD. Both superstition and scrupulosity have fertile ground on which to sprout and grow.

To state the obvious, many of those with OCD continue to struggle to resolve the issues of early childhood; it is *not* that they are childlike, or "childish." Some with OCD are at the developmental stage characterized by oral needs; this is illustrated by alcoholism and the spectrum disorder of anorexia; most persons with moderate OCD are at a higher level of personality development. Certainly there can exist a vulnerability to OCD, such as being an introvert rather than an extrovert, but the question cannot be avoided, "Why obsessions and compulsions?" Regardless of the personality characteristics of the person suffering from OCD, why should the obsessions and compulsions—considered as a "package"—resemble the characteristics of early childhood? Why, if the characteristics of OCD can be generalized as an amplification of traits in the personality, is it almost invariably preceded by overwhelming stress or recognizable trauma?

Now consider how a depressive personality is described in the *Diagnostic and Statistical Manual of Mental Disorders* (DSM-IV):

persistent and pervasive feelings of dejection, gloominess, cheerlessness, joylessness, and unhappiness . . . overly serious, incapable of enjoyment or relaxation, and lack a sense of humor . . . tends to brood and worry, dwelling persistently on their negative and unhappy thoughts . . . views the future as negatively . . . doubt that things will ever improve, anticipate the worst . . . harsh in self-judgment and prone to feeling excessively guilty for shortcomings and failings. Self-esteem is low and particularly focused on feelings of inadequacy.[5]

It is clear that any child who does not resolve the developmental issues appropriate to ages one-and-a-half through five will likely have an affinity for depression; no surprise either that with OCD there will also be an affinity for depression—half are reported to be depressed and many will experience a major depression. "Doubt" and "ambivalence" are notable in both the depressive personality and OCD.

The question is: do most persons with OCD get "stuck" developmentally in this period, or do a statistically significant number resolve those issues positively, only to regress later, at the age of the first overtly identifiable experience of OCD? You might regard this as whether the chicken or the egg comes first, but experience with OCD sufferers suggests that both happen. If we accept, however, that the average person with OCD is more "intelligent" than the general population, then most of them in their non-OCD daily living have moved from the concrete thinking of early childhood to the ability to think abstractly—it argues, intellectually, that the OCD sufferer has achieved a developmental level from which regression is possible.

Furthermore, if the percentage of persons with OCD who obtain driver's licenses lacks statistically significant difference from those without OCD, it argues that the premorbid condition of persons who later have OCD is not characterized by low risk taking. So many with OCD have terrifying obsessions associated with driving; yet relatively few quit driving, which argues that characteristics such as timidity, shyness, and inhibition are more associated with the OCD experience than with their normal lifestyle. That they are low in novelty seeking may well be associated with avoidances imposed by OCD and its symptom creep, such as depression, rather than a dislike for new experiences.

The following theoretical arguments are of significance:

1. If the premorbid personality was a "normal" one, then a reasonable goal of treatment is symptom resolution.
2. When there was a "normal" personality development well into the adolescent years before experiencing OCD, similar circumstances exist to those that make brief psychotherapy successful. Exposure/response blocking techniques are both successful and sufficient for symptom removal. In combination with cognitive techniques the sufferer usually can be significantly helped.
3. Since there are different developmental issues to be resolved between the oral, anal, and oedipal stages, different treatment techniques need to be considered.
4. When characteristics such as timidity, shyness, dependence, and people-pleasing not only are part of the OCD experience, but also characterize the major personality traits of the person and constitute significant difficulties in the person's life, they deserve to become targets of treatment, as well as the obsessions and compulsions.
5. If OCD is a regression to the one-and-a-half to three, or three through five age group developmental levels, *there are qualities to those periods that can be utilized in treatment and which need to be incorporated in the treatment program, as we will see.*
6. Because of the impact of OCD on personality development, such aspects as a depressive lifestyle and poor interpersonal relationships need to be addressed in the treatment sequence.
7. Since religious feelings are a natural part of the latter part of the developmental periods, for persons with OCD, religious feelings need to be acknowledged and considered as part of the treatment process.
8. As the early childhood stages are at a developmental level where a person experiences emotional handicaps in the adult world, a positive outcome to treatment is not limited to symptom removal, but includes growth toward a higher level of

emotional functioning, in keeping with one's intellectual development.

Again, let me reaffirm what is being said: a person with OCD is not being childlike, much less "childish." We are rather discussing a *regression* to that evolutionary stage of human development when persons most resembled the characteristics of today's children in the personality developmental stage of early childhood. This explains why persons with OCD most frequently have their first episode after a traumatic experience or inability to continue to cope with the buildup of stress. As the post-traumatic stress disorder is regressive, so is the obsessive-compulsive disorder. It is reminiscent of the sentiment a wife shared with me, "Someday they will find a cure, and it will give my husband back to me"—a hope that, even in a most severe case, the adult person will emerge from a most severe regression.

Once the older system with its programming for survival takes over, it will alter the response to sensory data by either *trivializing* it or *canalizing* it. In the instance of trivializing, it will include too much, making evaluations vague. This is illustrated by hoarding: anything and everything is likely to be perceived as valuable—"I may need it"—and consequently nothing is of value, all values are leveled—such as being able to have grandchildren stay for their vacation as opposed to keeping bulging bags of "things" blocking the bedrooms. Scrupulosity appears to be the fraternal twin of hoarding because anything and everything may be perceived as "sinful"; guilt levels the values of all experiences. In canalization, the initial response is in accord with the survival programming—recheck that lock, be sure the stove is really off—but immediate data then are excluded, as if the memory were defective. *Both trivializing and canalizing processes may cloak themselves in religion, but are areligious in their rejection of assigning hierarchies of worth.*

Creative advances in career and relationships stumble haltingly after the OCD outbreak. Life gets tiresome—very tiresome—a monotone of life with biological manacles. It is not that the person has lost her or his intelligence; it is that in this monotone sensory data have largely lost their meaning, blending into a sameness of experiencing. Stimuli are rejected out of fear they will provoke a startle response. It is inadequate not only for a person to say, "Stop it. You can if you really want to." It is also inadequate to criticize the sameness; most of all, it is inadequate to go along with the OCD "program" of avoidance to evade a "scene." The object of it all is creative advance—growth.

PERSONAL DEVELOPMENT

The "personality profile" sought for those suffering from OCD has not been a productive undertaking. Little wonder in that from an evolutionary perspective, we are looking at a process extending from whatever was the beginning, to the mammalian, and then to modern men and women. Those "modern men and women" as individuals have all sorts and sizes of personality development; however, using Erik Erikson's scale of solving crucial issues, it looks like this:

Infancy	0 to 1.5 years	basic trust versus mistrust (hope)
Early Childhood	1.5 to 6	autonomy versus shame and doubt
		initiative versus guilt (purpose)
Childhood	6 to 12	industry versus inferiority (competence)
Adolescence	13 to 21	identity versus role confusion (fidelity)
Young Adulthood	21 to 35	intimacy versus isolation (love)
Adulthood	35 to 60	generativity versus stagnation (care)
Maturity	60+	integrity (wisdom) versus despair

As may be seen in any OCD support group meeting, there is no developmental pattern among the participants: one person at one level, one here, there, and everywhere. Often a person will share that she now recognizes she had symptoms for a long time, but was coping well with them until some trauma led to an acceleration of obsessions and the shattering of self-esteem. After the shattering of self-esteem and the obsessions and rituals enlarge, then the developmental stage characterizing the interior of the OCD experience leads to a greater uniformity of subsequent "personality." One may be unable to hold a job, another will be a high achiever.

A pattern does appear, however, one that any parent may recognize. There is a natural time for the need for repetition to appear. We all know how it is: "Read it again!" And again. And again. If you get tired, change a word, or leave out a page, you will hear about it. Reading that story has to be *just right.* This may explain why OCD is often found in the lives of those with an early childhood strep infection: high fever + a natural phase in which repetition occurs = OCD.

Now you get a pattern and a differentiation of patterns. Participation in the group—after the introductory phase—is marked by a different level than you would expect for someone with OCD. Outside of the OCD experience, the life of the individual is often not what you would expect with someone with OCD; personality greatly varies. *Inside* the OCD experience a far more uniform personality pattern exists: insecurity, egocentricity to the point of blocking out others' needs, often a dependency need, doubting, negativity, hostility, and, as in hoarding, anality.

Concepts such as weaning and toilet training make for helpful diagnostic differences here. Oral needs—such as too much or too little eating, or substance abuse, probably indicate unresolved needs more related to a developmental stage even earlier than early childhood. Often treatment has to be considered in the form of hospitalization in order to effect "weaning." Self-control and boundary setting are central issues. Just withholding, saying "No," is identity-forming. An unresolved need for the maternal may result in needing reassurance over and over again; when upset, this need can seem a bottomless pit.

This is a time of special wounds. The first of these is a failure to hope, of giving way to despair: "I will never be able to get my life in order"; "I am so shamed of having OCD; what's the use of trying?" There is a cyclical movement, as in the borderline personality syndrome of improvement and regression: less stress and it gets better, more stress and "here we go again." There may be narcissistic wounds so deep that self-love is turned into self-loathing, or even self-mutilating.

This is the age for the basic family, "my"—or "our"—kind of people. This is marvelously portrayed in the cartoon strip *Calvin and Hobbes;* the "club" is really important, especially which member is most important—and "girls keep out." It is a time when a feeling of independence is highly cherished, although its reality is limited and unrealistic from a "grown-up's" point of view—or the judge's, if there is a lawsuit about some club's membership.

It is a time of rapid brain development, particularly of connective tissue. In OCD, the brain development continues, but there is less connecting tissue (the white matter connecting the gray cells, the carriers of "intelligence"). Consequently, a vulnerability to superstitions occurs when stress accelerates, a potentiality to regress to the point where an ability to grasp relationships is precarious. In cognitive behavioral therapy, the natural process of developing the connectors within the brain is utilized in challenging superstitious avoidances and to grasping relationships.

In the grip of the OCD experience, there is a value system that Freud would have considered "primary process thinking" regarding what is pleasurable as good and what is not pleasurable as bad, as in very early childhood. Fear of getting caught and punished is present; you could reflect on morality and conclude there is none, just a desire to be reassured as "good." Shame is experienced, but not guilt. Until after about age three, when guilt feelings stir resulting from identification with a father figure and internalization of parental norms, you will not find much reality in being "moral." Avoidances and consequent inhibitions may portray themselves as "moral," but most often find expression in being "moralistic."

There is an orientation toward punishment and obedience to rules and that strange sense of exception. If an absence of authority occurs, the child will do as he or she pleases because "It's not wrong if I don't get caught." In the cartoon strip, Calvin discusses his Christmas list with the stuffed tiger, Hobbes, and he is totally truthful about his age group: you have to figure out what you can get away with and still get the gifts.

Authority becomes a big issue in the transitions from maternal to family to daddy. Big people have special privileges. Wanting to please is a big issue; being good is deferring to the big person who loves you. Later, age four or so, there will be a striving to be a "good boy" or a "good girl." Then appears a need to help Mommy and Daddy, to take responsibility and "look at what I can do." It is a time of magical thinking, of an invisible playmate, of superstitious fears, and of Santa Claus.

At about age three the child begins to identify with, and internalize, the father. This begins the formation of an internal authority—to adequately develop a "conscience." The child begins to set rules and becomes a law and order demander. People have to play by the rules. Everything is either black or white, right or wrong. The developmental ability to analyze and reason may result in the proliferation of rules, which children at play often make up as they go along.

In OCD we see "superstition," but this is an adult word. Something that is more descriptive of a child naturally indulging in magical thinking is the cartoon child, Calvin, when he shifts into "Spaceman Spiff," usually in response to anxiety. It is a time for splitting, a means of coping, when the ability to have an imaginary playmate will, under severe abuse, result in a dissociative disorder (one form of this used to be termed "multiple personality").

The child may rebel in early childhood, as Calvin does, and in consequence a big person can be terrorizing to such a little person. If such logic has credibility, then those of us without a clinically significant level of OCD can assume that experiencing OCD feels as overwhelming and beyond control as a small child feels with an adult who is totally out of control.

Thinking will demonstrate difficulty in distinguishing between fact and fantasy, as with Calvin and Hobbes. An animal, even a stuffed one, can be real to the child. Death is recognized, but the death of a pet will be more real to the child than the death of a person, such as a grandparent. Conflict may be enjoyed, as when Hobbes always jumps Calvin when he comes home, but no one ever really gets hurt. Socialization will be difficult, particularly for boys, and Calvin is mean to the girl in his neighborhood.

They can count, but not classify; a sense of proportion is yet to be developed. Lacking experience, there is no foresight. Religion is present, in the form of a projected image of the (usually) father figure, existing in an intuitive rather than a conscious form. It is a time of big questions.

Diagnostically, at the stage of ages two to three, the child is largely presympathetic and the OCD sufferer is likely to fear contamination from others. At ages four and five, he or she is afraid of contaminating others. In this later period, he or she will also suffer from counting and perfecting, which are unimportant accomplishments to a younger child. It sometimes helps to think about Santa Claus: at age one, the child is stimulated by the lights on the tree; at age two Mommy tries to help the child pronounce "Santa Claus"; in preschool, they are ready to sit on Santa's lap and tell all; at age six and in school, they classify as to who believes and who knows who Santa really is, and who wants to share that secret among friends.

About this time, the parents and day school teacher agree on the child's preschool readiness and some peer interaction. Children at this stage will play alongside one another, but not really *with* one another; true interrelation takes place only after the oedipal conflict has been resolved. The child is able to sympathize with someone who is hurt, but cannot as yet empathize because there is no way he or she can imagine how the other feels or thinks. On that evening when a group member first bursts out with empathetic understanding of another group member, it is a time for a consultant to lead in the burst of applause and admiration for a display of a new level of maturity.

In due time, about age ten or so, the brain changes. Systematic collecting begins, not just aimless gathering from curiosity (although a mother going through her son's pockets before washing may not think so). Empathy comes, logic comes, and symbolic thinking begins. Empathy develops and "fairness" becomes a virtue, due to the interactions on the playground. The ability to think abstractly will develop—usually about the time of learning long division; algebra appears in the class about the time of the capacity for symbolic thinking. Unfortunately, other things can happen as the chemical processes take place, such as the recognition of ADD. Learning disabilities become clear and again usually occur earlier in boys.

To summarize, OCD is a regression into a human past when that portion of the brain was evolving. The development of an individual's brain follows the evolutionary pattern of the specie: early childhood reflecting early humankind and regression in today's adult is marked by that paralleling. How better to interpret the sudden emergence of this disorder when it occurs most frequently after a trauma or extraordinary accumulations of stress? We are seeing a continuum of that regression: in its most catastrophic form, it is interrelated with autism and psychosis; in a slightly less severe form, it will be frequently interrelated with the spectrum disorders. It is this regression, this splitting of consciousness, that gives OCD its peculiar trancelike quality. When a sufferer speaks of "zoning out," this points to regression.

The line of reasoning, then, is that OCD is not bizarre; it is a continuation of a developmental stage of early humans. This stage is reenacted in early childhood. Ordinarily, persons grow and move on to further stages, but under extraordinary stress or a particular startle stimulus, vulnerable persons can, and do, regress in various ways. Obsessive-compulsive disorder is one of these situations; in OCD, coping with overwhelming stress and anxiety consists of thinking patterns and behaviors that characterized the early humans. We would expect to see a sequence of techniques to undo regression as anxiety expresses itself in the form of avoidance. These would have a treatment goal of modifying these from:

- ***SCARY, Scary, Scary***, *Scary*, *frightened*, agitated, a passing feeling of upset
  or
  PERFECT, Perfect, Perfect, *Perfect*, good enough, OK
  and
- the utilization of the positive qualities of early childhood, particularly in relationship to the "family feeling" in the support group

Health versus Pathology

"Health," then, may be defined in terms of the person's normal sequence of personality growth, which may, of course, have starts and stops according to circumstances and which can be arrested. The assumption here, *my* assumption, is that treatment leads broadly from a feeling for "my kind," in a sequence of resolutions to characteristic issues in living, to identification with and caring for "humankind."

PATHWAYS TO CHANGE

Exploring individual change, when we consider the implications of the first case story cited, "Nancy," and given the two memory systems, we can appreciate why healing is a process. We are struck with what William James described as "conversion" in *The Varieties of Religious Experience,* in which there is an integration of previously conflicting command structures in the brain. It also brings to heart and mind, "the more things change, the more they remain the same." In the evolving of personality, there is a biological continuance with its related issues. Change occurs, but not often in a unitary way; issues most often have to be resolved one at a time, probably because they must be integrated biologically in the person.

What we know is that OCD is enormously resistant to change. The explanation is recent and grounded in two memory systems, and even freedom from one does not mean remission from the other. In the matter of vacations, it is sometimes observed that OCD symptoms decline because one memory system is flooded with fresh stimuli and is refreshed while the other goes into remission— until returning home. Appropriate medication for the OCD condition may work wonderfully well in some cases even without exposure/response therapy—until the person goes off it for about six months. If change is to have a lasting quality, both memory systems have to be addressed.

The question comes up, however, as to whether OCD "ever burns itself out." In the natural course of events, it seems that it doesn't, although three exceptions occur. The first exception has to do with when it is taught. Scrupulosity seems to result from auditory sensory input, often enforced by anxiety-provoking means, perhaps by guilt-inducing teachers in a religious setting. When the individual is removed from those conditions, what Ciarrocchi termed "developmental" scrupulosity dissipates. This probably is the case for many students who experience scrupulosity; once out of school, an individual who has been biologically programmed for a preferred source of sensory input, other than auditory and scrupulosity, may go into remission. The second exception involves a young mother with several children. The needs of the children overwhelm the need to straighten and clean. The exhaustive demands of motherhood are great exposure and response therapy. The third exception is also about cleaning and straightening rituals, particularly if a woman learned them from her mother. After thirty years of repetitious, laborious, boring housework and the shine is off the value. Exposure takes place, takes place, takes place, so that the response—while not blocked—is so flooded eventually the ritual is moderated. The homemaker decides she likes the orderliness, but is not driven to it. She decides upon the level of cleaning and straightening with which she is satisfied and this becomes a comfortable new self-identity. Probably a trauma can, however, reactivate the OCD if life is unkind.

If a person wants to change his or her OCD, it requires a high degree of intentionality; spontaneous remissions exist in a host of mental conditions, but rarely in OCD. The reality of that is grounded in the neurobiological condition, a feedback loop within the individual's brain involving it almost in its entirety with a patterning of impulses along a well-used pathway. To this degree, OCD does resemble a habit. It is a habit that functions like an old mule used for grinding; when it is turned out to pasture, it finds a tree in the pasture and continues to walk in a circle around it.

It is that "mule" in the brain that must be addressed with the full force of a person's intentionality. The issue is similar to an apocryphal story told about John Dewey, the father of the American philosophy of pragmatism. A friend saw Dewey observing his grandson standing in a mudpuddle. "Mr. Dewey, don't you think you ought to get him out?" Dewey replied, "I am trying to think of a way to make him *want* to get out."

The change must occur on two levels, just as we have been discovering that a combination of treatment approaches is most effective. A remedial approach is needed for the midbrain's memory system and a growth approach is essential to the working memory of the individual's forebrain. Because we have to start somewhere, a tactic much favored by carrier pilots is:

> When in danger, or in doubt,
> Run in circles, scream and shout.

Telephone the OC Foundation, your doctor, your pastor, your . . . well, start by looking in the newspaper to see if a support group exists. Find out what is available. Use the Internet; there are at least two Web sites for OCD information. Check in the back of this book.

The remedial opportunity is to employ exposure and response-blocking techniques. The situation is that of the mammalian memory system having an imprinting of emergency imagery. If it sets off false alarms frequently enough and creates enough interference with daily living, then exposure response is the best current remedial procedure.

The exposure part may properly be characterized as an *incineration* technique. Instead of teeth grinding and jaw clamping, the sufferer actively challenges the OCD, but on his or her terms. The challenge—such as putting one's hand in the dirt, if that is the avoidance—sets off the chemical response. The challenge and its predictable response is preselected by the individual to be on a manageable level. The glucose burns and the person lets it burn. All treatments are part mythology because we are so lacking in understanding, but what seems to be happening is that, if the DNA has a trauma chemically etched into it, then the response must be blocked by the alleviating ritual. As a result, glucose will burn the imprinting out of the DNA. If terror comes when standing on a rug at the foot of the stairs, the person stands there, letting the glucose come and go, and before too many such sessions the glucose diminishes; whatever triggers it has been "satiated" or extinguished. For example, feed a pigeon a grain of corn when it rings the bell and it will ring the bell; quit giving it the grain of corn and the pigeon eventually quits. Obsessive-compulsive disorder functions on that level.

In exposure/response blocking, the way to eliminate a contamination fear is to attack the avoidance; let it burn and it will begin to literally incinerate the memory in that part of the mammalian memory system. This is using the mind to help modify the brain and thus free the working memory. Behavior modification techniques work because they were developed on animal models and what we have to modify are animal responses: dog hears bell, gets fed; dog hears bell, salivates. Dog is next taught that it will not be fed when the bell rings and eventually salivation ceases because the response has been extinguished. These procedures are well understood and we just use them on that part of our brain that functions on a similar level. If a false alarm goes off about contamination, and no washing follows, the amygdala will eventually quit responding to false alarms.

In reality, the chemical etchings on the person's DNA probably are being addressed, perhaps literally incinerated by the repeated exposure response and the naturally high rate of metabolizing glucose in the OCD episode. The images in the mammalian system probably are never completely extinguished, but certainly are greatly reduced in their ability to respond to misread stimuli. Actively challenging OCD is a more secure path than is extinction only by resistance, but both will modify the mammalian memory system; both work best together.

Sometimes, sensory input is so overwhelming that it must be remedied. The proper medications—the selective serotonin reuptake inhibitor family, or Anafranil (although of a different chemical family)—serve to make stress tolerable. They are not a cure, but they do buy toleration for treatment. Reduce the stress responses to the tolerable and the false alarms become more tolerable, more controllable, and more distinguishable from a real emergency. At the most extreme, electric shock treatment and even psychosurgery are needed to remedy the physiological condition. The obsessive-compulsive disorder is maintained by a recurrent sense of crisis, in which the startle response and subsequent obsessing in which there is a rush of energy by the well-photographed flooding of glucose to the brain.

What is to be avoided is a false homeostasis, in which a balance has been struck to keep the pathology in place. Obsessive-compulsive disorder is maintained by a sense of crisis—the startle response and subsequent obsessing—in which a rush of energy is generated to meet the emergency and glucose floods the brain. To relieve this flooding, the ritual is performed and in a measurable length of time it dissipates the glucose (and other chemical emergency team components).

It is a closed system, which is highly resistant to change: when the episode is over, the person is exhausted—for the glucose available to the body is exhausted—but the person experienced relief from "zoning out." The closed system is set to recycle and perhaps the person has to eat chocolate to generate more glucose! The recycling operates much like rechambering a round in the rifle and leaving the safety off, ready to "fire" at the next startle response. The treatment is to simulate an emergency, a controlled emergency agreed to and effected in a treatment program. A contrived stimulus is offered and the physiological reliever that actually resets the pathology is blocked.

On the level of growth, and addressing the need for change in the working memory, conceptual revision plays a key role. This cognitive level is demonstrated by Step One in *Brain Lock*, because "it's my OCD, it isn't me."[6] It never is purely cognitive, of course, as we are dealing with a feedback loop and there are always physiological consequences. In this case there is no exposure, but simply blocking responses. It is a technique used in several forms of psychotherapy: "reframing" the issue, as in Step Two, because "it's just a chemical thing in my brain."

Now it is possible to see how treatment works. An incineration occurs of the traumas burned into the DNA. On another level, this is assisted by the appropriate level of serotonin so that one nerve ending connects to the next nerve ending and facilitates appropriate communication within the brain. With that, both broader relationships and cognitions are encouraged so that the corpus callosum, that strip connecting the two hemispheres, functions better. The dominating hemisphere then begins to balance out, giving intellect access to feeling and emotions access to cognitive evaluations. On another level, a relating to those near and dear—as in a support group—occurs so isolation is not so intense that it feels like the end of one's world as an entrancement occurs and reality fades. The sufferer feels more "real."

The "rules of the game" regarding sensory input are important here. These are referred to as "epigenetic rules" by Edmund Wilson.[7] They are those experiences of pain and pleasure—and survival—internalized in the two memory systems. The primordial system with its learned pain and pleasure continues to exist because it is reinforced by the contemporary system. Feel terror, start checking; feel anxious, start cleaning, changing clothes—whatever. It is an interlocking feedback system. Change the rules about a startle response, instead of going into the emergency mode; slow everything down and take in stimuli more slowly—feel the muscles, smell the smells.

The issue is that the contemporary conscious rules help preserve the unconscious ones: they codependently sustain the primordial one. Change the rules—"do the opposite," as Ignatius counsels—and change occurs. Change begins when a sufferer realizes, "When I get anxious, I straighten and that gives me relief—and also makes my life miserable." The person begins reconfiguring the rules of the game for pain and pleasure. Part of that reconfiguring is redoing one's life to a manageable level of stress; if stress is overwhelming, so too is reality—and dropping out into another stratum of memory has greater pulling power. Better the torment that is false than the torment of what is all too real.

First, the change being effected is what Whitehead termed "conceptual revision." In the instant of time that we term "the present," all our inheritance of heredity and environment, which goes into making us what we are, is brought together. In that instant, there is a freedom in which cognition reevaluates this summation of data; some up, some down. All the stimuli offered to the instantaneous moment cannot be absorbed; below the level of awareness, simplification occurs. Whether studying a computer screen or absorbed in a sunset, something gets ignored. A new thing emerges in the new instant that did not exist in the instant that passed into the momentary present, until that "present" passed into its successor. Change occurs—always. When the interjected thought strikes, do not respond in knee-jerk fashion, but evaluate.

Next, what we are offered is a freedom that we humans may choose in which, by *valuing,* we can intentionally—somewhat—choose our future. Consciousness is only a flicker on the pinnacle of the massive size of biology, but it is our prize and our joy as humans. We can only modify that future; we cannot revolutionize it by "jumping over our own shadow"—and the attempt most frequently is an invitation to disaster by denial—but we can participate in *evolving* our future. There is always the possibility, on the level of awareness, that we can *choose.* In OCD, the person has to choose before the whole body goes on "full alert" to a nonexisting emergency, but practice in choosing makes much more perfect than does trying to get it all to feel "just so."

The third pathway is through new data, new perspectives: the Twelve Step Program of OCD Anonymous demonstrates that daily, as do support groups. There is acceptance, trust, and bonding so that the formerly closed system begins to open. Stress and threat closes the individual's system; now, a less restricted pattern of knowing and belonging helps the person to open up to changes in believing and behaving. A sense of "inspiration" occasionally occurs, particularly in group existence, an "aha" that marks more of the brain being activated. The old patterns of knowing, which locked in contradictory modes of processing information—"I have to wash down the refrigerator again, but I know it is clean because I have just washed it"—begin to give way. Acceptance by the group leads to acceptance of the group, and that opens up new pathways for sensory processing and grasp of relationships, both about objects and with other persons. It is the usual experience for persons with OCD to come to a group with an intense feeling of absolute aloneness and most often with thoughts of "I must be crazy to think and do these things." In the sharing of stories, and particularly in the sharing of laughter, there comes a therapeutic distance from the dysfunction.

A change is now possible in relationship to what is one's reality; it absorbs one's attention when about to descend into hell. The biological agitation that the OCD experience conveys serves to reinforce one's sense of excluding reality so greatly that it severs the sense of relatedness to one's primary reference group. For example, the mother ignores the kids' supper when obsessing; the father staring at the lock on the door is oblivious to the kids' anger in the car. This severing, at the same time, brings a terror as primary relationships fade. The ability to change is reinforced by opening the door to relatedness and that is often done through the experience of a support group: "First time in my life I ever felt I belonged"; "This group really feels like family to me." Effective therapy is never individual, it simply occurs in the context of a group of two in which acceptance is mutually experienced by counselor and counselee; only then is the behaviorist granted permission for behavior to be modified.

Once the person starts "opening up," change occurs on several levels. On the bonding level, the right hemisphere becomes more functional. On the level of accepting group feedback, the left hemisphere probably becomes more activated, particularly in the development of psychological connections, and consequently biological connectors. The greater activation of both hemispheres encourages the utilization of new circuits as new relationships are formed. More of the brain is being utilized and no treatment strategy is going to finally work that does not accomplish that.

On another level, facilitating change is the issue of what draws us toward fulfillment: sperm and egg to fetus, fetus to adulthood, *Homo habilis* to Neanderthal to *Homo sapiens sapiens*. On the most mature aspect of this "drawing toward" St. Augustine offered this thought as he wrote, "Our hearts are restless—*our being is agitated*—they find their rest in Thee."

Chapter 8

Learning from Effecting Change

Above all, trust in the slow work of God. We are, quite naturally, impatient in everything to reach the end without delay. We
should like to skip the intermediate stages. . . . Yet it is the law
of all progress that it is made by passing through some stages
of instability. . . . Let your ideas mature gradually, let them
grow, let them shape themselves, without due haste. Don't try
to "force" them on, as though you could be today what time
(that is to say, grace and circumstances acting on your own
good will) will make you tomorrow.

Pierre Teilhard de Chardin
letter to his cousin, July 4, 1915
at the front in the sand dunes east of Dunkirk
The Making of a Mind, 1965

The state of the art, in OCD treatment modalities today, can be
summed up in a one-liner: *The Expert Consensus Treatment Guidelines for Obsessive-Compulsive Disorder.* The book comes in two
forms, one as a guide for patients and families and one for professionals to be kept in the office for handy referral. Both may be
obtained from the OC Foundation, whose address is listed in Available Resources at the back of the book. Having said that, we may go
on, as any guidelines are constituted by consensus of committee and
the "state of the art" is a moving target.

WE HAVE MUCH EXPERIENCE
WITH WHAT DOES NOT WORK

We have known about OCD for a long time. Attempts to cure it
have illustrated the truth that, if you want to understand something,
just try to change it. It has been similar to Thomas Edison trying to

design the electric light. He knew about light and electricity, he then found 999 ways to make an electric light that did not work. What we now understand about OCD is built on 999 good-faith efforts. This is not to deny—in hindsight—wacky treatment attempts such as exorcisms, inappropriate hospitalizations, the administration of inappropriate medications, or the resurrection of 2,000-year-old surgical procedures. The advancement in psychotherapy is a lot like making sausage: it is not for the faint of stomach. We need to salute, not condemn, all the efforts to discover something that would work. What succeeds now was developed through honorable, yet painful, failures and only partial successes.

It was only 140 years ago that the explosive data appeared in print proposing the theory of evolution; 100 years ago we had the notion of relativity—what exists does not have inherent qualities, but rather is defined by relationships. Fifty years ago, we started probing, graphing, and even illuminating the brain. By 1969, Anafranil was created as the first effective medication for OCD; a quarter of a century of certain behavioral modification techniques began to work with it. Only about ten years ago, in the mid-1980s, did a National Institute of Mental Health study cause us to understand how widespread OCD actually is. Now that we can appreciate what did not work, we begin to partially grasp what will. The knowledge explosion at work!

We have had some effective psychotherapies this century; unfortunately, in reference to OCD, the right questions were not asked because there was little appreciation for just how basic those questions had to be. When we found a human skull, it was as if we started speculating about the mind, instead of asking, as in the case of identifying an animal, what the incisors for ripping and the molars for grinding might tell us. Other psychotherapies failed by excluding the animal in us; OCD treatment started succeeding by capitalizing on animal studies in behaviorism.

We have had many effective medical treatments developed, but usually because the sufferers said, "I can't stand the pain," and the mental health folks could not stand the uncertainty of cause and cure. With OCD and its particular need for an exposure/response blocking approach, help begins with the assumption that pain has to be endured and uncertainty has to be accepted on principle. Even the medications are not for symptomatic relief, but for toleration of the exposure/response methods so as to strengthen the endurance of symptoms so that they might be modified.

More than partially, failures resulted because our conceptual model of the world was inadequate. Philosophically, the assumption was a Newtonian one: what exists has inherent qualities, such as gravity. We referred to "the diabetic" rather than a person having diabetes; you can go through the roll call, "the epileptic," "the hypochondriac," "the schizophrenic," etc. The model described people as objects and the disease was treated, but not the person. This created a fundamental subject/object split, an "us-and-them" perspective—of which the medical model for illness is a good example: there is a "doctor," a "nurse," and a "patient." It has been literally a "can't see the forest for the trees" situation. We have looked for OCD and a treatment for it . . . and it is Us.

Failure also occurred because we failed to implement notions having to do with "growth," psychologically, spiritually, and developmentally. Techniques enhancing the several dimensions of growth in adults were being explored, but we never adequately addressed the needs of children; only a start in play therapy appeared. A generation ago, "growth" was being explored, then medical costs went up and demands were made to curtail these costs. The medical model of illness was back "in" and "growth" for persons, out. It is as if we are demanding that illness in a person stands still so we can get a good shot at it, defying awareness that nature is relational and reality is process.

This becomes awkwardly clear if you conceptualize OCD as a regression to early childhood. If you have a disturbed child, age two to five, you have a treatment problem: the child is frequently regarded as too young for play therapy and too young for "talk" therapy. This is usually resolved by working with the parents. If the child in question has OCD, therein lies the problem: the child chronologically may be age eight, but the OCD experience, developmentally, is about age two. So, verbalizing does not help, insight does not help, and logic does not help. At age eight, the child does not have enough outside-the-home experience to become sufficiently uncomfortable with the rituals and sufficiently motivated to be treated effectively. Complicating that, if the outbreak of OCD is at age eighteen, if the treatment requires the self-parenting of willpower, we are requiring a great deal more maturity than can be reasonably expected. Complicating this is that any child of eight who has OCD is—externally—likely to have a biological parent with OCD. These sorts of issues have slowed the development of treatment considerably.

WE NOW HAVE SOME EXPERIENCE
WITH WHAT WORKS AND WHY

The Biophysical Process

An interesting level of preconsciousness sometimes can be probed, although never completely to one's satisfaction. Occasionally, someone can respond to the question, "Do you have any sensations immediately prior to the OCD flaring up?" As one teenager said, "It's like I am squeezed in my middle and then there is a shudder that goes all the way up." The "Anne" of that case story in Chapter 5 reflected, "It's like a buzzing noise." Usually the OCD gives some space after waking until the anticipation of stress develops, then multiple clothes changes or multiple showers may take place. In some instances, upon waking there may be a need to start touching, almost with the return of consciousness. The physical basis of what we term a "neurological" disorder becomes clear here: with that need to touch likely comes an awareness of nausea.

Obsessive-compulsive disorder is an involuntary, automatic process—a physiological process on a level where it is impossible to readily differentiate chemical from electrical. Once this reality is accepted, OCD becomes less difficult to manage. The mind is beginning to cope with the brain, even though mind is an expression of brain. Slow learners, we; after thousands of years of knowing how to alter consciousness by dulling or "expanding" it, we are at a period in history where we are beginning to learn how a person's mind may choose to positively alter its housing.

Usually the stimulus for the first experience of OCD is initiated by trauma; the panic of being caught by her mother as with seven-year-old "Nancy," or the classic trauma of hormonal change in a woman having a baby. It can be an accumulation of stress, however, as in the case stories of "Lou" and "Mary" in which a neurological pattern is set in motion. Many times, however, there is no awareness of an impending OCD experience. A stimulus, perhaps below the level of consciousness, will evoke a startle response. In the case of a startle response, the sensory data are registered in the brain, not the mind, at levels far below thought and matching patterns forwarded through the medium of the body's emergency system. The vulnerability to OCD lies both in accumulated stress or in an anxiety that is aroused when a pattern is matched with a life-threatening memory. Either may set in motion a prepared program for survival of fight/flight/stillness.

We will probably never know how that ancient imprinting works, any more than we understand the chemical imprinting on the brain in post-traumatic stress disorder. In some fashion, however, we may surmise that ancient trauma has been chemically etched—perhaps by amino acids—into the proteins making up the DNA molecules.

A veterinarian researcher sounds much like a researcher in OCD among humans:

> After varying periods of expression, the compulsive behavior becomes emancipated from the original context and may be performed in other situations when arousal exceeds a critical threshold. We hypothesize that at this point, neurochemical changes have occurred in the central nervous system, thus producing a pathological condition.[1]

When the alarm sounds, the startle response places a demand on the whole body. There is no subtlety here; the OCD entrainment response has the appearance of "battle stations!" on a navy ship. The brain, on a sensory level, has matched up a here-and-now stimulus to a pattern of a threatening silhouette. The mind may, however, offer a second opinion as to whether the immediate situation actually corresponds to that silhouetted memory. The second opinion is a questioning one, but in OCD there is an override of anxiety. Sensations focused on survival become interjected thoughts thrust from the brain into the mind and the "doubting of doubt" becoming second thoughts about the first "second thoughts."

The older system is unconscious, experienced, not learned, almost instinctual; the "modern" system alone is consciously aware, both participating in what might be termed The Survival Feedback Loop. In a person with a "normal" level of anxiety, there must be a shutoff valve somewhere. With OCD, the person is going to have to create—through treatment—his or her own backup system. A rabbit checks, runs fast, stops, checks, runs fast again, or settles down to browse—a natural termination. The OCD sufferer goes through a similar checking process, but recycling is continuous because the feedback loop is extended into the forebrain, thought is engaged, and obsession often begins as a loop. If the cycle is to be broken, it has to be consciously learned and enforced by decision: *I will manage this; it will not manage me.*

One way to get at this is to ask, "How long does your OCD attack last?" With a teen's physical condition it may be fifteen minutes; with an older body, longer—probably not two days, although anyone can experience a lengthened episode. It helps to time it and then to graph it. The startle response sets it off, the chemicals squire in response, but then they start to dribble. They can only carry on at full strength for a measurable length of time; the body then dissipates them through natural means (i.e., lungs, liver, and kidneys). Rooted in animal alertness, it never *totally* goes away, but through treatment it can be reduced from a full-blown chemical attack into what most sufferers describe, in electrical terms, as background static.

It is almost a bad joke—as we are discussing animal responses—that an egg timer is invaluable to anyone with OCD: all you have to know is how long a particular OCD attack routinely keeps a particular individual anxious, and then outlast it by one minute. The person just blocks the response one minute longer than the OCD chemical can maximize its stay in the brain. That is all, but that is enough, and it is downhill all the way for that attack. In exposure/response treatment, cry "wolf" too often and the OCD volume turns down and out.

This is not rocket science. The system was designed to help a person climb a tree with a bear after them; sit on a limb and the bear will eventually go away, and you can climb down. Bodies differ in their ability to produce the "juice" for an emergency. Just look at a watch and time how long a particular "bear" stays under the tree before going away: how long the "stuff" stays in the system. Drink more water and take longer walks because processing chemicals is simply processing chemicals. It may take a medication to bring the agitation down to a manageable level, but there is a sewer system provided to us all for the disposing of toxic wastes.

We are all, to a certain degree, commentaries on the organic. This is not an affirmation that "we are nothing but" a physical body. It is to affirm that each of us exists in a physical body which has inherited the past in coming into being, and that our bodies are organized to respond to the present. Genetically and environmentally, we are the mammals who talk. To entertain this notion of being co-creatures, if you do not have a dog, in imagination, I will lend our Frances. She is a mammal, specifically a yellow Laborador, who is named after our household saint, St. Francis. If, from this "loaner," someone develops treatment procedures from this discussion, why not call these procedures the Rules of St. Francis? Neither the saint nor the dog will take offense; it will be an insider's joke on OCD.

We, the Mammals

Frances is a good dog; she knows how to behave. If a dog does not, it can cause a lot of rug cleaning. So it is off with the two of you to obedience school (known in some circles as "This is me and this is my OCD"; *Heel!* by any other name is still *heel!* and has to be taught by repetition). Here the mammalian midbrain and the "wish-I-was-the-master" new brain, together with trainee, meet with a trainer. It will be clear by the end of the first class who is getting trained.

The first principle of obedience training is grounded in the acknowledgment that a dog is a member of a pack. The owner is part of that pack, even if he or she dresses the other pack member in scarf and baseball cap for the cutest picture to show friends. The question—for which somebody is paying out good money—is, "Who is the leader of the pack?" That has to be settled. If the dog is the leader of the pack, the household has a "bad dog."

Next comes obedience school where there is unlearning and relearning on the part of owner and owned. It is precisely that issue to be settled in the first therapy session: mammalian brain and new brain, the "me and my OCD"—"codependency" being just an extension of "who trains who."

Some consider exposure/response techniques to be a variation on the theme of "bronco bustin'" and there is some reality to that. The bronco buster gets on the "hurricane deck" of a horse to be broken and does not get off (voluntarily!) until the pitching stops, the quivering starts, and the relationship is clear. Anyone who has singled out an OCD symptom as a target is also clear about that process. It works, too.

There is a little more to the discussion about OCD and modifying behavior, of course. One of these points is something that any parent with a child with OCD has learned:

> If the desire to exhibit the offending behavior is present, despite restraint, punishment, training or incarceration, the condition is present. If the control is removed and the animal can commit the behavior, he will commit the behavior.[2]

For many centuries, anyone connected to OCD could have told you, in detail, what *does not work:*

> We advocate that the owner never rebuke or punish the dog for engaging in the behavior. Inconsistent, unpredictable punishment is likely to worsen the behavior.[3]

If your library does not have the volume to check this footnote, show up at any support group meeting with your questions and do not commit yourself to being home at a certain hour.

Some suggestions that veterinarians make for working with their mammals will sound familiar to working with the mammal of us, but not all points are equally relevant:

> Most behavioral modifications involve counter conditioning and desensitization. In counter conditioning, an animal is taught another behavior that is more enjoyable or pleasant to exhibit in the presence of the stimuli that elicits abnormal behavior. The animal must first be taught in benign circumstances before it can be taught in a stressful one. The substitute behavior can be as simple as teaching the dog or cat to sit or lie down and look at the client, relaxing and appearing calm and happy, in exchange for a food treat or attention. The period in

which the animal is expected to remain calm should be gradually increased, until it lasts thirty minutes. The animal is then ready to have the trigger event introduced at some attenuated level, this level will gradually be increased to teach the animal to habituate the stimulus.[4]

A different suggestion could well be as an illustration of the third step in the treatment procedure taught in *Brain Lock* of a rehabituation technique used with trichotillomania.

The dog should first be trained to perform a behavior that is incompatible with the compulsive behavior. Then, as soon as the dog shows intentions to perform the compulsive behavior, it should be distracted using a novel sound (such as a whistle) and commanded to perform the alternate behavior; it should be rewarded for doing so. To be successful, it must be used every time (the compulsive behavior happens).[5]

Strong parallels are suggested here between a two-year-old child, a dog, and your OCD. The dog may be ten but the brain of that mammal is limited to about age two of the child. All three have limitations on the ability to think at that level; all three have limits on language. The vocabulary of the child and the dog will be about 125 words, and if you try to reason with any of the three, the limitations are severe. If you want to talk to the child, your dog, or OCD, you have to limit the vocabulary. *If you intend to do "self-talk" to your OCD you had better keep it brief, simple, and to the point. Be consistent and persistent with dog, child, and OCD: no negotiation, no pleading, no whining.* Pack leader, say it and mean it, or learn to clean carpets.

CLEAN, CLEAN, CLEAN YOUR CARPET, GENTLY DOWN LIFE'S STREAM

Developmental Psychology

Probably everyone feels that their lives are mostly low-grade melodrama, but people with OCD have a right to take a curtain call. Regardless of what their lives are *outside* the OCD experience, *within* it are the unresolved early childhood issues and enough symptom creep to contaminate the rest. Even one hour a day inside it leaves a bad taste in the mouth for the other twenty-three. The next step is again a diagnostic one; to fail to continue to diagnose is to fail to treat. In this instance a time measurement is used, only the variation is not an hour or greater, but ages and stages. Erikson's categories are, once again, useful when dealing within the OCD regression.

Orality is characterized by the issue of trust versus mistrust, and if the therapist cannot be trusted, no therapeutic alliance will form, no work proceeds. If an eating disorder is present, boundary setting on OCD symptoms takes a backseat to whether the person will starve to death or go into a potentially fatal heart rhythm due to potassium deprivation. If orality is marked by substance abuse, no work proceeds until that is resolved because OCD is trance enough without a chemical fog. Only after weaning from the bottle—excuse the pun—may the next step be considered.

This stage of anality is often characterized as the "terrible twos" in parenting books, and the therapist will have to be clever not to be caught by a ready "*no*" to everything. Doubt, negativity, despair, lack of hope, shame, and ambivalence all run together. The counselee may have been badgered by family into an appointment, but a quick termination follows unless a way is found to take advantage of the urge to use "*no*" on something appropriate to treatment. Since depression may not only accompany OCD, but precede it, it is a condition often found in this stage. If a depression existed prior to the outbreak of the disorder it likely has been integrated into the structure of the personality. It may be wise to consider getting a psychotropic program effected prior to psychotherapy rather than adjunctive to it.

In the anal stage, we are using a term from Freud—out of fashion, but marvelously descriptive! For Erikson, the issue is hope versus despair, autonomy versus shame and doubt. The child has separated from mother, but is not ready to bond with father. This is the time of the basic family.

When the sufferer is ready to deal with OCD, it often is marked by the great "Aha!" or "I thought I was alone with these thoughts/ behaviors, but now I know what I have and I am not alone." It may have happened after reading a magazine article, but this experience is most often found in a support group; this is where the readiness to celebrate basic family feelings flourishes. Those feelings thrust forward a treatment progression—personality development growth—a truism developed in Alcoholics Anonymous over a long time. That growth carries the person forward toward awareness of others, sharing, fairness, empathy, and, eventually, intimacy. All adults chronologically pass through these ages, but some never developmentally pass through the stages. It is in passing through these stages in successful treatment that gifts the young student with OCD. It is not the appearance, but the reality, of greater maturity than his or her peers.

The characteristics of this stage may be used to one's advantage. Language is being learned: "It was such a relief when I finally knew that what was wrong had a name." It is just like the Rumpelstiltskin fairy tale: learn the name of the "elf" and you get power over him. "Hoarder," "straightener," "washer" are not put-down names, but tools to use in classification, just as naming things delights a child of two. It is a delight to a person whose OCD reflects that developmental level to be able to give a name to its various "flavors."

Once objectified—"It isn't me, it's my OCD," or given a nickname, as in "How I Ran OCD Off My Land"—then the separation of "Me" from OCD starts taking place. Hostility can then be better managed and the toilet training/self-control/boundary setting has begun—the saying "no" to OCD. The therapist teaches that it is neurological, not a defect of personality. There is no need for shame by the sufferer, and every reason not to be shaming, by the parents. Weekly participation in a group and the sharing tends to smooth the roller-coaster ride of emotional ups and downs as acceptance is integrated. Celebration of the small successes is learned.

This dynamic can be used to advantage in therapy. Independence in this phase is running a short distance, perhaps into the next room, but quickly coming back to mother. In therapy, the homework assignment is made, and a report brought back to the next session. In the context of basic family feelings, the support group often is verbalized explicitly in family terms and can be extraordinarily healing, as a result of moving from feelings of alienation to acceptance.

This is anality, but graduate courses in Freudian thinking should not confuse us. The quick response to "anality" is "toilet training," but in OCD the cleaning and contamination rites do not belong here, but to the next stage, when the "good boy" and "good girl" love to please Mommy and Daddy and can show they know how to do it. The stage of age one-and-a-half to three is neutral in regard to the therapist. The prior stage will be influenced by the maternal and likely to be characterized by dependency. The subsequent stage will be influenced by the paternal and likely to be characterized by conformity to authority. What may be conformity early in the period, however, may very well turn to conflict later in it.

We see this developmental stage also reflected in a common treatment prescription: "Your OCD is like a spoiled brat. In a grocery store he will grab for the candy. If you say, 'No,' he will yell louder. If you get embarrassed, next time the yelling will start at the same level that was effective to work against you the last time. The only way to win is to say 'No' and mean it and let the brat yell. It will try to intimidate you a few times and then give up."

Diagnostically, it is possible to differentiate between the anal and oedipal stages. Developmentally, the child of three or four—who may be chronologically thirty-three—will probably display the superstitious characteristic of OCD. Developmentally, the child of four to six—who may be chronologically sixty-six—may well use the language of religion. At two, the child/adult will probably not be sharing with a group the fact that he or she is hearing interjected thoughts; at four, the child/adult will be more apt to share the pain of scrupulosity and similar interjections.

You will also see the characteristic of deferring to the "big person" in the standard procedure with scrupulosity. It is very effective with Catholics and has been used since Ignatius of Loyola: accept the priest's judgment on the matter of a defective conscience. Thus, utilizing the characteristics of the preschooler can be an advantage in treatment. The quandary of a Protestant pastor is how to have the authority of a spiritual director.

It is also a time of wanting to be able to do things, such as learning to tie a shoe. In treatment planning, the implication is to choose the tasks that are simple to accomplish; be concrete, specific, limit the objective to what is achievable, and build on success.

Again, this is not because the sufferer is "childish." Obsessive-compulsive disorder is a regression to early childhood and you work *at* the OCD in this context; the counselor works *with* the sufferer—of whatever chronological age—in a manner appropriate to that age (firm with one, respectful with the other). With the OCD, the tactic is to break up what is essentially a trance—an altered state of consciousness; with the person, with whom the counselor works, the strategy is to take full advantage of the conscious awareness.

It is in the late anal and oedipal phases that the extraordinarily high success rate of exposure/response treatment appears. The issue for this period is initiative versus guilt as values are being internalized and conscience is formed. The therapist suggests making a list of symptoms and ranking them while the person feels it as an opportunity to demonstrate initiative and the ability to classify and quantify. Guilt is explored and shame questioned. Since a characteristic of this phase is respect for authority, the therapist may suggest, "Why don't we talk to your priest/rabbi/pastor about this?" The phase is ripe for role models; St. Ignatius suggested a solid, practical person be found to whom uncertainties could be addressed. The therapist coaches and parental figures in a support group are brought in to be a "team." The "child of OCD" is ready to begin to learn to read and the group and therapist support that with suggestions for reading.

When the OCD sufferer, in the midst of the treatment experience, exclaims "Look what I can do!" everyone applauds. Growth is encouraged, similar to when Daddy stands the child against the door frame and makes a pencil mark to show how much Sonny has grown. The beauty is that, in a support group, everyone has a chance to be in the role of both child and parent: opening up one's self as a child, and when the next person opens up, to be the good mother and/or good father in order to assist in mutual growth.

At this stage, the treatment flows *before* the starting gun sounds. When the therapist suggests charting the problem, making a list, weighing the relative intensity of each, taking initiative (the things that go along with being the stage of age three to five), it is really unfair to compare exposure/response to other therapies. The "child of OCD" wants to be a "big boy" and "like Daddy." When he has contamination fears the therapist demonstrates putting his or her own hand in the dirt and encourages the client to do the same.

Wanting to please struggles with fear, so that when the need to please comes, it is at an appropriate time and group acceptance of the person results in applying salve to the wounds of shame.

The child in this stage of personality development thinks concretely, rather than abstractly or symbolically. The support group can become weighed down into a "pity party," and be just as uselessly wordy as "insight therapy." Objectives need to be specified and the OCD "elephant" is eaten one bite at a time.

The "child" developmentally enjoys the other kids at preschool—school or office—and a therapist usually recommends a support group rather than individual treatment. The counselee may be into magical thinking, yet also has precious religious beliefs outside of what can be identified as OCD. The therapist consequently identifies the superstition, differentiates the mature beliefs, sets up a "double dare you" challenge, and watches the belief and fear fight. It often is particularly effective, with a high-functioning person with OCD, to identify a superstition as the very first homework. Perhaps it is unsporting of a therapist to stack the deck by pitting her or his belief that God is in Charge of My Life versus number 13 or 666 triggering avoidance. It will occur to some to question whether God is in Charge of My Life is just another example of a superstitious belief. Until a better tactic comes along, even a nonbeliever as a therapist can "set a thief to catch a thief."

The developmental stage can make a treatment difference: the two-year-old is difficult to assess verbally, the five-year-old is less so. For the five-year-old, authority is something more easily accepted, particularly as it involves reading; many playroom arguments are settled by "it is in a book." The use of books on OCD is highly valuable in treatment; the authority figure, whether as therapist or the group, may be successful in suggesting to the "hoarder" that those cherished mountains of old newspaper can be useful in recycling. The male "cleaner" may just rinse it twice if an expert homemaker in the group says, "I use Lysol and that does it. Just do it once."

When "the child of OCD"—of whatever adult chronology—wants to ask all the Big Questions of Life, the therapist leans back and asks, "Have you read 'Step Four, What's It All About' in *Brain Lock*?" If they are not into abstract thinking, never mind about evolution. If a counselee wants to use terminology, such as The

Devil—a therapist may or may not think like that—but can accept, utilize, and/or respect it. We are not going to cure OCD as long as we are human anyway and healing is a gift that is out of our price range. We are just the fortunate participants and recipients. What is important is to take seriously The Big Questions/The Big Picture, emotionally as well as intellectually.

The Effective Therapies

Viewing the present state of treatment, in which exposure/response and the Four Steps have track records of successfully modifying OCD, it would seem that exposure/response does well in three areas: (1) its primary strength is to extinguish the "silhouettes" in the older security system memory bank that sets off false alarms; (2) exposure/response indirectly addresses personality traits, such as being timid, that tend to make the sufferer vulnerable to anxiety by utilizing techniques such as attacking and avoidance—the consequence is increased self-esteem; (3) exposure/response tends to promote growth-enabling persons to move beyond the developmental issues of ages one-and-a-half to three. Its weakness is that a behaviorist may focus on (1) extinguishing, (2) ignoring, and (3) neglecting, which gives exposure/response a defensive posture in regard to attribution and quality of life issues.

We have begun to learn when behavior modification succeeds—when it works with the mammalian part of the brain. We have learned that it is with difficulty that behavior modification is directed toward mental rituals, which logically would be in the newest sections of the brain and unrelated to the mammalian brain. Unless we differentiate what exposure/response can and cannot do for an individual, it becomes a "procrustean bed" upon which a patient is stretched or cut to fit the size of the treatment we have available.

We need to keep in mind B. F. Skinner's (the father of American behaviorism) last participation in the radio program sponsored by the Unitarian Universalist Church, known as *The Cambridge Forum*. It was shortly before his death and by chance I was listening as he proclaimed that he no longer believed in behavior modification on the grounds that it did not do justice to the fullness of that which is human. Moving toward incorporating cognitive issues and techniques is a response to this in behavior modification and undoubtedly will continue.

To bring the Four Steps from *Brain Lock* into focus, they are (1) using the formula, "It isn't me—it's my OCD"; (2) reminding oneself that OCD is simply an experience of some chemicals in the brain; (3) refocusing one's attention; and (4) keeping the perspective of what is truly meaningful. A criticism of the Four Steps, which approach OCD from a cognitive perspective, might be that they only indirectly attack the silhouettes of the mammalian brain. It does something, however, that exposure/response, in spite of its behavioral model, fails adequately to do as symptoms are addressed singly. The Four Steps confront what *maintains* the dysfunction; symptoms are often cloaked in shadow and their *reiterated* identification in Step One and *objectification* of symptoms in Step Two brings them into sharp awareness. Attribution theory is applied: the symptoms are *chemical* no more, no less. Step Three, refocusing, addresses the initiative issue to be resolved by three-year-olds; there can also be consequences of personality growth moving toward broadening underutilized parts of the brain, as well. Step Four, on the meaning of life, directly addresses the development issues of ages four to six when the big questions are asked that dumbfound Daddy so he sends the boy to ask his mother.

I believe an issue that will emerge in the Four Steps and become focused is, "It isn't me—it's my OCD." This is the subject/object split that has dogged Western philosophy and Western science for a long period. To cite "it is me" and to separate that from "my OCD" is to cut a person off from a part of themselves. There is no cure for OCD and, if the thesis of this work is correct, never will be: OCD is part of our humanness. It is a part of "my body" and to disclaim a relationship with it is to disclaim part of the self—unless we accept a dualism of body and mind. Religiously that has not worked since the Gnostic Heresy of the first centuries. As a counselee—a Christian who is very sophisticated theologically—said to me: "I cannot reject my OCD, it is a part of me and I must take full responsibility for it, just as for all my actions." If we split OCD from "me," in effect we are naming it as an alien force in us, and since we cannot reject it—cure it—then there is forever a part of the self that is alien. If we, as some conservative religious persons do, attribute OCD to a literal "devil," the reality of no cure is the acceptance of permanently incorporating evil in our very being. The only advantage to bonding OCD and "the devil" is that since we can cause OCD, for research purposes, by administering glucose to a willing sufferer, for the first time we really have the devil at our mercy: we can snap our fingers and he appears, in response to a massive dose of glucose and ready to jump as high as we ask.

Returning to the subject/object split, there can be an impossible philosophical conflict leading to a therapeutic impasse. This indicates a need for a well-thought-through understanding—not rejection—of Step One: "My OCD is an inherent part of my physical self; it was—and sometimes is—a good thing out of control upon which I have to set reasonable boundaries. I am learning to be objective about this aspect of myself and consequently more free to make choices and live more in balance." In treatment, we are getting down to that basic: "Why am I?"

"Humanness" is the crucial issue in OCD and it is clearly indicated when psychosurgery is employed as a treatment of last resort. Psychosurgery does not dehumanize the patient, but the ability to relate in the fullness of the human is curtailed. As the OCD response in the emergency security system is disconnected, however, it also disconnects a significant part of the human potential because the mammalian brain and the new brain are so interconnected.

To get at the "truth" of how best to treat OCD, the issue of the adequacy of a treatment approach is best reached by exploring a variety of perspectives, each of which has some validity and none of which has total adequacy. The consequence of this is that we currently know that a combination of therapeutic media works best—behavioral, cognitive, and frequently medication. With that as a starting block, we can look at other possibilities.

We all have periods of trance as an expansion of the normal: Dad is just lucky the house never burns down when he gets into a good murder mystery. The continuum of clinical and subclinical OCD is one of an alternated state of consciousness with varying intensities, consequently necessitating a further differentiation of treatment strategies. We now know part of unraveling the mystery is that there are two memory systems, a twist of the tale that would have intrigued even Agatha Christie.

Another aspect of the continuum is the similarity between OCD and posttrauma states. "Zoning out," described in trichotillomania is also dissociation; another extreme is what used to be referred to as "multiple personality." Depersonalization and derealization are others and perhaps the "out-of-body" experiences of some persons, as well.

Hypnosis is an intentionally induced out-of-body experience and OCD certainly resembles a trance state in some ways. The boy actor in *The Touching Tree,* a video available from the OC Foundation, in the sequence about hand washing, did a marvelous job of depicting the trance state of a compulsion. In terms of two memory systems, prelife experiences in hypnosis certainly deserve credible research.

The realization of the two memory systems is helpful also in that it enables a person to differentiate between fear and anxiety. The older system was begun with an actual terror or deadly fear and because it is housed in the mammalian brain is inaccessible to consciousness. It has become transformed into a biological basis of the startle response. It is somewhat similar to post-traumatic stress disorder in that both may produce interjecting sensations or thoughts. Fear or worry, on the other hand, are related to the newer memory system and are accessible to consciousness. The older memory system is subject to responding to extinction procedures, especially when rank ordered so as not to overwhelm consciousness. The newer system is more subject to positive response to cognitive procedures based on experiential learning.

This differentiation has its religious implication; "the just shall live by faith alone" is a general truth relevant to OCD. Its applicability, however, will be less to the unconscious process and more to the later one. It is addressing the anxiousness and worry that bedevils us so faith can lift the person to a new and better level of living. As the case story of "Nancy" indicated, there is often a needed interrelationship between the "born again" and treatment—combining psychotherapy and medication—for a profound change in biological programming.

STEP AHEAD

More thought has to be given to the flick of the switch between the stimulus, obsessive thought, and the start of compulsive behavior. The principle is *timing is crucial*. No one is going to prevent interjected thoughts. They are. The question is, "How am I going to handle them?" That requires preplanning. Part of what needs to be learned is to *fight a sensation with a sensation*. What has limited applicability with OCD is to try to fight a sensation with a thought. The primitive system operates by sensation; the newer system by thought. The sensory sensation is in a code that is decoded—interpreted—by the new brain, according to its environment—such as driving a car, not visualizing a camel. Thought switching does not work because changing one interpretation to a reinterpretation—all the while the startle response has evoked all kinds of sensations over the security network—is fiddling while the glucose burns. What works many times is to switch sensory systems, moving from an auditory system caught in a startle response, for instance, to a better-coping tactile system. For at least some persons, if trapped by a tune that repeats and repeats, this suggests going to the piano and playing the tune—shifting systems. If listening to the baby breathe causes the glucose to go crazy, take that glucose out and let it respond to rollerblading for a while, letting the endorphines augment the serotonin; it is all chemical "up there," and exercise is one way to get a better chemical flowing. In HeartMath, in the next chapter, an additional alternative will be suggested.

As we are dealing with two hemispheres with different capabilities, remember that any treatment strategy not involving both hemispheres is doomed to failure. We can find the feedback loop of OCD in a vertical dimension, as illustrated in diagrams in various books; what is suggested here is that treatment must also encompass a horizontal dimension. If the person is dominated by a right hemisphere style, it will be helpful to begin to read on OCD; if the difficulty is in reading, perhaps something of sufficient interest to the right hemisphere—can arouse that capacity—a mystery, a western, a light romance. If the person is dominated by the left hemisphere, try painting. If the person lacks some ability to use both, starting to write poetry can be helpful—words for the left and rhythm for the right.

A helpful treatment principle is not only "do the opposite," but to take advantage of the opposite. As we will discuss in the next chapter, increase your brain power, utilize unused portions of your brain, and stimulate circuits and data banks not involved with your OCD. There is an enormous part of all of our brains we do not consciously utilize. Glucose floods most areas of the brain when an OCD attack occurs, as the PET scans indicate. Reason suggests we involve all those parts as a conscious treatment effort to counter this; what can be flooded, can be used.

One of the things suggested by an understanding of hemispheres, is that it is perhaps wise to clear one segment in order to get at another segment. One segment may be using all the energy for the entire system and some "slack" may have to be obtained there in order to have energy for other treatment needs. It may be that the emotional hijacking is so overwhelming that the new brain's full capacity is unavailable to assist in treatment. We commonly see this in the improvement in grades of a student when a couple of OCD symptoms have been worked through and more energy is available for conscious direction.

This double bind is apt to be a relational symbol of security and trust, such as a "loving God," who is at the same time forcibly presented as a "judgmental God." Consequently the person combines an experience of both attraction and anxiety. Those contradictory messages could drive a person "nuts." This often can be countered by an authority figure, usually a trusted priest, who can help a believing Catholic to accept that the priest will take upon himself the "sins that are not sins." The person does not sort out the double bind, just accepts that it has been resolved. All of us need to be more clever in identifying the double binds of OCD and intervening in them and utilizing different sides of the brain's function in those interventions.

A type of double bind, with developmental implications and perhaps for the role of the hemispheres as well, is when the person has had bad parenting and longs for a power-giving, loving God—a gap not easily bridged. Religion is a potentially powerful stimulant for growth, but setting the stage as a part of treatment for that is a void yet to be filled by psychological and theological thought.

We also need a reminder how often in support groups persons will share how, in the OCD "zoning out" experience, their minds seem to race ahead of their thoughts. While feeling "weird" to them, it appears to be a natural phenomenon. Time speeds up when a person is anxious: remember the first plane ride, the first of most anxiety-filled experiences; you are there, think, remember, but as a blur—although it can slow down, as in some car wrecks. Perhaps this is true of OCD when it takes the form of slowness. The experience of time is relative.

What matters here, as we consider treatment, is the "old pro" quarterback effect: if you have been there, been there, done that, done that, the anxiety lessens, becomes manageable, and time moves at its normal pace. The "been there, done that" is a flooding of experience, washing clean the anxiety, wringing dry the obsession so that it is modified, if not nullified. This is exactly what happens in exposure/response blocking treatment: it does not take ten or fifteen NFL (National Football League) years of experience, simply sustained behavioral homework assignments that are completed.

"Lou" (Chapter 5) demonstrated one way to cope: slow everything down. Experience your hand reaching out, experience your fingers touching the knob. Smell. Look, now directly, now off center. What taste is in your mouth? How does the floor feel under your feet and your feet in your shoes? Delay and absorb new data, flooding with intentional sensory awareness is tactically sound.

The problem is how to stay in the present, when an interjected thought is commandeering immediate reality with its own sense of what is happening. This suggests that some of the self-messages that need to be given are *"get real,"* stay in touch, and be present. To be real, to be in touch, to be truly present is to experience a religious dimension of life, both in relationship to others and to ourselves; if God, as Paul Tillich writes, is the "Ground of Being," this further adds and enriches a life with both horizontal and vertical dimensions.

When working with personality development, we realize that we deal with security from cradle to grace: from trust versus mistrust when our mother presents a breast, through doubt and despair, to whether we choose to be risk taking and creative when we cross forty, to whether we can surmount the crest of the mountain and see the world as "humankind," rather than grouchily as "my kind." At each step a security issue must be successfully resolved or our vulnerability to regression strengthens.

THEORY INTO SCENARIO

Let us construct a preposterous scenario. Joey Von Taylor, Eagle Scout and Sunday school teacher, is tormented. When he passes a scrawny third-grade girl, he has the tumultuous feelings he had when he was first in puberty and fantasized about a Marilyn Monroe clone under a palm tree on a South Sea island. Intellectually, as Eagle Scout, Sunday school teacher, and going steady with a lovely woman his age, he has a firm grasp that a scrawny third grader is not an appropriate sex object. The forbidden thoughts keep rolling and roiling and now he has developed a full-blown hobby of self-accusation as a consequence: starting with A for "asshole," B for "bastard," C for "crud," D for "damned," he has gone through the alphabet, even learning some new languages when confronted with X, Y, and Z. His creativity in name-calling about those horrendous thoughts is such that the tail feathers even droop on his Eagle Scout badge.

Now, Joey Von Taylor is one of the 1,111 linear descendants, 222 generations later, of Igor the Tailor, who came over with the Saxon horde to Britain. Igor never met an Englishwoman he did not rape and his motto was, "The younger, the more delicious." Now Igor is long since in the death registry, but his DNA lingers on. Some people would hope he is now in the fires of hell, but his DNA still causes some bizarre electric spikes in the brain, and these have become interjected thoughts, and the glucose tormentingly burns in the brain of Joey, whether or not Igor's soul is on a pile of burning coal.

Joey is not about to act on those interjected thoughts, which disgust him, cause him to view himself with contempt, by which he frightens himself and questions his personal identity . . . and, incidentally, causes him to wonder if he is crazy. The options begin to look like a life of fearing the fires of hell or a shotgun barrel in the mouth. There is a third option, however: Joey can march into a behavior-modification expert's office and announce: "If you have an exposure technique that I can use to command the glucose to burn on *my* terms I will find a way to block the response and cremate those imprinted horrors and those hellish anxieties they carry with them." It is the beginning of finally getting those anxieties laid to rest. In a support group a non-Irish kind of "wake" gets underway.

This whole scenario is a preposterous proposal, of course—but maybe not to people named Joey—or Joey's son, who never may have to fight such fears . . . or even hear about them.

PLANNING FOR PRACTICE

A treatment model might be an immediate treatment *target* focused on the false alarms set off in the security system:

> The target is broken down into sequential steps. These notions are grounded in process philosophy; they entail assumptions that a present "something"—such as a counselee—must house his or her past, that all things are characterized by their relationships—such as a body, a family, a career—and the best interest of all things are best served when they harmonize.

with an *objective* of enhancing the security system:

> At each stage of personality development, there are issues to be resolved before the next growth stage is readied, and treatment incorporates these, most often in the sessions while the homework assignments are being carried out.

and a *goal* of participating in the fulfillment of the potentiality for humanness by that individual:

> The person never loses sight of the ability to maximize human potential in whatever way heredity and the situation allows.

In anticipating the direction of future developments in treatment, it seems we are already well grounded. One begins with the question: To what do you *attribute* this condition? The attribution is *neurobiological* and that perspective sets an appropriate neutral tone for beginning treatment. The notion of "evolution" need not be explored with a counselee, for instance, but that reality in reference to the evolution of the brain certainly has a bearing on what treatment entails. The further treatment progresses, the more the treatment will predictably become involved in the basic human questions of existence and relationships; the initial success in treating—moderating—symptoms often opens more profound issues for resolution. The technocrat therapist of the opening movement will have to be a more subtle and sophisticated person if subsequent themes are to be effectively explored.

WE CLIMBERS NOW HAVE A GOOD FOOTHOLD

The Swiss mountaineers have a saying that "they climb on the backs of their fathers," and it is true in psychotherapy. Reading "It's not me—it's my OCD" is reminiscent of much earlier building blocks. Sigmund Freud wrote of pathology being "ego syntonic"—accepted as part of one's self—and therapy turning this into "ego alien." A little later, an American psychiatrist, Harry Stack Sullivan, proposed that we should work with terms such as "not me" and "real me." Since OCD has as many dual diagnoses as alcoholism, techniques from other mental health areas are justified, as Jeffrey Schwartz indicated in the second half of *Brain Lock*.

We can celebrate that today we have an earlier recognition of OCD. Let us imagine a ten-year-old boy with an appointment. The scene is set for where we climbers are with our present hand- and footholds.

In that first session, after an OCD checklist has come and gone, it is history-taking time involving the whole family.[6] Overtly, it is necessary to find out about the developmental "milestones" such as walking, talking, how toilet training was accomplished, when the symptoms began to visibly erupt, discipline problems and disciplining, how the child relates, and how school is going.

Covertly, the therapist is probably trying to determine the unwritten laws for that family, such as the "golden rule" or the "pathogenic rule." Many parents and spouses strictly adhere to the pathogenic rule, "Once you are fully satisfied what won't work in the family, redouble your efforts in doing it." If a whack on the you-know-where does not stop closing the door, closing the door, closing the door, try two whacks; if that does not work, try four, try eight—any discipline that fails a half dozen times deserves a second chance to stop repetitive, frustrating behavior. In such cases, the course of treatment may be more visible; you help the persons identify those unwritten pathogenic rules—which were usually learned in their own families (which they hated and now duplicate) and often that resolves some difficulties.

Unfortunately, with the "golden rule," the official standard may be "to do unto others as you would have them do unto you," and it will not appear for a while that this can open the door to codependency. In this case, "goodness" may mask "permissiveness" in giving in to rituals or avoidance. Denial, in these instances, may be no more than a gossamer gleam, sometimes dissipated just by asking how often the kid misses the school bus because of those last dozen showers or three changes of clothes. Mom has to drive him to school and being late to work herself is a great incentive to forthrightness. In either instance, OCD being what it is, whatever enlightenment brought them in will be intermixed with emotional heat, and the first step is to neutralize it. This is best done by presenting OCD as a neurobiological condition.

Since it is a child who is the occasion for the intake, it will be a relief to everyone to learn some of the psychiatric possibilities the parents have been whispering about to each other may not be central to their child's problem. Depending upon severity, OCD is frequently more of a "kissing cousin" than a blood relative to psychiatric concerns. Assisting in determining this is taking a case history: who passed on what to whom; was there a strep infection early on? It usually is a big relief to know that usually depression is more of a hangover from the night before. Each question is an educational component; parents trying to recollect often helps in quietly decontaminating the emotional situation.

The first homework assignment probably is for the whole family to watch a video from the OC Foundation. Not everyone has a family available, and not all the available families are positive influences, but the point is that a person is defined by relationships—first of all by the systems of the body—and since the "self" is a social creation, this has to be taken into account and, if at all possible, used to advantage. If it can be done, it is best to invite the whole family in, start that way in the beginning, and conclude that way. OCD has a way of being at the beginning and, all too frequently, at the ending of a family.

The truth as *shown* is usually more helpful than as told. Color photographs of the brain before and after an OCD episode (such as on the dust cover of *Brain Lock,* in many of the videos on OCD, or in a booklet from one of the drug representatives of a company marketing a serotonin reuptake inhibitor [SRI]) are useful. A picture of the glucose going crazy here, there, and everywhere during an OCD episode is highly educational. It is hope filling to show what is concretely intended by treatment: with the brain we intend to take the red out (as in glucose being hypermetabolized), and here is how we will do it.

Seeing the here, there, and everywhere of glucose metabolizing at a furious rate also demonstrates visually what everyone knows about OCD: its symptoms dance like a deviant drunk. "It" manages to turn up the color from warm to hot, then hotter, to "you wouldn't believe this" in a most miscellaneous manner. A holistic approach of body, mind, and spirit is an easy clinical hunch, and looking at OCD from several perspectives is what we will do.

While the immediate treatment will doubtless be behavioral, the context must be kept in mind. That context may well be best presented by subscribing to *Kidscope,* published by the OC Foundation; here, kids exchange information. Most people with OCD have active minds and it helps to offer more and more information; after a few weeks into treatment it may be appropriate to discuss how the brain evolved (but evolution as a theory need not be introduced as a complicating offense to someone's belief system). Since intelligence and OCD do not make strange bedmates, most individuals are glad to share in whatever you know. In no other field of psychotherapy is bibliotherapy more popular, better utilized, and gratefully accepted. The reason is, as the kids say, a "no brainer": with OCD the brain is long on gray matter and short on white—the connectors. What is accomplished cognitively is to activate more of the white cells.

It is always best to start where the person is. In the case of boys, they love to play the computer game "Mortal Kombat," and military metaphors help. After the symptoms are identified, an island is drawn on a large sheet and given the boy's name, such as "Bob's Island." The symptoms are listed and given that proportion of the island; the symptom-free areas—perhaps "when I play sports"—are shown as belonging to Bob; the rest is enemy controlled and given the name used for his OCD. The proportion of time during the day is then visually represented and can be referred to as treatment progresses. A no-man's land is shown between the areas: symptoms under partial control and those listed for attack. The strategy is outlined in military terms; the enemy is stronger so you have to be clever and use guerrilla warfare, attacking the weakest point. Always focus your attack, never attack the strong points, and always fight to win. A weak point to attack is identified for the coming week.

In the case of fearfulness in going beyond sight of home and always forcing the family to drive in a familiar route, get on the bike and start exploring the neighborhood. A competitive dynamic is set up: a "double dare" is a pretty irresistible challenge to a lot of kids, including those with OCD. Coaching helps: if you circle the block by always turning right, you come out where you started. A child may be so anxious that this never occurred to him. A treatment sequence evolves and the game progresses. The line is moved as "Bob" controls more of "Bob's Island."

A helpful element in treatment is a school visit, if the teacher is judged helpful and open to it. Most are; most are grateful. That helps set the stage for when more time and energy is free and available as symptoms dissipate for grades to move remarkably upward. Sometimes the discussion has to deal with test phobias; if the boy can be coached to shoot a free throw with a basketball under pressure, he can learn to relax and take a test. That has a marvelous effect on everyone's morale. Sometimes a parallel movement can be obtained: muscle building is esteem enhancing; sometimes sports success is reflected in that enough of the brain's energy supply can be shifted from straightening a locker to remembering the plays.

In treatment, there is no perfection of accomplishment; it is important to make a reasonable judgment and affirm "this is good enough; not perfect, but good enough." An 80 percent gain usually indicates that it is time to move on. For a client to look for a magic point of perfection in treatment is clearly not to have explored adequate treatment. In balancing perfection and acquiescence to mediocrity, "excellence" is a word for both counselor and counselee to weigh.

To accept this is to accept that gains have to be maintained; no one with OCD rests on a plateau, although the time comes when regular sessions cease. What is expected—three weeks, three months, three years—is that stress eventually builds up and OCD flares to some degree. It is, however, a lapse rather than a relapse. With adequate treatment, the physiological condition upon which the startle response rested is incapable of ever fully recovering to its original state.

When a lapse occurs, the OCD treatment drill of exposure/ response blocking is reinstated. There is no saying in OCD support groups, as there is in Alcoholics Anonymous, about "take one drink and you are a drunk." The person figuratively becomes a safety inspector and simply restarts ordering safety drills. If the theme is contamination, then touch the door handle, touch the floor, and touch the toilet—whatever the drill is to provoke the OCD into physiological overresponse and the inevitable subsequent eroding. The drill is the same: figuratively, every time the OCD crew settles down to lunch, conduct a safety drill. Every time they lie down to sleep, have a safety check. Then go for the kill: down in the mess hall of the basal ganglia, when they are exhausted and finally sitting down to eat, someone will look up at the monitor hooked up to the optical nerves and yell, "Mah Gawd! Look at what she's doing again" and everyone grabs for a barf bag. When it comes to a lapse, it usually is sufficient for the person in recovery to open the mess hall door when they start to eat, and yell, "What's for supper?" Emotional Antabuse; playing dirty does it.

GAINING WISDOM FROM OCD

Exposure/response works; it illustrates utilizing intelligence, but it is not wisdom. Caught in superficiality, such as having to re-arrange the shoes in the closet every morning before going to work, "It" is the original "Johnny One Note" who sings—with a lack of gusto. In the overwhelming intensity of fearing there are scissors in the house, it is wisdom that inspires a person to an awareness of how little this terror expresses the essential Self. In the minutiae of anguish in an OCD attack that seems to last for hours, wisdom finally emerges to demand more to life.

For the compulsive shopper, "intelligence" means only knowing the best price; "wisdom" raises the question of voids that acquisi-tions cannot fill. Reason struggles with the resistance of breaking out of the entrapment and provides the basis of support by which life can be lived better and better. Intelligence, the How To, in the form of exposure/response blocking guides the sequences of steps, which reason supports and moves toward the freedom to which wisdom beckons. The problem of having OCD—and what we need to learn from it—is that the issue with the sufferer is not intelligence. The issue is having *wisdom* because without that there is no vision and the sufferer perishes.

The person with all the inhibitions of OCD—the avoidance it entails, the wasted time, the wasted energy—has intelligence. The raw sensations, however, act like cutworms on a plant. Reason is so cut off from its emotional roots that it cannot perform its function of leading to the best of the satisfactions possible, given one's heritage and situation. It is *wisdom* that makes a break for freedom from the prison cell of repetition, in its awareness of how enfeebling the monotone of obsessing really is. Wisdom is the sense of lack, of what is missing, and *potentiality*. It is wisdom that supplies the motivation for treatment and sustains it.

Exposure/response illustrates an intelligence accumulating a knowledge of what "works"; wisdom systematizes that knowledge and defines the limitations of that knowledge, then points into what is not, but can be. Treatment only goes so far, and it is that "so far" that needs to be recognized and the lacks in one's life explored. Since no one is going to be cured—not only of OCD but scarcely anything else, more especially death—it is well to consider how we can be healed. Sin/sickness/disorder/disease/pathological habituation/neurobiological dysfunction—however "It" is conceptualized—whatever motivation and effective treatment techniques are suggested by intelligence and supported by reason, nothing escapes quality of life issues. This is the *wisdom* to be learned from OCD.

Chapter 9

OCD and the Quality of Life

When an evil spirit goes out of a person, it travels over dry country looking for a place to rest. If it can't find one, it says to itself, "I will go back to my house." So it goes back and finds the house empty, clean, and all fixed up. Then it goes out and brings along seven other spirits even worse than itself, and they come and live there. So when it is all over, that person is in worse shape than he was at the beginning. This is what will happen to the evil people of this day.

Matthew 12:43-45

Since the human is the only animal to know that he or she must die, if a person meditates on how she wants her tombstone to read not many would choose,

Janie Smith
Born a human being
Died a straightener and a cleaner

Enter, however, the proverb of the psychiatrist:

The patient wants to be comfortable.
The patient does not want to change.

Successful treatment has all the problems of forced early retirement; it is one thing to fantasize about more time to do what you want to do, another thing to have it. Persons are well warned by the proverb not to ask God for something in prayer, lest they get it. Simply to achieve symptom moderation is a happy thing for the young—their grades usually go up—but for adults, more time and disposable energy raises the question of what they really want to do with their lives. "Not much," would be an honest answer in many cases. The parable quoted from Jesus at the beginning of this chapter is something to ponder. Like the alcoholic who has achieved sobriety, the person with OCD is always in "recovery" and, like the alcoholic, in need of a positive program that leads to the development of personhood.

There are a number of sequential steps in this development. "Marie," in the third grade, faced the developmental challenge of creating successful peer relationships; fortunately, at that period, a characteristic of the elementary school child is the playground virtue of "fairness," and she and I successfully appealed to that with her classmates. "Nancy" faced the developmental challenge of commitment in her early adulthood in regard to mothering her children. "Lou" faced the issue in older middle age of continuing to work with integrity when he was passed over for promotion. Life not only presents developmental challenges, however, for situational ones arise, as when "Mary" lost her beloved grandchild, even as retirement complicated her life. It all points toward the needfulness of successful treatment—and that more than successful treatment is needed by a person who has OCD.

In this chapter, we will consider a passage of Scripture as a positive program:

> Love the Lord your God with all your heart, with all your soul, with all your strength, and with all your mind; and, love your neighbor as you love yourself.

Luke 10:27

To begin at the end—which is a very good beginning—in the matter of "loving yourself," there are three important elements in this for those with OCD. The first is to be *merciful* to yourself; having interjected thoughts is a terrible burden, one that the sufferer never invites and should never willingly host. The practice of beating oneself up for these ought to have gone out with Martin Luther and his flagella in the monastery. The second of these is to have *respect* for yourself in all your efforts, large or small, successful or the least of treatment building blocks. The third is what St. Francis learned, perhaps too late in his foreshortened life, *to be kind to*

Brother Donkey, the body. We, too, need to display that kindness to our bodies. Building on a reasonable self-regard—the "love yourself"—we are in a position to accord that to everyone else.

The love of neighbor is the summary challenge to love humankind. The saintly almost always have echoed this teaching, as the Quakers are fond of the proverbial saying of George Fox, "We should walk through the world gladly, seeing the image of God in every man."

Perhaps one of the most striking examples of the love of neighbor, as an example of the triumph of the spirit to which we all should aspire, comes to us from the founder of modern Turkey, Kemal Atatürk. Of the ordeal of the Gallipoli campaign in World War I—perhaps almost equaling Verdun in horror, length, and cost—Atatürk wrote:

> Those heroes that shed their blood
> and lost their lives
> You are now lying in the soil of a friendly country
> Therefore rest in peace
> There is no difference between the Johnies
> And the Mehmets to us where they lie side by side
> Here in this country of ours
> You, the mothers
> Who sent their sons from far away countries,
> Wipe away your tears
> Your sons are now lying in our bosom
> And we are in peace.
> Having lost their lives on this land they have
> Become our sons as well.

If only we could achieve such a spiritual level as this poem displays, doubtless there would continue many ills of the body, but there could be a healing of the mind. The little question of the sufferer, "Why me?" could be transformed into "Why not me?" and yet into "Why anyone?" Let us turn now to the issue of ways in which a sufferer might develop a positive program for healing that not only might maintain the gains of treatment but also move beyond them.

LOVING WITH YOUR HEART

To love with all your heart is an interesting admonition, for the "heart" has been regarded as the center of a person's being in most times and climes. A universal folk insight is not to be easily disregarded: to be good-hearted, pure-hearted, kindhearted—to avoid being coldhearted, hard-hearted. These sayings may not have been highly regarded for accuracy by the scientific minded, yet when paying a compliment to a colleague they would sometimes use the metaphor, "His heart is really in the right place."

More recently, less metaphorically, there is the recognition that each cell in our bodies has a capacity for mental activity and that the heart, considered as an electrical unit, is more powerful in output than the brain. The brain may use more energy, but is far less powerful than the heart. When the brain goes flatline, that is it; the heart more usually carries nobly or ignobly on, and on, and on.[1]

This approach is of interest in the area of OCD, perhaps not for treatment directly, but rather in the area of prevention. Many persons with OCD are sufficiently out of touch with themselves so, when stress builds to an attack, it takes them by surprise. Part of learning to cope with OCD is to sense accumulating stress. The interjected thought, for instance, can be—and ordinarily should be—dismissed. In one ear and out the other: accepted for what it is and on its way. The interjected thought, however, can be a warning that the boundary line between the two memory systems is weakening. That is when a HeartMath technique is worth practicing, for it offers impulse control over the startle response. There are a series of techniques that are well worth researching for OCD, but let us look at just one.

The central technique is that of "freeze-frame"; it is what mammals often use when a startle response occurs. For a split second or so, they are in total attention. Then they run or return to feeding. In freeze-frame it is much the same for people because it is somewhat like pushing the pause button on the VCR. For a moment—six seconds is the recommended time—everything halts, then the action proceeds in whatever way is relevant. This expands what is already known: delay is often the appropriate tactic when the OCD chemicals squirt in a startle response. Buy some time and they pass.

In the moment of consciously "freezing" when the interjecting sensation hits, and before the thought plays loop the loop, *the shift is from the head to the heart* as an alternative *practiced* response strategy. The "head," as illustrated by scrupulosity, is the site of a "defective conscience." The shift away from cognition—so easily entangled by the startle response and beginning the feedback loop with various many-splendored superstitions—is a preprogrammed decision that goes from head to heart.

Instead of tamely submitting to emotional blackmail, the person takes six seconds—no more—and centers on the heart, in effect practicing a specific conscious sensation. By embracing an alternate reality—the simplicity and unification of heart-centeredness instead of the swirls of sensations starting in the feedback loop—two things happen simultaneously. The first is a countersensation that has been posed against the mammalian memory system's sensation. The second is, since the spinal column only carries messages one way at a time, the cordial message center is being controlled by the focus on the adjoining heart. Activating the heart co-opts the cortisol center, according to HeartMath research findings, thus preventing the activation of much of the emergency response system. The heart "entrains" the body's systems due to being a more powerful source of electrical energy, about two and a half times greater.

The sequence of this "way of the heart" is: (1) Be aware of your accumulating stresses. (2) When a stress-induced sensation erupts, go to "freeze-frame." (3) Take six seconds—no obsessing, please!—to focus on the heart, becoming consciously aware of it. (4) Shift from the sensations of a heart focus to a preselected heartwarming memory. This could be of holding your baby on his or her first birthday, being with your best friend on a camping trip, a sunset in the Rockies, or a precious moment on the beach. Evoke a warm, beautiful, emotionally stirring image as a countermemory you have selected to displace the OCD sensations. A technique of "anchoring" may help—much as is done in hypnotic treatments—by placing in a billfold pictures that evoke powerful positive images. (5) Move into a positive mind frame of gratitude, not just intellectualizing about being thankful, but getting fully *into* being thankful. (6) From this, when you are ready, move on to what you need to learn from this experience so that coping skills are steadily developed. It is a rehabituating from years of running in the brain's "ruts"; it takes practice, but it can work for you. The "method" actors use such a similar process successfully for their purposes; so can you.[2]

As another suggestion on the theme of quality of life, what is next needed is for the person to begin to organize life around what folk wisdom has passed on to us: good-hearted, kindhearted, warm-hearted. The thoughts may be contaminated, but trust in the *will* to be pure of heart. Mother, if your hormones have somehow become twisted, listen to your heart, you can trust that; husband, your head may spin around with obsessions of knives and/or sex, but listen to your heart.

A chemical happenstance may occur in the ten million or so synapses in a brain; God knows if the heart is right. What we have learned from OCD is that the interjection of a bizarrely interpreted sensation may not initially be controlled, but intention can be con-trolled. A scam sensation may scream for attention, but we have the power to modify behavior—if it takes medication, so be it. To believe in a Creator is to acknowledge He accepts the responsibility of how we are put together—amygdala, hippocampus, right and left hemispheres, and all the neurons that run hither and yon—and if He can love us, we can love us.

If God is love—which is the personalized expression of creativi-ty—then to love Him with all our heart, is to intend what John Wesley, that great saint, had to say. "If thy heart is right, as my heart is right, then give me thy hand" and our relationships will move in the right direction. As in modern architecture, where "form follows function," if the mind demands an appropriate form of behavior, in due time that will induce the function of the brain to be more appropriate, as well.

LOVING WITH ALL YOUR MIND

Obsessive-compulsive disorder, taken as a whole, is a pattern of tamed perfections—such as the clothes hangers arranged "just so" and the handles of the coffee cups aligned to perfection—that uti-lizes terror to ensure submission. If a scholar wanted to write an encyclopedia on emotional abuse, he or she would be well advised to start with a study of OCD, rather than the classic fairy tale of a wicked stepmother. The way to break up this repetitious pattern is through the introduction of discord created by opposing sensations. These contrasts are, of course, behaviors that constitute the "refiner's fire" that incinerates the obsessions, and, as anyone knows who has worked with exposure/response blocking, that is no ease-taking experience. When that pattern is forcibly "modified," as in exposure/response, the issue then becomes how to maintain that lowered level of intensity.

The new understanding of the brain adds a whole new possibility to the ancient injunction to love God with mind and strength because we now know how to strengthen the mind. The idea is to live in an intellectually challenging way—and certainly reading everything you can get hold of on OCD is a good start (but a poor ending, of course). The suggestions in articles for strengthening the mind run the gamut from doing crossword puzzles to taking dance lessons, to learning to fix things if you are "all thumbs," to learning a musical instrument, to making new friends whose interests open up all sorts of stimulating avenues to explore.

Interestingly, the director of Art United in Fort Wayne, Indiana, cites research concluding that students who become interested in classical music improved their SAT scores.[3] We know that different languages utilize different parts of the brain, with multilingual persons using a somewhat larger portion of it than persons who speak a single language. Probably every suggestion made here also utilizes a different part of the brain: if OCD has created "ruts" in a person's brain, there are ways to get around them. The brain is like a computer in this regard; there are several means to an end.

Persons with OCD are long on gray cells and short on white connectors—superstition-prone, relationship-phobic—the crucial question for those with OCD may very well be, "Why not?" There is nothing to lose but the various avoidances. The terror used by OCD is a bluff: no one ever died from being dangled over its pits of hellfire. This is not to deny that the Master Illusionist is capable of making it feel so: no one creates a stronger hypnotic trance than OCD.

There is always an avoidance commanded as a posthypnotic suggestion to inhibit the freedom to which wisdom beckons. The problem of having OCD—and what we need to learn from it—is that the issue with the sufferer is not intelligence; the issue is having *wisdom*, without it there is no vision and the sufferer perishes.

It would seem the part of wisdom, in seeking to fulfill the potentiality of the mind for healing, is to focus upon five qualities, turning them in sequence into behaviors, as "process thought" suggests.

The Willingness to Adventure

What it is all about is "creative advance" from the first molecule floating around in space, to our latest breath, to the final atom whenever. Attempting to live out a person's life, when it is based on avoidances, is a form of existence dependent upon a defensive strategy and doomed to failure. If a life makes such a faint imprint, it offers vagaries to subsequent life. It may not be sin, but it certainly is pathology. If a person is to attempt to love God "with all one's mind," and the nature of God is creativity itself, then we must be prepared to find the courage to adventure, to ever press the limits imposed by anxiety. In this way, we fulfill our potentiality by joining in the creative advance that marks our world.

A Determination to Be a Searcher for Truth

To be victimized by the doubting disease is to have a compulsion to achieve absolute certainty, to be condemned to anxiousness and sustained by perfectionism. To love God with all one's mind is to accept the limitations of "mind," to have a willingness to be a searcher for truth, willing to be a practicing realist engaging in a pilgrimage foregoing certainty.

Obsessive-compulsive disorder surely is a stern teacher in one regard to the locked brain, the notion there is only one way to look at things; existence has one dimension and one only, and truth is black and white. "My way or no way; all or nothing at all." If we have learned our lesson from trying to cope with OCD, there are as many dimensions to truth as there are relationships. The greater the number of perspectives considered, the more likely our opinion is to have a sounder relationship with reality, that multifaceted creation of the moment. If we know the truth, we know it in its relationships, whether of family, friends, medications or meditation, heredity or circumstances . . . and how clean is acceptably clean for the toilet!

The measure of "truth" is certainly not in some abstract dogma as to scrubbing or rubbing; what exists has various perspectives such as, "Does my scrubbing drive my kids nuts?" There is a beauty to truth, but it does not reside in absoluteness and its fraternal twin, certainty, but rather it resides in an acceptance of whatever excellence of understanding we may gain rather than in some absolute perfection. It comes down to judgment, whether of a statesman regarding an international treaty or a woman looking at marks left by her sweep on the rug: what is wise?

In essence, the willingness to love God with all our minds, in regard to having a commitment to the Truth, is to have a comprehension of relationships and to be a loyal lover of reality—whose foundation rests in the mind of reality, our hope for guiding and guarding our world.

The Will to Be a Maker of Peace

Peace is not the quiet of the grave; it is the hallmark of *fine thoughts and fine actions*. Process thought, at this point, can learn from OCD; thoughts can be interjected without consent (as the Catholic Church has always recognized in differentiating these from a mortal sin). The obsessions with blasphemy, of sex and violence, of course, are anything but "fine." What we learn is will, intention. If we refuse to entertain the obsessions—that is, *to be entertained with fantasizing,* there is no sin. The issue is, "What kind of thoughts do you treat as honored guests?" The fineness of thought is in having a personal philosophy encompassing the realities of sin and suffering, of evil and inequalities, in a sufficient acceptance of life, while also encompassing and affirming a vision of the overarching goodness of life. The fineness of actions is our determination to do something about the sin, suffering, evil, and inequalities within what scope of influence we have. As Martin Luther is reported to have said to Melanchthon, "Trust God and sin bravely." This is wisdom: a peace that does not necessitate perfection of thought and accomplishment. It is a peace that accepts limitations but is committed to doing the best we can, granted what we know and the given situation.

If we have learned our lessons from the study of OCD, existence cannot be equated with quietude; it is the militancy of doing and giving one's best and then resting it in God's hands, for earth offers no certainty but in that resolve. In a universe where perfection only rests in the primordial nature of God, the only perfection open to us is the beauty coming through a peace that accepts reality and echoes it with a resolution to set our faces toward excellence.

A Commitment to the Art of Living

Here Alfred North Whitehead might well have added "beauty," by which he meant an appreciation of contrasts. Anyone with OCD can applaud that notion: grasping the contrast between the excludingness of an OCD attack—such as repetitively washing the bathroom floor for hours, with ears deaf to whatever else is going on—and the richness of data in normal conscious awareness such as the children needing to be fed. Whitehead believed *expression is the one fundamental sacrament,* that what we say and do is sacramental in nature, and the expression is always in response to stimuli—which may be from our DNA or from the environment. What a travesty is made of this, for instance, in scrupulosity when the person repeatedly demands reassurance from a frazzled spouse relating to forgiveness of "sins that are not sins" or sensations that sabotage a parent's love for his or her child in giving in when going on vacation to returning to check the electrical switch one more time. The nature of OCD itself is not that of sin, but rather a denial of beauty in the art of living. It is an intensity so great it alienates us from our truer selves or avoidances that are so pervasive and are such vagaries that they deprive both self and others of the nourishment of stimulation.

Edmund Wilson, in *Consilience: The Unity of Knowledge,* has presented an option on Whiteheadean thought worth noting as to what we can learn from OCD. *To express oneself is an art form and the artistry of life is to express oneself truly and fully.*[4] What we are to learn from OCD, as pathology, is to make the deed truthful. If a sufferer hits a bump and stops and searches, the truth is that it is because of sensations of terror and unrelated guilt, much, much less in caring. There is no virtue in circling the block excited by terror. Virtue lies in being a caring person.

If a man's brain initiates "hiccuping" with violent thoughts, is that the *whole* truth of who he is? If a woman has sexual thoughts, is that the truth of how she chooses to relate to others? The differentiation of what is OCD and what is truly "me" to some degree must lie in the length and severity of interjected thoughts; however, the possibility of living in a way truly sacramental rests on *how we express ourselves rather than on how we experience ourselves.* Perfectionism insists on a black-and-white mode of pronouncing a sentence on the self. Correcting that distortion of reality begins as treatment, but moves to an artistry of expression based on a person learning to evaluate thoughts and deeds and finding the wisdom to balance these as to who he or she truly is.

It is truth that the sufferer of the doubting disease seeks, as Bunyan truly wrote about Christian and Faithful imprisoned in a cage at Vanity Fair. The essential issue is less objective reality—"Did I back over a person?"—than it is a subjective reality—"Are my actions motivated by a will-of-the-wisp terror or do I express my life in the context of caring for others?" That, rather than color-coordinating the house, is artistry. That is what we are seeing in the undeniable grace and beauty in the responses that people in support groups make who have paid the price of effective treatment and moved on from seeking a cure to being healers.

Will to Live in Harmony

Whitehead considered the "aesthetic" the ultimate category of what is of worth, but for the purpose of what is to be learned from OCD, the less august term of "harmony" may be better suited. Probably anyone who has paid the price of modifying the biology of OCD has acted out of the motivation of "harmony": softening the raw, rough edges of frustration with oneself and those who are loved. On the other hand, perhaps a noble word such as "aesthetic" is more descriptive of anyone's character who has risen to the challenge of OCD.

LOVING WITH ALL YOUR STRENGTH

There is an undeniable attitudinal contest to OCD when it comes to "strength." A saying, popularly attributed to Frederick the Great (1712-1786), is worth considering: "Whatever makes a man" (and today we would amend that to "person"), "whatever makes a person strong is good," OCD included, or, as "Anne" would say, "Life is for learning."

Part of the needful strength for those with OCD is the ability to assess stress, acknowledge what is tolerable, and accept the necessity to live within those limits. Within this disorder is a two-year-old brat ready to break out in the fashion of all two-year-olds when they are too tired, too hungry, or too sleepy. No one is around to parent those with OCD except themselves—and if a cranky "kid" is apt to begin whining and acting out, that "kid" has to be able to appropriately parent himself or herself in the one-on-one challenge of willing and willfulness.

Being a permissive parent to oneself, when a person has OCD, is certain to bring its own reward . . . and so is the strength and wisdom of good parenting. The classic Greek motto was "to know thyself," to which we may add, in the context of loving the Lord thy God with all thy strength, know how to "no" thyself appropriately.

LOVING WITH ALL THE SOUL

If the experience of OCD by its very nature raises religious questions, various alternatives become considered; if OCD is central to the human experience, then what does an organized religious system offer? Each religious approach constitutes an understanding of human existence; each in some way deals with mammalian physical structures we each incorporate. In the light of OCD, we have a right to inquire how a particular religious approach affects the pathological distortion of exaggerations in thinking and behavior. We have a right—perhaps an obligation—to inquire how a particular religious approach affects the development of our human potential, as well as setting limits on what is our mammalian heritage and what care we are to give our bodies.

The pantheistic religions, in general, offer the way of blending with the universe. The Self becomes at one with nature: we live, we die and we are part of earth and sky. Another option is seeing life as a cycle of existence, a series of incarnations, from which we seek the pathway of escape. Through the suppression of desire, we find cessation of repetitions. In others, we are extensions of our family who went before us and trustees of those who come thereafter. In the philosophies of ethical living, we are offered a wisdom by which life can be well-lived and finitude accepted. In America, on Sunday mornings, one is offered a way of perceiving life as a time between heaven and hell, and existence is hooked to a hope for eternal bliss in the hereafter and an avoidance of you-know-where. With a channel changer we can even flip around to a philosophy of "Be Happy and How To." With a movement of the finger on the channel changer we can learn where to buy a prayer for our healing and a spiritually potent handkerchief. On a rainy afternoon, when it is too soggy to do anything more than be a couch potato, for those who are of that religious persuasion a golf game is going on someplace.

The religiousness of the "New Age" addresses some of the feelings and flashes of religious intuition. In spite of limited experience with New Age religion, I will venture one observation as angels are a topic of popular religion. I know some spouses who believe in angels, but any person with OCD who has gotten better—of whom I am aware—seems uniformly to have a belief system built around the "doctrine of sweat equity." Linking suffering and curing, or trauma and survival if you have OCD, to the intervention of an angel has the same probability as winning a million dollars playing a slot machine in Las Vegas.

Each religious system, and there are many more than have been listed, has its kernel of truth. We are part of nature: mammals, born alive, nursing young. Our bodies are carriers of DNA, then, now, and for most adults, after our deaths, in our children. Suffering is real. Meditation offers little solution; philosophy offers small consolation; if some types of religion are opiates, then some "doctor" certainly underprescribed. If OCD is humanity writ large for all to see, it is legitimate to test the philosophical and religious alternatives that are offered. If life is a School for Learning, OCD is arguably a postgraduate course in Suffering 403 in which we take notes for a test on Living with Creditability.

If each system—despite its kernel of truth—falls short of the needs of a person with OCD, it is reasonable to suggest that all systems are still evolving, hopefully in a direction of greater adequacy for those who suffer and to which learning from OCD has something to offer each. For those with OCD, however, there may be an even greater relevancy to be a religious searcher and seeker.

The OCD experience is itself a form of religion that has both system and organization. Its obsessing is systematic and the compulsions are duly organized; no organized religion can claim a greater devotion to its rituals than the unfortunate sufferer. What dedicated churchgoer do you know who has a faith to rival that of the most ordinary practitioner of the superstitions of OCD? On the religious level, OCD competes with great success in preaching doubt, and when scrupulosity becomes a social contagion, its evangelistic successes boggle the mind.

Some may shrug at such a proposition that OCD may be regarded as a form of religion, but is not the loving practice of hoarding in a search for total security rising against one's human need? A person can indeed "shop until you drop," but is it not a searching for salvation arising from feelings of deepest human anxiety? Scrupulosity is not religious; it is a religion, as is checking and washing and so on. Every ritual is in effect a prayer and every superstition, an Article of Faith.

How do these, however, compare to a cup of coffee with a friend, to talking to your roses so they sense you are grateful, to the smell of fresh sheets upon the bed, or to lying back to back with someone you love when the night is cold? You might ask, "What do all these have to do with religion?" and then reply, "A great deal." Religion concerns the assigning of values and behaviors reflecting the evaluation of what is of worth or worthy of worship. Obsessions and rituals reflect values that are religious as much as the saying, "There—but for the grace of God—go I."

Religion is a quest for meaning, climaxing in an expression of one's ultimate concern. To be creditable—at least from what we can learn from the study of OCD—such a quest has to be a vigorous approach to a particular situation, a determination to achieve whatever the potential for living in that situation and its environment allows.

From Paul Tillich, we learn the essence of living religiously: to identify and commit to one's ultimate concern by valuing, assigning of worth. That is why hoarding, as much as scrupulosity, dons the cloak of a religion as it organizes a person's life. In direct opposition to this, I once knew a black preacher in a growth-group setting.

I have long since forgotten his name, but his belief is engraved on my heart: "I have come to love reality." When Tillich offers the "Ground of Being" as one of the names of God, I hear the echo of that black pastor: a love of Reality. *Be Here, Live Now.*

If we are to say what we have learned from OCD in the matter of religion, it is the basic message: *Get real.* What the frustrations and intolerable boredom of OCD have to teach are made apparent in the board game of Trivial Pursuit.

QUALITY OF LIFE: THE NEED FOR A ROLE MODEL

Role models are always in short supply, they are the wrong gender half of the time and never completely adequate any of the time. But they are most needed with a dysfunction that is characterized as being the doubting disease. The Church's wisdom in treating scrupulosity recommends that the sufferer find a person of solid common sense for the measurement of what is real and reliable.

In this light, Father Teilhard de Chardin is worth considering for anyone with or without OCD. This good Jesuit just never could have it easy: As a young paleontologist he was taken advantage of, as a man of impeccable integrity, by being invited to be a part of the follow-up discovery group of the Piltdown man. That turned out to be a hoax perpetrated by someone who combined the top half of the skull of an ancient man with the ancient jaw of an ape. The find area was "salted" with other bone fragments and Teilhard de Chardin was invited to the party. He did not have OCD, but he must have become very familiar with the suffering that can be caused by an illusion presented as reality.

He served continual years as a stretcher bearer in the French lines during World War I. He came out with two commendations for bringing men in under fire and yet never suffered a scratch. He did have a problem, nevertheless. Instead of writing about miracles he started writing books on evolution. The church "powers that be" were not happy that he combined priesthood with paleontology nor were they happy about his theories of evolution that meddled with established Catholic doctrines.

He was one of those priests who would insist on writing one too many books, so he found himself in China between the world wars, hoping to find valid a tentative promise from a church superior to publish more of his works when he got back—some day. He did not make it.

Let us join such a man in celebrating Mass in China with what was available to him:

> Since once again, Lord—though this time not in the forests of the Aisne but in the steppes of Asia—I have neither bread, nor wine, nor altar, I will raise myself beyond these symbols, up to the pure majesty of the real itself; I, your priest, will make the whole earth my altar and on it will offer you all the labours and sufferings of the world.
>
> Over there, on the horizon, the sun has just touched with light the outermost fringe of the eastern sky. Once again, beneath this moving sheet of fire, the living surface of the earth wakes and trembles, and once again begins its fearful travail. I will place on my paten, O God, the harvest to be won by this renewal of labour. Into my chalice I shall pour all the sap which is to be pressed out this day from the earth's fruits.
>
> My paten and my chalice are the depths of a soul laid widely open to all the forces which in a moment will rise up from every corner of the earth and converge upon the Spirit. Grant me the remembrance and the mystic presence of all those whom the light is now awakening to the new day.
>
> One by one, Lord, I see and I love all those whom you have given me to sustain and charm my life. One by one also I number all those who make up that other beloved family which has gradually surrounded me, its unity fashioned out of the most disparate elements, with affinities of the heart, of scientific research and of thought. And again one by one—more vaguely it is true, yet all-inclusively—I call before me the whole vast anonymous army of living humanity; those who surround me though I to not know them; those who come, and those who go; above all, those who in office, laboratory and factory, through their vision of truth or despite their error, truly believe in the progress of earthly reality and who today will take up again their impassioned pursuit of the light.

This restless multitude, confused or orderly, the immensity of which terrifies us; this ocean of humanity whose slow, monotonous wave-flows trouble the hearts even of those whose faith is most firm: it is to this deep that I thus desire all the fibers of my being should respond. All the things in the world to which this day will bring increase; all those that will diminish; all those too that will die: all of them, Lord, I try to gather into my arms, so as to hold them out to you in offering. This is the material of my sacrifice; the only material you desire.

Once upon a time men took into your temple the first fruits of their harvests, the flower of their flocks. But the offering you really want, the offering you mysteriously need every day to appease your hunger, to slake your thirst is nothing less than the growth of the world borne ever onwards in the stream of universal becoming.

Receive, O Lord, this all-embracing host which your whole creation, moved by your magnetism, offers you at the dawn of a new day.

This bread, our toil, is of itself, I know, but an immense fragmentation; this wine, our pain, is no more, I know, than a draught that dissolves yet in the very depths of this formless mass you have implanted—and this I am sure of, for I sense it—a desire, irresistible, hallowing, which makes us cry out, believer and unbeliever alike: "Lord, make us *one*."

Because, my God, though I lack the soul-zeal and the sublime integrity of your saints, I yet have received from you an overwhelming sympathy for all that stirs within the dark mass of matter, because I know myself to be irremediably less a child of heaven than a son of earth; therefore I will this morning climb up in spirit to the high places, bearing with me the hopes and the miseries of my mother; and there—empowered by that priesthood which you alone (as I firmly believe) have bestowed on me—upon all that in the world of human flesh is now about to be born or die beneath the rising sun I will call down the Fire.

Opening section
"The Mass on the World"
in *Hymn of the Universe*

You may think to yourself, what a loss to the world when his life and work faded. *But.* If you are a guessing person and unsurprised by church history, rumor has it John 23rd, Pastor of Pastors and of gracious and beloved memory, had been reading that good Jesuit and paleontologist prior to calling an ecumenical council. *Renewal will always find resources.*

Chapter 10

Theologizing
in a Neurobiological Age

The deeper piety is, the humbler are its claims with regard to the supersensible. It is like a path that winds between the hills instead of going over them.

Albert Schweitzer
Out of My Life and Thought, 1931

A tourist from Jupiter might empathize with a story recounted by a tour guide on Cyprus, Greece. As she went up and down the bus aisle answering questions, she noted one British tourist was always busily writing in her diary. Glancing over it, the tour guide noted that frequently the only note entered was "ABC." Curious about it, she asked. Looking her straight in the eye the tourist replied, "It stands for 'Another Bloody Church.'" However a person feels about it, organized religion was, and will be, a fundamental factor in human history; religion is not going to go away. Tillich was right in characterizing it as one's "ultimate concern" and an ultimate concern of which we may come to realize is the hallmark of our specie.

The issue is what "religion" must be reckoned with, as the jokes about golfers and their wives will testify. As a matter of conjecture, looking at the magazine racks in drugstores, you might surmise the gods of mythology have not gone to sleep, but into publishing. Bacchus is still partying with wine, Mars continues to exalt military glory, Venus has her loving devotees of feminine beauty, Neptune never had it better with the sea-engrossed yachting fans, and Mercury would delight in the new forms of computerized communication. Vulcan, the technocrat, evokes long theological discussions about horsepower. Astrology in all the ancient world never had the number of devotees now buying those magazines. Need a lucky number for the lottery? Consult the stars. Only Athena, goddess of wisdom, seems to have slumbered through the publishing and ratings wars.

With such competition for becoming an individual's ultimate concern, we might regard it as curious that the National Institute of Mental Health celebrated the 1990s as "The Decade of the Brain." Not only does neurobiology have a profound effect on mental health, it also points toward theological implications, as well, that merit discussion as we enter the twenty-first century. The study of the brain can provide a stimulus for new perspectives that help focus a person's ultimate concern with greater relevancy. In fact, one might say that, for theology, neurobiology is a good deal like a complete autopsy: a lot of the superficial is cut away and it quickly gets down to fundamentals and what we really need to know.

Neurobiology, as it keeps evolving, is not going to go away either; it is—and continues to be—a challenge both in the mental health field and in theology. One option for Christians is that today we can take our stance in the tradition of St. Francis and affirm our oneness with Brother Sun, Sister Moon, and the creatures Francis loved, including Brother Donkey—our bodies.

Christians are not strangers to the fundamental, "the Word made flesh." This is to theologize, not in pantheistic fashion, but in the midst of the Knowledge Explosion while standing accepting and unshaken. We can rest secure in the validity of raising questions about what is the individual's ultimate concern and in the healing power of spirituality—as the healing power of twelve-step programs illustrate daily.

Of the many theological implications of this "Decade of the Brain," only three will be explored: our past, present, and a sense of the future.

OUR PAST CONTINUES INTO OUR PRESENT

One of the doctrines of creation is that it proceeded as "creation from nothingness." God, the Houdini of Creation, produced the world and all therein with a flourish of the hand. Creation, as it were, by card trick. We, the contemporary audience, are to be awestruck, asking "How did He do that?" Is there more religious value in marveling at a Creator producing a world as if by sleight of hand, or the awesome accountability and responsibility of a heritage coming to us over inestimable eons overseen by a Creative Power, in a simile affirmed by many as a caring Father?

When we reflect on that little family group on the African plains discussed in Chapter 2, we are filled with awe that we are trustees of uncountable lives. Looking over our shoulders, and unknowable to them, the very brain is a gift with which I write and with which you read. The brain we exhibit is a result of process and will be in process. Facing forward, you and I have reason to be awestruck by being trustees of those who are to come. What is truly awe inspiring is that our brains are in the process of developing even as we dialogue between our minds and *because* we dialogue. That awe inevitably has a religious quality, a concern finally more ultimate—as we look at our children and grandchildren—than what we are to eat and what we are to wear.

As that endangered little family group closes in together, clutching their sticks, we recognize in them:

- an environment stimulating concern with violence
- the centrality of survival needs
- the predominance of fear
- preoccupation with safety
- communal centeredness around food and drink
- continual fear of being poisoned by food or drink
- interdependency
- breeding needs

Doubtless someone will reflect that the family who eats supper around the television, absorbed in its sex and violence, has not come very far, in some characteristics, in these millions of years. On the other hand, their "breeding needs" have become our intimacy needs and their central concerns were the origins of our sacraments. God, no magician He, seemingly prefers that we know how He did it.

It is easy to recognize how these concerns, reflecting their circumstances, could evolve from a primary family group, to my clan, to my tribe, to my country. It makes it easy to relate to the basic family theme as characterizing early childhood/early humans, and "my country, right or wrong" in a later, parallel context. My race, my age, my sex, my religion are but extensions, primary narcissism to secondary narcissism, as Freud would categorize it. What an awe-inspiring developmental leap to move beyond a concentration on "my kind" to a concern for "humankind," even now evolving into a concern for our co-creatures—for *our world* is their world, too.

To theologize neurologically—to develop a "neurobiology"—is to own a perspective of what it means to be human that not only encompasses humanity, but also acknowledges our co-creatures. Limiting our discussion to what we have set out to explore, however, we are more immediately concerned with the developmental stage when we no longer see life in terms of "my kind"—or my tribal god—but rather identify with humankind. To someone with OCD, this is what is rightly experienced in a support group: "In my individuality I am unique, but I am not alone; in my very suffering I am one with both humanness and with these newly discovered brothers and sisters—I am Me; I am one of the co-creatures, I am of the specie Human."

> No man is an *Iland*, intire of it selfe, every man is a piece of the *Continent*, a part of the maine . . .[1]

It becomes clear, as we consider the circumstances of the far, far ago, why their limited concerns would be enormously focused as to what was really happening and of what was of value. It is also clear why, in the less far ago, these concerns should gradually have taken on a religious aura in an evolution from supersition into the "higher religions." In some ways, there is as much gap between the focused concerns of that Not Yets/Will Be family group and the higher religions of today as there is between the chimpanzees and ourselves. There are similarities, but also enormous differences.

Learning from OCD can broaden hunches about organized religious groups focusing on rituals. Humans obsess about anxiety, humans create rituals to relieve anxiety, and over time these become structurally integrated into religious tradition. Neither the religious group nor the individual worshipper would be pathological, just a reflection on how a pious practice to relieve anxiety became emulated custom, hardened into ritual, gradually integrating into self-identity, finally maintained by peer pressure arising itself from the anxiety of not being of those who "belong."

Similarities appear, too, in the experience *when trapped within* a person's OCD today and the Not Yets/Will Be group who lived several million years ago. The similarities actually are no more remarkable than that we have an appendix and a little toe on each foot. They also gave us a thumb with which we can grasp, so let us be aware of it and be appreciative; if we have moved along technologically, a great deal is owed to that factor of a wiggly, yet able fifth digit. If we still struggle with some of the same issues, we have evolved enormously and will evolve further. They exhibited an ultimate concern—survival—had an overwhelming feeling tone—fear—and had no option. We have an option: to choose what shall be our ultimate concern and we are open to a variety of feeling tones, although for some the one still predominating is fear. We have something they did not have, not for several million years: we have an expanded skull and an enlarged (although at one point not necessarily heavier) brain. With that, we can make a difference—if we choose.

Perhaps choices are unduly limited by anxiety. It has been said, "There are no atheists in foxholes," and it may be that fear is a mighty incentive to religious feelings. It may be as natural as the body clustering blood in its protected middle when danger threatens. We are however, even in the midst of severe anxiety, participants in that specie marked by an ability to *choose*.

Central to most Christians' beliefs is the Lord's Supper, called the Eucharist, the Thanksgiving. Is it not a marvel that, from the primitive beginnings, such as the struggle for survival by a little group of Not Yets/Will Be, that such a ritual arose? A ritual in which there is an acknowledgment of the reality of suffering, of being forgiven and forgiving, and where there is an affirming of goodwill toward all persons and a determination to live a better life. What could be more appropriate, given the sweep of timelessness and history, than characterizing the ritual as the Thanksgiving. This experience and the sensations it can evoke sum up much of what can be learned from having OCD and meeting its challenges successfully.

IMPLICATIONS FOR LIVING
IN THE PRESENT

To state the obvious, in OCD—the doubting disease—the person is tortured by a lack of certainty. The question of what is true, what is real, is of vital importance, not just to philosophers and theologians, but to hurting persons such as those who have shared their case stories. What we know is that it is not only those suffering from the doubting disease who are pressed for certainty; this is a universal issue and one which is continually pressing to the religious and nonreligious, for OCD is humanity written in script large enough for everyone to read.

Obsessive-compulsive disorder is a pathological distortion of the connectedness within the human brain resulting, usually, in a conscious dubiousness of one's relationship to reality. At the same time, the very exaggerating nature of OCD results in a magnification of the human condition so we may better understand it. In particular, the OCD experience illustrates the problem in religion of the gap between appearance and reality.

It is the gap between appearance and reality that is so "crazy-making" in the experience of OCD. This is illustrated by the thought, "I must be crazy to have such feelings and thoughts" that violate both my sense of reality and value. It is this sense a parent with OCD feels when the interjected thought strikes about harming his or her much-loved baby; "I must be 'mad,'" as in that feeling about the obsessional thought, "This is maddening." No wonder that at the extreme, some bewildered doctor has said, "Anyone who thinks like this needs to be in the 'madhouse.'" Some part of the person, an animalness, more primitive it would seem than the animal nature we ordinarily experience today, seems to present itself. We are not only bipeds, we are binatured because of our evolving. The human mother horrified by alien sensations to hurt her baby is just one example.

To believe in a Creator is to accept not only that we are creatures but that finally the Creator is responsible, and accepts responsibility, for what has been created. It is believing this creative power is at work perfecting creation, and, ultimately, "perfecting" is the Creator's task, not the individual's. Ours is to accept the realities of being creatures, accountable for our moment in time in a larger scheme of things.

Sensations grounded in anxiety may lead to the assumption that the sufferer has grasped the truth, achieved certainty, and can act with authority, or *must* act. There are several variations on that theme. The first is reliance on "Scripture alone," that is, I read the Scripture, it reveals the mind of God, therefore I know, and I act. The possibilities for pathology are obvious; anyone with OCD knows the sensations deal with intellect. If no broader criterion for the truth exists—for reality—than just my own thinking, sensations can lead me into strange pathways indeed. The history of the Church is full of such stories and stone tossers.

One of the things to learn from studying OCD is an appreciation of the historic role of doubting, seeing it as a contemporary dysfunction, but recognizing that it has been a tool of creative advance and continues potentially to serve that purpose. In an exaggerative mode, it is dysfunction, but without doubt playing its proper role, there is no creative advance.

What we can know about God—the mind undergirding reality—comes through the brain of a person.[2] Even when we surmise the mind of God through the judgments apparent in cause and effect—smoking and lung cancer, the consequences of ravishing the forests and the sea—that surmise still comes through the medium of the human brain. This is the reality to which *all* human understanding conforms: the world-renowned theologian no less than the sufferer from religious forms of OCD, the statesman of the Church no less than the convictions of the psychotic troubled by the "unforgivable sin." What we believe reflects the "Mind of Reality" is interpreted by the human mind and its dependency upon tissue. There is no center in the organic brain that serves as a receptacle for God's communications. What we believe to be the will of God is interpreted by human biological processes, as they function in feelings and logic in response to environmental stimuli.

Concepts such as "infallibility" are understandable when announced to a world grounded in Newtonian physics in which an entity has inherent properties and environmental conditions are believed to be static. In a world of physics grounded in the thinking of Albert Einstein, in which an entity is characterized by its relativity to other entities and environmental conditions are recognized as always in flux, infallibility is thinkable, but unthoughtful. Infallibility also would have to be attributed to the interpreters trying to manage an applicability to "eternal principles" when conditions have inevitably altered. The only conclusion today's physics offers—and this assumption underlies religious truths—is that *all* the relevant questions are always unforeseen. If we have learned well from a study of OCD, it is that the attempt at perfection results in pathology: a claim of perfection in Scripture, followed by an unconscious assertion of perfection in interpretation is something to gulp over.

In the avoidance of doubt, the matter of authority on which religious—and other—truth is asserted, some would look to Scripture alone, some to Scripture and Church tradition, and some to a specific form of personal religious experience. From a neurobiological basis, this begs the question not only how the mind of God was expressed through the mortal authorship, it also does not address how the organic brain of the subsequent followers, who invariably must interpret, also are to be infallible. *What we affirm as the infallibility of a primary document is also the infallibility of the necessary updating by the commentators who come after. Infallibility is a projection in the minds of those who originated the notion and those who perpetuate it: two sides of a coin, Icarus and Narcissus.*

When we speak of "God," this Ultimate Reality and Mind of Reality, we color our interpretations through the medium of the body. We know appearance and we offer interpretations and perspectives. Since what we experience, or "know," always involves simplification, we cannot grasp all of the relatedness of the data composing "reality." We grasp what we can; we judge some factors more important and others less so. A sense of importance is always involved in our consciousness, otherwise persons feel crazy and behave a little "crazy" because OCD is a stern master teacher here. The questions for the individual are *What is my ultimate reality? Perfection? What is my ultimate concern? Certainty?*

What we have learned from OCD is that persons must learn to live with uncertainty if they are to aspire to health. If, too often, persons desire certainty to keep their hands from quivering, too often a leader has offered it to keep his or her voice from quaking. Mortal tissue of nerve and synapse set boundaries of mortal vision, mortal insight, set the limits on all our pronouncements, a statute of limitations on all we deem to announce as without future qualification. We humans long to soar to certainty, much as Icarus was flooded with joy when he discovered the power of the wings he had created—before soaring too high led to plunging into the sea. So our need to reach infallibility lends itself to becoming entranced with our own beauty—as it did Narcissus, even as he toppled downward into the pool's depths.

"Hubris" would be the kind way of indicating that some person speaks on behalf of God, ventriloquist fashion; original sin, organic and situational limitations, however, always factor in with all our religious understandings. Immanuel Kant wrote that we should make our decisions "under the aspect of eternity." Alas, we have no such position as humans, for we must make use of, and be accountable for, our biological dependency. This is not to deny the inspirational nature of Scripture, church council, or the saintly sharing of spiritual struggles. This simply sets a boundary on the absoluteness of certainty. We are all of the earth—earthly—with no exceptions. We pray for the gift of discernment. We never can take a doctrine, prophecy, or promise to a notary public to get it authenticated as the will of God.

Here we are, as the British would phrase it, experiencing a very "sticky wicket." The first is "What is truth?" philosophically, and the second is "On what authority?" religiously. Two conditions help illustrate the importance of these. The first is someone prayerfully begging, "Please God, deliver me from these hellish torments of sins that are not sins!" Treatment and theology often intersect in OCD—and sometimes collide, especially if we researched the broader effects of some religious teachings, such as "be therefore perfect," and "if a man thinketh in his heart he has . . ."

Another of these sticky wickets is when the person suffering from OCD has a compulsion to "witness" to others (about Jesus or taking pictures of the Wailing Wall on the Sabbath or anyone of a hundred expressions of fraternal scrupulosity). These can get to the point that when others see this person coming to urge holiness on them, they respond with an urge to call an emergency medical squad.

The relevancy of this to OCD is apparent in the way in which sensations overwhelm the intellect. Intellectually, the person knows the lock is locked, but the sensation—fearfulness as a physical sensation and not an emotion interacting with awareness—bulldozes through, resulting in check, check, check. The person intellectually knows to quit praying and go to work or quit counting so he and his wife are not late again for the hundred and first time. The woman fearing contamination knows it is irrational to throw away a new purse because it became polluted by the rain. Raging sensations are a human dilemma, of which OCD supplies ample illustrations. The problem of sensations is not new to the Church Universal and the religious communities can learn from the OCD experience why their intellectual grasp of what they believe to be true is so often overwhelmed. The preaching of morality and ethics is not treatment. They affect the mind but not the brain because the affecting of the brain is the province of therapy. What theology can do is supply a broader context of healing than can therapy: the two interact.

Both unite in the conviction that the closer in relationship our interpretations are to reality, the better off we are—more in touch with reality. Our interpretations are never reality itself, of course. What we try to achieve is for our interpretations, our consciousness, and our perspectives, to be in the best possible truth relationship to a reality of which we only consciously can surmise. The consequence of this for the person with OCD—or just plain John or Jane Doe, Practicing Human Being—is rich. Theologizing in a neurobiological context means that the mind of the Creator comes in only one way: through the medium of the organic human brain into the mind of the person, with all the happenstance of the "flesh" this implies. Eternal verities enter our existence through moral means. As those with OCD who sacrifice certainty in exchange for healing, we must face our anxieties and give up the infallible and assent to that ancient understanding of reality, the interrelationship of very God of very God, very man of very man. "The Word made flesh" as the Gospel of John phrases it—with all its relativity, uncertainties, and mortal process—is the implication in this affirmation of the duality and unity of brain and mind. "The just shall live by faith alone," as Paul affirmed in his Letter to the Romans and to which OCD-suffering Martin Luther gave his hearty consent. This may not meet the need for absolute certainty in characterizing OCD suffering and the needs of some of us humans, but it beats those options of absolute certainty that come to mind.

While the compulsion to religious expression in OCD is not readily amenable to reason, reason is the tool we have to work with, both as counselor and counselee, pastor and parishioner—or parishioner to pastor—depending on who has the OCD. Religiously, we do need to reason—and share—together. Consensus may be a blunt instrument in trying to cobble together a grasp of the truth, but we can trust the Mind of Reality to disclose realities that will sharpen it.

WHAT THEN CAN WE AFFIRM?

On the night that Jesus was betrayed, he is said to have told his disciples,

> I have much more to tell you, but now it would be too much for you to bear. When, however, the Spirit comes, who reveals the truth about God, he will lead you to all truth.[3]

He spoke truly, it has been a long and fruitful quest over twenty centuries, and continues to be so. Considering that we attempt to comprehend creation as we sense a Creator through the instrumet of an organic brain in response to environmental stimuli, we will undoubtedly continue to add new faces to the many faces of God. What then can we affirm of the old and new?

1. When some persons look at the process from the perspective of recorded history, the question is arguable as to mankind's advance, decline, or cyclical movement: the rise and fall of the Babylonian, Roman, British, whatever empire, whatever nature of the individual. Looking at the process from the perspective of the total existence of the earth, however, and the arguable becomes less so. Picture that tiny embryo with what appears to be gills, floating in the oceanlike fluid of the human mother's womb; picture that miraculous transition from oxygen transmitted from that oceanic fluid to the shock of taking breath in our earthly atmosphere; picture the little band of Not Yets/Will Be on the African veldt five million years ago—and be con-

scious of yourself as you sit in your chair reading this. When considering "the more things change, the more they remain the same"—checking then, checking now—consider, too, that although some continue to fear that others will contaminate them, still others experience the illness in the form of fearing to contaminate others. Twenty years ago, a sufferer with OCD had little chance at effective treatment, but the choice is real now. We can affirm the continuing miraculousness of Creative Power.

2. Whatever we experience is in process, from the pictures on the morning TV news show, to the local weather forecast based on a photograph from an orbiting satellite, to getting out the old pictures of vacations when the family gathers at Thanksgiving. The process is characterized by relationships, down to the coroner on the evening news at the latest crime scene estimating the time of death by the particular insects that have come to the feast. Whether we estimate the size of the universe in its apparently unimaginable continuing expansion, to watching a farmer plant corn, it all has the hallmark of creative energy; all is in process; all is in relationship.

From the perspective of neurobiology, what we can know of reality is that our world is very old and our specie is very old, and derived from life-forms that are still older. This offers us a "higher power," such as in the beginning of healing in all the forms of the Twelve-Step programs, and a sense of the magnitude of its creative power. We know our reality through recognition of a *process*. This process seemingly involved both freedom and order, and its interrelatedness emerges in a vision and experience of creative power. It is this creative power, whose personalized form is a "love," to which we appeal when we suffer and which appropriately suffuses us with gratitude when we contemplate it.

3. Among the many facets of God, there is judgment; it is a necessity to creative advance. As Tennyson wrote in the *Idylls of the King* about the passing of a golden knightly age,

> The old order changeth, yielding place to new
> And God fulfills Himself in many ways,
> Lest one good custom should corrupt the world.[4]

It is this judgment that so many persons with OCD over-experience biologically. The proneness to anxiety is so out of proportion as to produce a sense of God that is false. The judgment is an aspect of God that has a place in the dynamics of creativity, but the overriding whole of what we sense to be God is most aptly expressed by "God is love," or creativity. It is not too much to write that part of what is clarified by learning from OCD is that religious leadership which places an out-of-balance emphasis on the judgment of God, unbalances and perhaps falsifies God as creativity, and consequently, "God is love." In the Bronze Age it was proverbial that "the fear of the Lord is the beginning of wisdom," but in the Information Age it is more likely the start of OCD. All children need structure in order to limit anxiety, but in the anal developmental period, where punishment precedes the integration of a consciousness of right and wrong, the outcome can truly be "anal" by continuing stuckness.

4. What we also affirm is the reality of *suffering,* and what we can learn from suffering—including OCD—is that the "Almighty" has limits imposed on Himself by the very nature of the creative process itself. "Creator" does not imply "all powerful." Alas, the Creator in His efforts, it would seem, is the ultimate politician in practicing "the art of the possible." "Creator" simply asserts the general characteristic of "all creativity": that power combining chaos and order in such a way that creative advance emerges, but always within the reality of freedom. With the assertion of "almighty" and attempting to unite it with a notion of loving, as in "Father," we do not have a paradox or contrast, but we experience painful contradictions. What we learn from suffering, not just the suffering of OCD but of all suffering, is that we have to "bite the bullet" theologically. When we are affirming a belief in a loving, creative God, we are affirming *all the power consistent with the reality of creativity itself. When we affirm "all loving" as a part of creativity the trade-off is clear: all powerful, all knowing.* To move on from this "almighty" and the "all knowing" and the other "alls" attributed to deity in the past, will strike many as giving up too much perfectionism. Walking away from a mass grave, however, if a person

has had a belief in God having *total* power, is indeed a massive "walking away" that every believer has observed in friends.

5. We can affirm the reality of *evil*. In the course of human development, the tribe was the ultimate experience of fellowship, all others were strangers; in the course of personality development, many persons never move beyond the sense of basic family and nothing beyond has potentiality for empathy. The tribal gods continue to exist and be worshipped, visible in Africa as tribes continue their age-long hatreds and slaughters, no less apparent in many areas in which historic hatreds exist. For example, in a holiday dedicated to celebrating one's Scottish heritage, one re-enactor, axe in one hand, shield in the other, hit shield with axe and exclaimed with historic and histrionic accuracy, "But it's a better sound when an axe hits an Englishman's skull." Few parts of our earth do not experience religiously the resurrection of dead hatred and new killings.

6. In a time of neurobiology, it seems rational to reflect on process as Arnold Toynbee has done and made religious reference to that creative energy we see at work and use the symbol, "the Mind of Reality." Whatever we do will be pure assumption, but assumption is not projection arising in mortals about an immortal process. Far better to assume a summation we call "God": the best minds of our race have explored that term; to reject it is to at least fall back upon assumptions with an ambiguous track record of accomplishment.

Some would not characterize Ultimate Reality, in Tillich's terms, or Mind of Reality, in Toynbee's, as the common source of all creativity; some would not personalize it as did the author of the letters of John in the New Testament: "God is love." However it is, whether watching the stars from the fantail of a ship, photographing a flower with your best close-up lens, or talking to the little girl from across the street who has come to visit her grandmother and wants to help you weed the garden, it does not seem a stretch of the assumption to maintain that whatever force set all this in motion had a considerable sense of the aesthetic. However it may be, it seems appropriate to affirm *a sense of wonderment in the human heart.*

A one-on-one competition between a time of spiritual meditation in the evening and being on the roof adjusting the satellite dish to get all 500 available channels is a real "no brainer." It reminds me, however, of a World War I British cartoon. Old Bill, a grizzled sergeant, and a scared young "Tommy" were in a hole up to their knees in mud with shells bursting all around. Old Bill looked at him and said, "If you know of a better 'ole, go to it."

THE DIRECTION OF HUMAN POTENTIAL

We might have Siegfried Sassoon, a British poet and "Tommy" in World War I, summarize our human situation:

> In me, past, present, future meet
> To hold long chiding conference
> My lusts usurp the present tense
> And strangle Reason in his seat.
> My loves leap through the future's fence
> To dance with dream-enfranchised feet.
>
> In me the cave-man clasps the seer,
> And garlanded Apollo goes
> Chanting to Abraham's deaf ear.
> In me the tiger sniffs the rose.
> Look in my heart, kind friends, and tremble,
> See there your elements assemble.

And what of *evil*? An exaggeration of order might reduce our planet to lifeless dryness; a large meteor and all would be chaos. Again, Sassoon addresses this in "The Ultimate Atrocity":

> When the first man who wasn't quite an ape
> Felt magnanimity and prayed for more,
> The world's redemption stood, in human shape,
> With darkness done and betterment before.
> From then till now such men have multiplied;
> From then till now their task has been the same,
> In whom the world's redemption dreamed and died—
> To whom the vision of perfection came.

> I hear an aeroplane—what years ahead
> Who knows?—but if from that machine should fall
> The first bacterial bomb, this world might find
> That all the aspirations of the dead
> Had been betrayed and blotted out, and all
> Their deeds denied who hoped for Humankind.[5]

This poem was written in 1933. Soon, Japan would invade China and Hitler would send weapons to be tested in Spain.

So much destruction was started then, so much destruction and more may begin again. And what of *providence*? Alfred North Whitehead had lost a son, a pilot on the Western Front, and he had thought through his loss as father, philosopher, scientist, and believer, writing of a "teleology," a pulling power operative both in nature and in the individual human that draws us toward a fulfillment of ourselves and the purposes of the Creative Power. For Whitehead, objective immortality might be seen through some such agency as DNA, although this term was not current during his lifetime. There is, however, an immortality in which we and those values for which we have striven are enclosed and absorbed into the very nature of God, an immortality in which nothing of value perishes; all virtue, all sacrifice is not only not vain, but is cherished and preserved.

It may be, of course, that atomic blast, radiation from the sun, some unknown bug against which we have no defense, or some happenstance meteor will blot out everything. If a life raft is floating around, however, given the creative nature we call God—and if there are a couple of raccoons, a pair of squirrels, and a pregnant rabbit or so with which to work, all is not lost; it is simply a new construction project. And, if You will allow a vote, Dear Lord, please include a set of golden retrievers and you may have better luck next time than with the boatload that Old Man Noah collected. From long experience, knowing the love of practical jokes the Dear Lord seems to cherish, He probably would include some mice from a research laboratory just so they would have the last laugh on us.

We cannot know, but in five hundred years, five hundred generations, or ten thousand, perhaps only a small group of upright creatures will be moving across a vast plain, shorn of doubt, bereft of logic, unable to count, cleaning, straightening, perfecting—all meaningless—even language foregone. Our only identity with them is fearfulness, check, check, check, be anxious about anything new that you eat or drink.

With a catastrophe, it could all begin again with such a small group who had survived. In that beginning there could be little ability to think as we know it, all the survivor fears and insecurities present. There would be the insecurities manifested in fears and avoidances, with the ability to doubt not yet. The symptoms of OCD as we generally know them would be still to come: symmetry, perfecting, guilt, blasphemy, superstitions, horror-filled fantasies of harming one's child. What comes, however, when we move in our fantasies beyond our own immediate time, when we are "the real people" as the Native Americans phrase it? Will there be a rounding of the circle so that what was, will be, or will the ascent continue, however waveringly, in a direction we can now discern? Will the chemical imbalances of brains be less severe, sections of brains less discordant? Will the intensity of feelings of guilt move in the direction of more ethical conduct? Will the compulsion of symmetry, cleaning, straightening, and perfecting evolve into a more harmonious and aesthetic world civilization?

To ask these questions is to acknowledge that there is no certainty of answer; it is so similar to the questions, "Do you believe in God?" and "So?"

What we have is Now, and in this Now, two passages of Scripture would seem to speak to those who suffer the "symptoms" that are, in actuality, the telling of our human saga. First a challenge:

> Then Jesus said to his disciples, "If anyone wants to come with me, he must forget himself, carry his cross, and follow me.[6]

and then a promise:

> Come to me, all of you who are tired from carrying heavy loads, and I will give you rest. Take my yoke and put it upon you, and learn from me, because I am gentle and humble in spirit; and you will find rest. For the yoke I will give you is easy, and the load I will put on you is light.[7]

Appendix

Available Resources

Anxiety Disorders Association of America
PO Box 631409
Baltimore, MD 21263-1409
Literature orders, (301) 231-7392, attn: Michelle Alonso
(registry for clinical resources, literature, national convention; includes resources for OCD)

National Association for the Mentally Ill
PO Box 753
Waldorf, MD 20604
Telephone (for literature catalog) 1-800-950-NAMI
FAX (301) 843-0159
(This is the national membership group for those suffering from mental illness and is the chief lobbyist for the mentally ill. They include literature resources for OCD and their newsletter carries reviews of new books, research findings, and reports on medications.)

National Institute of Mental Health
Dept. of Health and Human Services
Room 7C-02
5600 Fishers Lane
Rockville, MD 20857
(The literature resource center of the federal government)

Obsessive-Compulsive Information Center
2771 Allen Blvd.
Middletown, WI 53562
Telephone (608) 827-2390
FAX (608) 827-2399
(The most complete literature resources in the world on OCD)

OC Foundation, Inc.
PO Box 70
Milford, CT 06460
Telephone (203) 878-5669
(There is a national membership, clinical registry of counselors, newsletter for adults and *Kidscope* for children and teens, as well as literature and video resources.)

OCD Web pages:
<http://www.pages.prodigy.com/alwillen/ocf.html> (home page of the OC Foundation, has complete listing of support groups)
<http://www.fairlite.com/ocd> (A well-run bulletin board for OCD sufferers)

Trichotillomania Learning Center
1215 Mission Street, Suite 2
Santa Cruz, CA 95060
Telephone (408) 457-1004
(For sufferers of hair pulling; newsletter, *In Touch,* and an excellent video is available depicting a group of sufferers)

Notes

Chapter 1

1. Collie, Robert, "The Obsessive-Compulsive Disorder: The Pastoral Knowledge Explosion," *The Journal of Pastoral Care,* Vol. 51(3), 1997, pp. 293-302.

2. Collie, Robert, "The Incidence of the Obsessive-Compulsive Disorder in North Indiana United Methodist Clergy," *The Journal of Pastoral Care,* Vol. 52(1), 1998, pp. 41-55.

3. Definitions will become more clear in Chapters 2 and 4, but for now "scrupulosity" derives from the root word "scruple" as a tiny stone in a shoe, and refers to ethical and moral nit-picking. Hoarding, cleaning, and straightening are colloquialisms used by those with OCD to describe various rituals. Hypochondriasis is being overly concerned with one's health, but it will become clear that it differs from being a "hypochondriac."

Chapter 2

1. The "body dysmorphic disorder" apparently was suffered by Charles Dickens, who spent a great amount of time combing his hair. Its cruelties can also be projected, as in Nathaniel Hawthorne's short story, "The Beauty Spot." This very dangerous condition is explored in Katharine Phillip's *The Broken Mirror: Understanding and Treating Body Dysmorphic Disorder,* New York: Oxford University Press, 1996.

2. The "spectrum disorders" of OCD include Tourette's disorder, hypochondriasis, trichotillomania (hair pulling), anorexia and bulimia, and kleptomania (compulsive stealing). When associated with OCD they may be differentiated from other compulsive behavior—gambling, alcoholism, sexual addiction—by the latter initially giving pleasure; the spectrum disorders are never enjoyable.

3. The older veterinarian literature indexes OCD under "perseverance" or "stereotypical behavior." Sometimes intriguing subtopics are also listed that are relevant, such as self-mutilation in horses. Recent literature indexes OCD similarities as "OCD." A useful introduction to the field is Karen Loverall's *Clinical Behavioral Medicine for Small Animals,* St. Louis: Mosby, 1997.

OCD literature generally does not explore the relationship between that disorder and animal behavior, but rather alludes to it, as in hoarding: Penzel, Fred, "Saving the World," *OC Foundation Newsletter,* August, 1995, p. 6, or in reference to fear of open spaces, as in: Ciarrocchi, Joseph, *The Doubting Disease,* Mahwah, NY: Paulist Press, 1995, p. 20.

4. Cuzzillo, Shawness L., "Historical Contingencies in the Evolution of Human Behavior and Psychopathology," *Psychiatry,* Vol. 54(2), 1991, p. 204.

5. Grandin, Temple, "How to Think Like an Animal," *The Utne Reader,* March-April, pp. 46-47. Ms. Grandin became autistic in her early teens; she writes that she now thinks in pictures as animals do, and experiences and understands their fears.

6. Petzinger, Thomas Jr., "Experts Draw on Past for Sixth Sense," *The Wall Street Journal,* reprinted in *The Journal Gazette,* Fort Wayne, IN, August 15, 1998, D1.

7. Schwartz, Jeffrey, *Brain Lock,* New York: HarperCollins, 1996, p. 51.

8. Ps. 108, Francis of Assisi, "All Creatures of Our God and King," *The Methodist Hymnal,* Nashville, TN: The Methodist Publishing House, 1932, and subsequently in many hymnals.

Chapter 3

1. Pindar, Steven, *How the Mind Works,* New York: W. W. Norton and Co., 1997, p. 21.

2. Nymberg, Jerome H. and van Hoppen, Barbara, "Obsessive-Compulsive Disorder: A Concealed Diagnosis," *American Family Physician,* American Academy of Family Physicians, 8880 Ward Parkway, Kansas City, MO, Vol. 49(5), 1994, pp. 1129-1137.

3. Yaryura-Tobias, José A. and Neziroglu, Fugen A., *Obsessive-Compulsive Disorder Spectrum, Pathogenesis, Diagnosis, and Treatment,* Washington, DC: American Psychiatric Press, Inc., 1997. Chapter 1, "History, Culture, and Clinical Aspects of OCD," is an excellent introduction to OCD.

4. Angela, Piero and Angela, Alberto, *The Extraordinary Story of Human Origins,* New York: Prometheus Books, 1993, p. 68. There is a similar picture in Ian Osborn's *Tormenting Thoughts and Secret Rituals,* New York: Pantheon Books, 1998, p. 87.

5. *Homo sapiens* indicates the broad category of "Early Man"; *Homo sapiens sapiens* is a narrower term used for later times when linguistic studies indicate symbolic language began to be displayed and consequently more directly related to modern humans.

6. Whitehead, Alfred North, *Process and Reality: An Essay in Cosmology,* New York: Harper Torchbooks, The Academic Library, Harper & Row, 1957, p. 341.

7. Angela, *The Extraordinary Story of Human Origins,* p. 72.

8. Walker, Alan and Shipman, Pat, *The Wisdom of the Bones,* New York: Alfred A. Knopf, 1996, pp. 280, 283ff.

9. Morris, Desmond, *The Naked Ape: A Zoologist's Study of the Human Animal,* New York: McGraw-Hill, 1967.

10. Auel, Jean, *The Clan of the Cave Bear,* New York: Crown Publishing Company, 1980.

11. Cuzzilo, Shawnee L. Wieder, "Historical Contingencies in the Evolution and Psychopathology," *Psychiatry,* Vol. 54(2), 1991, pp. 187-207.

12. Whitehead, Alfred North, *Adventures of Ideas,* New York: The Macmillan Company, 1933. No better book could be found to survey the process we are discussing. A more detailed discussion of the quest to live "better and better" is to be found in his *The Function of Reason.*

13. Asberg, Gustavsson M. and Schalling, D., summarized from *Acta Psychiatrica Scandinavica* in the *Harvard Mental Health Letter,* Vol. 15(4), 1999, p. 7.

14. From the poem "Euclid Alone Has Looked on Beauty Bare" by Edna St. Vincent Millay, 1923.

15. Paul Tillich, *Systematic Theology,* Chicago: University of Chicago Press, 1951. Volume I deals with the concept of God. God as "ground of being" is explored on pages 116-117; "ultimate concern" is explored on pp. 12-14.

Chapter 4

1. Booth, Father Leo, *When God Becomes a Drug: Attaining Healthy Spirituality,* (New York: G.P. Putnam's Sons, 1991), pp. 4-14.

2. *Homo religiosus* was a term coined by Joseph Campbell and Mircea Eliade, cultural anthropologists, to characterize those who began the Neanderthal burial sites, first dated 70,000 years ago.

3. Auel, Jean, *The Clan of the Cave Bear,* New York: Crown Publishing Co., 1980.

4. Genesis 3:16.

5. A thirty-year-old waiter who feared that he might cause his employer loss through fire, theft, or flood.

6. Three references are useful at this point: Kushner, Matt G., Sher, Kenneth, and Beltman, Bernard, "The Relationship Between Alcohol Problems and the Anxiety Disorders," *American Journal of Psychiatry,* Vol. 147(6), 1990, pp. 685-695; Eisen, Janne, and Rasmussen, Steven, "Coexisting Obsessive-Compulsive Disorder and Alcoholism, *Journal of Clinical Psychiatry,* Vol. 50(3), 1989, pp. 87-96; Dimitrious, E.C., Lavrentiadis, G., and Dimitrious, C.E., "Obsessive-Compulsive Disorder and Alcohol Abuse," *European Journal of Psychiatry,* Vol. 7(4), 1993, pp. 244-248.

7. Jeremiah 31: 29-30; Ezekiel 18:1-4.

8. Yaryura-Tobias, José A. and Neziroglu, Fugen A., *Obsessive-Compulsive Disorder Spectrum, Pathogenesis, Diagnosis, and Treatment,* Washington, DC: American Psychiatric Press, Inc., 1997, pp. 3-5.

9. Borg, Marcus J., *Meeting Jesus Again for the First Time,* HarperSanFrancisco, 1994. The third chapter is highly relevant to the discussion here. What is especially interesting from the perspective of the dating of the gospel of Matthew is that, if the thesis is correct about this gospel relating particularly to "scrupulous" conditions, it was most likely written prior to the fall of Jerusalem. If Matthew is addressed to the Jewish religious situation, then the age of the gospel writer falls within the range of a normal life expectancy of the twelve disciples.

10. Murphy-O'Connor, Jerome, O.P., *Paul: A Critical Life,* Milltown, NJ: Clarendon Press, 1996, p. 55.

11. Yaryura-Tobias and Neziroglu, *Obsessive-Compulsive Disorder Spectrum,* pp. 227-228.

12. Rapoport, Judith, *The Boy Who Couldn't Stop Washing,* New York: E.P. Dutton, 1989, p. 170ff.

13. Greenberg, David, "The Influence of Cultural Factors on Obsessive-Compulsive Disorder: Religious Symptoms in a Religious Society," *Israel Journal of Psychiatry and Related Sciences,* Vol. 31, 1994, pp. 211-220.

14. Margorie Miller's article originally appeared in *The Los Angeles Times* and was reprinted in the weekly section on religion in *The Journal Gazette,* April 19, 1997, p. C1.

15. I am indebted to one in the support group, who is a Jehovah's Witness, bringing to my attention an article titled, "The Castrati: Mutilation in the Name of Religion," from *Awake,* February 8, 1996, pp. 11-14.

16. Ciarrocchi, Joseph, *The Doubting Disease,* Mahwah, NJ: The Paulist Press, 1995, p. 18.

17. Osborn, Ian, *Tormenting Thoughts and Secret Rituals,* New York: Pantheon Books, 1998, pp. 53-59.

18. Erikson, Erik, *Young Man Luther: A Study in Psychoanalysis and History,* New York: W.W. Norton & Co., 1958.

19. McBrien, Richard, *Lives of the Popes,* HarperSanFrancisco, 1997, 264ff.

20. Yaryura-Tobias and Neziroglu, *Obsessive-Compulsive Disorder Spectrum,* p. 12.

21. A fun, rather than a tedious, way into this aspect of brain, is Marx, Kathryn, *Right Brain/Left Brain Photograph: The Art and Technique of 70 Modern Masters,* New York: Watson, Gluptill Publications, 1994.

22. Bunyan, John, *Grace Abounding to the Chief of Sinners,* New York: E.P. Dutton & Co., 1956.

23. Santa, Thomas (Ed.), "The Dilemma Department," *Scrupulous Anonymous,* Ligouri, MO, Vol. 35(6), 1998.

24. This same dynamic is to be seen in the body dismorphic disorder, when a loathing of one's body part(s) may become externalized and the loathing shifted to a loved one.

25. Durant, Will, *The Story of Civilization: Part I, Our Oriental Heritage,* New York: Simon and Schuster, 1954, p. 4.

Chapter 5

1. Rapoport, Judith, *The Boy Who Couldn't Stop Washing,* New York: E.P. Dutton, 1989.

2. Ciarrocchi, Joseph, *The Doubting Disease,* Mahwah, NJ: Paulist Press, 1995.

3. Van Ornum, William, *A Thousand Frightening Fantasies,* New York: Crossroad Publishing Co., 1997.

4. James, William, *Varieties of Religious Experience,* New York: Longmans, Green, 1919.

5. These have now been expanded and published in: March, John S. and Mulle, Karen, *OCD in Children and Adolescents, A Cognitive-Behavioral Treatment Manual,* New York: The Guilford Press, 1998.

6. Schwartz, Jeffrey, *Brain Lock: Free Yourself from Obsessive-Compulsive Behavior, A Four-Step-Treatment Method to Change Your Brain Chemistry,* New York: HarperCollins Publishers, 1996. Step 4, Revalue, p. 96ff.

7. Dumont, Reann. *The Sky Is Falling: Understanding and Coping with Phobias, Panic, and Obsessive-Compulsive Disorders,* New York: Norton.

Chapter 6

1. Ashbrook, James, *Brain and Belief: Faith in the Light of Brain Research,* Bristol, IN: Wyndham Hall Press, 1988. Dr. Ashbrook's professional life's work was to relate brain research and theological beliefs. His thinking in relationship to the role of the hemispheres of the brain to religion is highly stimulating.

2. "Addictions and the Brain," *The Harvard Mental Health Letter,* Vol. 14(12), 1998, p. 1.

3. "A Little Help from Serotonin," *Newsday,* December 29, 1997, p. 80.

4. Goleman, Daniel, *Emotional Intelligence,* New York: Bantam Books, 1995. Mr. Goleman, as the science editor of *The New York Times,* wrote a fascinating summary for laypersons of what was known about the brain.

5. Wilson, Edmund O., *Consilience: The Unity of Knowledge,* New York: Alfred A. Knopf, 1998, p. 107.

6. Kantorowitz, Barbara and Kalb, Claudie, "Boys Will Be Boys," *Newsweek,* May 11, 1998, pp. 55-60.

7. Greist, J.H., "New Developments in Behavior Therapy for Obsessive-Compulsive Disorder," *International Clinical Psychopharmacology,* Vol. 11, Supplement 5, 1996, p. 70. The problem is well stated: "what animals learn in one CNS (central nervous system) state may not be accessible in another CNS state." This is the problem of the transfer of learning we face within the brain.

8. Hales, Dianne, "The Female Brain," *Ladies Home Journal,* May, 1998, 128ff. In the tenth annual special health report of *USA Weekend,* January 1-3, 1999, there are a number of good short articles; one of special interest here is titled "Why a Female Brain Is Like a Swiss Army Knife," p. 8.

9. Angela, Piero and Angela, Alberto, *The Extraordinary Story of Human Origins,* New York: Promethcus Books, 1993, p. 146.

10. Jenike, Michael A., "Brain Structural Abnormalities in Obsessive-Compulsive Disorder," *OCD Newsletter.* The OC Foundation, Volume 10(5), 1996, pp. 1-2.

11. Bernstein, Borey, *The Search for Bridey Murphy,* Garden City, NY: Doubleday, 1956.

Chapter 7

1. Part I, "The Obsessive-Compulsive Disorder," *The Harvard Mental Health Letter,* Vol. 15(4), 1998, p. 3.

2. Krause, M.S., "A Reconsideration of the Nosological Status of Obsessive-Compulsive Disorder," *Neurology, Psychiatry, and Brain Research,* Universitätsverlag Ulm GmbH, Vol. 3, 1995, pp. 35-46.

3. Osborn, Ian, *Tormenting Thoughts and Secret Rituals: The Hidden Epidemic of Obsessive-Compulsive Disorder,* New York: Pantheon Books, 1998, p. 66.

4. Fowler, James, *Faith Development and Pastoral Care,* Philadelphia: Fortress Press, 1987, pp. 59-60. The work of Erikson has been expanded by persons such as Fowler, who are working on "the life cycle" of personality theory. His thinking is highly stimulating in regard to religion and the life cycle.

5. "Depressive Personality Disorder," *Diagnostic and Statistical Manual of Mental Disorders,* Fourth Edition, Washington, DC: American Psychiatric Association, 1994, p. 732.

6. Schwartz, Jeffrey, *Brain Lock,* New York: HarperCollins Publishers, 1996, p. 196.

7. Wilson, Edmund O., *Consilience: The Unity of Knowledge,* New York: Alfred A. Knopf, 1998, p. 197.

Chapter 8

1. Hewson, Caroline and Luercher, "Compulsive Disorder in Dogs," in Voith, Victoria L. and Borchalt, Peter, *Readings in Companion Animal Behavior,* Trenton, NJ: Veterinary Learning Systems, 1996, p. 154.

2. Overall, Karen L., *Clinical Behavioral Medicine for Small Animals,* St. Louis: Mosby, 1997, p. 220.

3. Hewson, C. and Luercher, *Readings,* p. 156.

4. Overall, Karen L., *Clinical Behavioral Medicine for Small Animals,* p. 23.

5. Hewson, C. and Luercher, *Readings,* p. 56.

6. Gravitz, Herbert L., *Obsessive-Compulsive Disorder: Help for the Family,* Santa Barbara, CA: Healing Visions Press, 1998. This is a "must" read on OCD and the family.

Chapter 9

1. *Research Overview: Exploring the Role of the Heart in Human Performance,* HeartMath Research Center, 14700 West Park Ave., Boulder, CO, 1997. This is potentially an extremely interesting aspect of research in the area of anxiety disorders. "Freeze-frame" is only one of a number of techniques developed at the HeartMath Research Center and others need to be explored, as well.

2. McCarthy, Rollin, Barrios-Choplin, Bob, Rozman, Deborah, Atkinson, Mike, and Watkins, Alan. "The Impact of a New Emotional Self-Management Program on Stress, Emotions, Heart Rate Variability, DHEA and Cortisol." This article is available from the HeartMath Institute and has been accepted for publication in *Integrative Physiological and Behavioral Science,* to appear in Vol. 33(2), 1998.

3. The director was referring to an article in the February 1996 issue of *School Arts,* p. 62. It reported that students taking four years of one of the classical arts did better in grades than students taking none. While this is not surprising, in that

it may be due to the expected differences in family backgrounds, it might be noted that some dairy farmers play gentle music for their cows during milking time in order to increase production. The mammalian brain is responsive to environmental stimulus, and, to some degree, that stimulus is programmable whether in hospital, home, office, or school.

4. Wilson, Edmund O., *Consilience: The Unity of Knowledge,* New York: Alfred A. Knopf, 1998. This is a work that should be read in its entirety as it sets OCD in a context of understanding what we presently know about ourselves. Whitehead, in the second quarter of the twentieth century, attempted to create a system of a general understanding of the nature of reality. Tillich, in the middle part of the century, attempted to do this in theology. After two volumes it was rumored that he gave up the attempt, but completed the third volume because so many doctoral students were doing their dissertations based on his work. Now, after another half century, Wilson is attempting a systematic grasp of what we can know, including evolution and the development of the brain.

5. de Chardin, Pierre Teilhard, from the opening section of the "Mass on the World," from *Hymn of the Universe,* New York: Harper and Row, 1965.

Chapter 10

1. There are a number of versions of John Donne's poem; I have chosen to quote these lines from Ernest Hemingway's *For Whom the Bell Tolls,* a story of a terrible civil war. That seems appropriate to this chapter.

2. Toynbee, Arnold, *An Historian's Approach to Religion,* London: Oxford University Press, 1956. The entire first chapter should be read in the context of gaining an appropriate perspective on OCD and religion. The phrase, "the Mind in Reality," is a beautiful one and deserving of theological reflection.

3. John 16:12, 13.

4. Tennyson, Alfred, "The Passing of Arthur," from *The Idylls of the King,* quoted from *The Complete Poetical Works of Tennyson,* Boston, Houghton Mifflin Company, 1898.

5. Sassoon, Siegfried, in Sanders, Gerald Dewitt and Nelson, Hon. Herbert (Ed.), *Chief Modern Poets of England and America,* New York: The Macmillan Company, Third Edition, 1943.

6. Matthew 10:38.

7. Matthew 11:29-30.

Index

Abel, 31, 43
Abraham, 42, 46-47
Achieving Peace of Mind, 93-94
Acts of the Apostles, 2
Adam, 43
Adler, Alfred, 40
Adultery, obsessional concern, 51
Adventure, willingness to, 218
Aesthetic worth, category of, 221
Afterlife, belief in, 34
Aggressive imagery, OCD symptom, 24
Agoraphobia, 154
Alcoholism, OCD symptom, 46
Alexander VI, Pope, 61
Alexander the Great, 49
Ambivalence, OCD, 163
American Association of Pastoral Counselors, 2
American Psychiatric Association, DSM-IV, 24, 147-148
Americans with Disabilities Act, 84
Amygdala, old brain, 126-127, 130, 142, 145, 174
Anafranil, SSRI, 175
Anal stage, OCD treatment, 190-193
"Anchoring," 215
Angela, Alberto, 137
Angela, Piero, 137
Anger, obsessional concern, 51, 70
"Angst," 152
Animal behavior, 16-17, 182
Anne, OCD case history, 86-88, 117, 221-222
Anorexia, 14, 29
Anxiety, 24, 137, 148, 152
    child development, 159
    evolutionary perspective, 151
    religious development, 232-233

Anxiety disorder, 13, 19
Appendix, human, 7, 233
Archetypes, 132, 143
Arousal, 132
As Good As It Gets, 5, 7
Ashbrook, James, 134
Astrology, 37, 229-230
Atatürk, Kemal, 213
Athena, 230
Attention deficit disorder, evolutionary perspective, 152
Attribution theory, OCD, 146
Auditory sensory input, 172, 199
Auel, Jean, 31, 34, 42
Australopithecus robustus, 26, 42
Authority
    childhood development, 168
    OCD treatment, 192, 200
    religious, 237
Autism
    evolutionary perspective, 148-149
    regressive disorder, 170-171

Babylonia captivity, 42, 48
Babylonian mythology, 44
Bacchus, 229
Baptists, 70
"Basic family values," attack on, 52
Beauty
    quality of life, 230
    sense of, 38
Behavior modification, OCD, 174, 195
Bible study group, 87, 89
Bipolarity
    evolutionary perspective, 153
    OCD, 151
Birth, among early humanoids, 31
Blasphemy, 118, 135

Body
  kindness to, 212-213, 230
  memory of, 28
Body dysmorphia disorder, 29
Booth, Father Leo, 40, 41
Borg, Marcus, 51
"Boris Becker was a really nice guy,"
  100
Boundary land, 37
Boy Who Couldn't Stop Washing,
  The, 57, 93
Boys, OCD strategy for, 206-207
Brain
  childhood changes in, 170
  connectors in OCD, 138-139, 149,
    168, 206, 234
  evolution of, 18, 27, 30, 32, 33,
    34-35, 124-125
  hemispheres
    differences of, 61, 62, 67,
      134-135
    treatment and, 199-200
  in neonatal, 137-138
  OCD, 38-39, 124-137
  startle response in, 18, 129-130
Brain lesion, 153, 159
Brain Lock, 98, 138, 176, 189, 194,
  196, 204
Brain stem, 34
Broca area, of brain, 27, 134
"Bronco bustin," 188
Bunyan, John, 64-68, 74, 119-120

Cain, 30-31, 43
Calvin and Hobbes, 167-169
Cambridge Forum, The, 195
Canalization, 165
Carnivores, food preference, 31
Case histories
  Anne, 86-88, 117, 184, 221-222
  Lou, 92-94, 184-185, 201, 212
  Marie, 79-81, 212
  Mary, 88-91, 184-185, 212

Case histories *(continued)*
  Nancy, 75-79, 171-172, 184, 198,
    212
  Nanette Joyce, 82-84
  OCD, 74-75
  Paul, 95-113
Castration, for sexual fears, 58-59
Certainty, possibility of, 236-237
Chardin, Father Teilhard de, 181,
  225-228
Charles I, beheading of, 64
Checkers
  OCD, 124
  poem about, 100-101
Child abuse, 83, 86
Child development
  developmental tasks, 75, 161,
    166-171
  OCD symptoms, 24, 160, 164
  religious dynamics, 85
Child sacrifice, 47
Children, brain stimulation, 139
Chimpanzees, behavior of, 26
Christianity, origin of, 50-56
Church tradition, belief in, 236, 237
Ciarrocchi, Joseph, 59, 63, 74, 172
Cicero, 70
Clan of the Cave Bear, The, 31, 34, 42
Cleaners, OCD symptom, 4, 25, 154
Clergy, OCD in, 6
Co-creatures, human beings as, 232
Cognitive behavior therapy, for OCD,
  9
Collie, Robert, 78, 79, 80, 94
Competition, origin of, 36
Compulsion, religion and, 46
Compulsions, OCD, 92, 145, 198, 237
"Conceptual revision," 177
Conscience
  childhood development, 169
  OCD treatment, 193
"Conscious sensations," 92, 215
Consilience: The Unity of Knowledge,
  220

Contamination
  OCD, 124
  religious taboos, 45, 46
Contamination fear, OCD symptom,
  16-17, 42, 49, 169-170
Control, childhood development, 169
"Conversion," 172
Countermemory, use of, 215
Creation stories, 27, 30
Creator, belief in, 234-235, 238, 241
Cromwell, Oliver, 64, 65
Culture, OCD expression, 24-25
Curiosity, early humanoid, 28, 35

"Dairy products," 36
Dante, 116
"Decade of the Brain," 230
"Decision tree," OCD diagnosis,
  148, 152
Defective conscience, 118, 215
Depersonalization, 198
Depression, 19
  emergence of, 74
  evolutionary perspective, 151,
    152, 153
  and OCD, 162-164
  treatment of, 17
Depressive personality, DSM-IV,
  162-163
Derealization, 198
"Developmental" scrupulosity, 172
Developmental tasks
  childhood, 75, 161, 166-171
  OCD treatment, 190-195
Dewey, John, 173
*Diagnostic and Statistical Manual of
  Mental Disorders* (DSM-IV)
  depressive personality, 162-163
  OCD criteria, 24, 147-148
Diaspora, Jewish history during, 56-58
Disorder of Paradox, 15
Dissociation, 198
  childhood development, 169
Divorce, obsessional concern, 51

Domestication, 36
Double bind, 200
"Double dipping," 160
Doubt
  early humanoid, 28, 35
  OCD symptom, 24, 163
  as tool, 235
Doubting Castle, 66-67
"Doubting disease," 60, 62, 65, 66,
  221, 234
Doubting Disease, The, 59
Dreams, in OCD, 140-141
Dumont, Reann, 117
Durant, Will, 71

Early childhood, OCD development,
  70, 118, 159, 164, 166-171
Early Church, OCD of, 54
Eating disorders, 14
Ecclesiasticus, 67
Edison, Thomas, 181-182
Education, on OCD, 205-206
Edwards, Jonathan, 64
"Ego alien," 204
"Ego syntonic," 204
Einstein, Albert, 235-236
Electric shock, OCD, 175
Emotional hijacking, 130, 132, 200
Emotional intelligence, 129
Emotional knowing, 128
Emotional memory, 129, 131-132
Empathy, childhood development,
  170
Epigenetic rules, 176
Epileptic episodes, OCD, 55. *See
  also* Seizures
Erikson, Erik, 59-60, 75, 161, 166,
  190
Esau, 68
Eve, 43
Evil, definition of, 25-26
Evolution, role of, 9, 25
*Expert Consensus Treatment
  Guidelines for Obsessive-
  Compulsive Disorder, The,* 181

Exposure/response blocking technique
    evaluation of, 193
    OCD, 89, 91, 159, 164, 173-176,
        182-183, 186, 188, 193, 201,
        208, 209
*Extraordinary Story of Human
    Origins, The,* 137
Extroverts, 40, 161
Eyebrows, pulling out, 76, 78
Ezekiel, 48

Faith
    affirmations of, 239-243
    salvation by, 56, 60, 69, 239
Family
    child development, 167-168
    early human, 231-232
"Favorite flavor," symptom, 14
Fear, basis for, 198
Feedback loop
    brain, 173, 199
    genetic/environment, 19
First Temple, 49-50
Flashbacks, PTSD, 130-131, 142
Flood, myths of, 44, 45
Fodhla, Ollamh, 37
Food taboos, 45
    Jewish regulation of, 55
Forebrain
    evolution of, 32, 33, 34, 67
    memory system, 173, 176-179
Four Steps, 195, 196-197
Fowler, James, 161-162
Fox, George, 213
Frederick the Great, 221-222
"Freeze-frame" technique, 214-215
Freud, Sigmund, 19, 190, 204, 232

Gamaliel, Rabbi, 55
Garden of Eden, 43
Gender
    brain differentiation, 134
    OCD, 24
    rise of dominant male, 36-37

Genesis, 30-31, 43
    Abraham, 46-47
    Cain and Abel, 30-31, 43
    flood story, 44, 45
    Sodom and Gomorrah, 47
Germ phobia, poem about, 101-102
Glucose, 198, 205-206
God
    definition of, 40
    knowledge about, 235-236
Golden rule, 204-205
"Goodness of fit," 33, 35, 38-39, 47
Gospel of John, 9, 118, 238, 239
Gospel of Luke, 9, 118, 212
Gospel of Mark, 9, 118
Gospel of Matthew, 9, 51-56,
        118-119, 211, 245
Grace, 115, 201
*Grace Abounding to the Chief
    Sinners,* 65, 67-68
Gratitude, 215
Greek mythology, 29-30, 39, 44, 229,
        230
"Ground of Being," 201, 225
"Ground of Reality," 40
Growth approach, OCD, 173, 176-179
Guilt
    inauthentic, 136
    OCD, 124

Handel, George Frideric, 153
Harm, fear of doing, 17
Harmony, quality of life, 221
Hartman, David, 58
"Healer of sore throats," 97
Health, definition of, 171
"Hearing voices," 8
HeartMath, 199, 214-215
Hebrews, history of, 30-31, 45
Herbivores, food preference, 31
Hillel, Rabbi, 55
Hippocampus, midbrain, 128-129

Hoarding
  animal behavior, 16
  OCD symptom, 10, 49, 69, 82,
    116, 120, 154, 191, 194
Homo habilis, 179
Homo religiosus, 33, 41-42
Homo sapiens sapiens, 19, 25, 26,
  33, 179
"How I Ran OCD Off My Land,"
  81, 191
"Hubris," 39, 237
Human beings
  evolution of, 26-29
  existence, religious view of,
    222-223
  mammalian characteristics,
    17, 19-20, 33
  sacrifice, 47
"Humility," 73-74
Humor, use of, 61
Hunting, invention of, 31
Hypochondriasis, 29, 136
  clergy knowledge about, 7
  poem about, 106-107
Hypothalamus, midbrain, 128-129

"I know. It's not easy to explain,"
  73-74
"I used to be God," 109
Icarus, 39, 237
Idylls of the King, 240
"If only my wife was a bit better
  looking," 105-106
Ikhnaton, Pharoah, 37
Incineration technique, 174-175, 176
Independence, OCD treatment, 191
Individualism, origin of, 36
Indulgences, sale of, 62
Infallibility, concept of, 235-236
Infanticide, in ancient world, 39
Inheritance, of OCD, 18, 88
Innocent VIII, Pope, 61
Inquisition, in Spain, 57, 62
"Inspiration," 178

Intellectual knowing, 128
Intelligence, and OCD, 24, 149, 163
Intentionality, OCD change, 173
Interdisciplinarian, 2
Interjected thoughts, 8, 9, 198, 199,
  201, 214, 215, 216, 219, 234
Introverts, 40, 161
"Is the chalk still squeaking there,"
  97-98
"It is Well with My Soul," 90
"It's nice to see the rain this morn,"
  113
"I've made lots of lists," 112

James, William, 79, 172
Jeremiah, 47-48
Jesuit Order, OCD relief program,
  63, 68, 92-94, 176-177
Jesus
  in Gospel of John, 239
  in Gospel of Matthew, 51-56, 245
Job, 114
Journal of Pastoral Care, The, 5
Judaism, post-biblical history of,
  56-58
Judgment of God, 240-241
Julius II, Pope, 61, 62
Jung, Carl, 132, 143
Justification, doctrine of, 69. *See
  also* Faith

Kafka, Franz, 70-71
Kant, Immanuel, 237
Kidscope, OC Foundation, 206
Kingship, emergence of, 37
Kleptomania, 16, 29, 78, 153-154
Knowing, types of, 128

La Bohème, 156
Language
  evolution of, 27, 28, 33
  OCD treatment, 191
Lapses, OCD therapy, 207-208

"Lawyer talk," attack on, 53
Left brain hemisphere, 61, 62, 68, 134
Legalism, origin of, 46
Letters to the Galatians, 55, 67-68
Letters to the Romans, 238
Life expectancy, in early humanoids, 31
Liguori, St. Alphonse, 59, 69
Limbic system, in midbrain, 128-129
Lithium, 151
Loki, 29
"Look at that building," 111
Lou, OCD case history, 92-94, 184-185, 201, 212
Loyola, St. Ignatius, 57, 59, 63-64, 65, 68, 176-177, 193
Luther, Martin, 55, 57, 59-63, 64-65, 67-68, 212, 219, 238

Maccabees, 49
Magical thinking
   ancient world, 38
   in children, 168
   in early humans, 32, 34
   OCD, 117
   OCD treatment, 194
Male, rise of dominant, 36-37
Mammalian brain, 125-133, 133-134, 140, 174, 187, 195, 197
Mammals, 17
Manual, Jesuit, 68, 93
Mapping, for OCD, 81
March, John, 81
Marie, OCD case history, 79-81, 212
Mars, 229
Marx, Karl, 74
Mary, OCD case history, 88-91, 184-185, 212
"Mary McBride just didn't like germs," 101-102
Masada, 49
Masochism, 50
Medical model, ODC, 183

Meeting Jesus Again for the First Time, 51
Melanchthon, Philip, 219
Memory system
   duality of, 9, 128-133, 171-173, 176, 198
   in OCD, 26, 171-173, 176
Mental factors, OCD, 148
Mental illness, evolutionary perspective, 148-152
Mercury, 229
Mercy, personhood development, 212
Messiah, 153
Methodists, 70
Midbrain
   evolution of, 30, 32, 33, 34, 125-133
   memory system, 173–176
   OCD modification, 187
Migration
   food supply, 30
   from Africa, 32
Milton, John, 116
Mind, strengthening of, 217
"Mind of Reality," 235, 236, 239, 242
Moreschi, Alessandro, 59
Morris, Desmond, 31
Mortal sin, Catholic conception of, 93, 119
Mosaic law, compilation of, 48-49
Moses, 37, 42
"Multiple personality" disorder, 169, 198
Mythology, ancient world, 29-30, 39, 44, 229-230

Naked Ape, The, 31
Nancy, OCD case history, 75-79, 171-172, 184, 198, 212
Nanette Joyce, OCD case history, 82-84
Narciso, Irala, S. J., 93-94
Narcissism, 232

Narcissus, 39, 237
Nariokotome Boy, 27, 30
National Convention, OCD, 4, 6
National Institute of Mental Health, 230
"Natural religion," 34
Natural selection, role of, 27
Neptune, 229
Neurobiology
   OCD, 2, 146, 203, 205
   religious implications of, 3, 230, 238
New Age religion, 223
New brain, 133-137, 187, 197
Neziroglu, Fugen A., 60, 63
Noah, 44, 46, 244
Norse mythology, 29
Not Stills/Not Yet, 157
Not Yets/Will Be, 27-31, 33, 40, 232, 233, 239-240

Obedience, childhood development, 168
Obsession
   origin of, 49
   persistence of, 159
   sources of, 51-52, 58, 124, 132
Obsessive-compulsive disorder (OCD)
   brain connectors, 138-139, 149, 168, 206, 234
   child development, 166-171
   definition of, 24
   differential diagnosis, 4, 146-154
   DSM-IV criteria, 24, 147-148
   evolution of, 9, 149-154
   experience, form of religion, 224
   genetic role, 18-19, 114, 153, 159
   human disorder, 1, 25, 197, 234
   inappropriate treatment for, 182-184
   learning from, 5-6, 20, 114-116, 208-209, 217-218
   in males, 135, 206-207

Obsessive-compulsive disorder (OCD) *(continued)*
   nicknames for, 81, 121, 191
   physical basis of, 8-9, 14, 142, 146, 153, 159, 184-187, 203, 205
   poetry about, 73-74, 100-113
   remission of, 172-173
   symptom suppression, 145-146
   symptoms of, 12-14, 24-25, 26, 58, 154-160, 217, 237-238
   theoretical arguments, 164-165
   treatment of, 7-8, 15, 171, 173-179, 182-183, 187-189, 190-195.
   See also Exposure/ response blocking, HeartMath, Mind, strengthening of
"Obsessive-Compulsive Disorder, The: The Pastoral Knowledge Explosion," 5
Obsessive-compulsive disorder (OCD) Anonymous, 177
Obsessive-Compulsive (OC) Foundation
   educational material, 205-206
   treatment guidelines, 181
Obsessive-compulsive personality disorder (OCPD), differential diagnosis, 146-147
Oedipal stage, OCD treatment, 192, 193-195
Oedipus, 37, 55
Oedipus Rex, 37, 71
"Oh, there's a nasty rumor," 106-107
Old brain, 34, 125-127
Olfactory system, 28, 32
"On Sunday nights we go to church," 98-100
Oral stage, OCD treatment, 190
Orderliness, OCD symptom, 24
Origen, 58
Orthodox Judaism
   OCD and religious practices, 120
   scrupulosity, 57-58
Osborn, Ian, 59
Ostracism, early humanoids, 33

Panic attack, 16, 126
Papacy, during the Renaissance, 61-62
Pathogenic rule, 204
Paul, 54-56, 238
    OCD case history, 95-113
Peace, quality of life, 219
Pentecost, 2
"People's Courts," 70-71
Perfectionism, 37-38, 39, 42-43, 44,
        82-83, 89, 118, 120, 135, 147,
        236
Pericopae
    of Jesus, 54
    in Jewish tradition, 55
Personality, in early humans, 28
Personhood, development of, 212
Pilgrim's Progress, 65-67, 69-70
"Pity party," 194
Play therapy, childhood OCD, 183-184
Post-traumatic shock disorder (PTSD)
    evolutionary perspective, 31, 153
    flashbacks, 130-131
    and OCD, 198
Prayer, compulsive, 86-87, 135
Priest, 36, 37
"Primary process thinking," 168
Procrastination, 84
Professional practice experience,
        OCD, 2, 3-4
Prometheus, 29-30
Promise, in *Pilgrim's Progress,* 66-67
Promises, obsessional concern, 51
Psychosis
    evolutionary perspective, 148,
        149-150
    regressive disorder, 170-171
Psychosurgery, for OCD, 175, 197
Psychotherapy, OCD treatment, 182
Punishment, childhood development,
        168
Puritans, 65

Rabbinical tradition, 55, 56-58
Raphe nuclei, old brain, 127

Rapoport, Judith, 57, 74, 93
Reason, emergence of, 35
Reassurance
    OCD, 132-133
    styles of, 132
Reframing, cognitive behavior, 176
Regression
    causes of, 159
    OCD, 18, 159-160, 162-171
Rehabituation, 215-216
Rehabituation technique, 189
Relativity, 235-236
Religion
    evolution of, 231-233
    and OCD, 1, 11, 115, 172
Religious conflict, 68-70
Religious experience, belief in,
        236, 237
Religious feelings, 33, 115
    expression of, 85
    OCD treatment, 164
Religious sensations, 120
    in childhood, 116
    in early humanoids, 33-34
Religious systems, truth of, 223-224
Remediation, OCD, 173-176
Remission, OCD, 172-173
Repetition
    in childhood, 159
    mammalian behavior, 114
    in ritual practice, 49, 59
Repetitious functional behavior,
        OCD, 42-43
Reptilian behavior, 17
Reptilian brain, 34, 125-127
Respect, personhood development,
        212
Retardation, evolutionary
        perspective, 150-151
Revenge, obsessional concerns, 51
Reverence for life, 23, 40
"Reverse engineering," 23-24, 25
Right brain hemisphere, 61, 62, 67,
        134, 178
    religious preferences, 135

Rituals
evolution of religious, 232-233
repetition in, 49, 59
of thanksgiving, 233
Rockwell, Norman, 95
Role models, quality of life, 225
Roman Catholics, scrupulosity in,
24-25
Rules, childhood development, 169
Rules of St. Francis, OCD
management, 187

Sacramentality, 220-221
Sacred numbers, among early
humans, 32
Sadism, 50
Samuel, 37
Sanctimoniousness, 50
Sanctuary
feelings of, 120
origin of, 33-34
storage in, 36
Sassoon, Siegfried, 243
Saul, 37
Saul of Tarsus, 54-56. *See also* Paul
Scarification, 47
Schizophrenia, 8, 154
evolutionary perspective, 150
School visit, 207
Schwartz, Jeffrey, 98, 138, 204
Schweitzer, Albert, 40, 229
Scriptures, belief in, 235, 236, 237
Scrupulosity
early childhood, 162, 172
in Ignatius Loyola, 63-64
Jesuit relief program, 63, 68,
92-93, 176-177
in Martin Luther, 59-63
OCD, 3, 5, 7, 9, 24-25, 49, 50,
53-54, 55, 68-69, 118-119,
135, 147, 165
in Orthodox Jews, 57-58
in Roman Catholics, 24-25
in Unitarians, 24-25

"Scrupulous Anonymous," 59, 69
Second Temple, 50, 56
Seizures, OCD, 60
Self-abusive behavior, Old
Testament example, 45
Self-control, child development, 167
Self-esteem
child development, 166
poem about, 111
Self-expression, as sacrament, 220
Self-love, 212-213
Self-mutilation, 47, 58
Self-pity, poem about, 105-106
Self-reflection, origin of, 28-29
Self-righteousness, 50
Self-talk, 189
Sensitivity training, 84
Sensory system, switching of, 199
Serotonin
deficiency, 28
dominant males, 36-37
in early humanoids, 33
OCD, 127, 140, 176
Serotonin reuptake inhibitors (SSRI),
151, 175
Settlements, establishing early, 35-36
Sexual imagery, OCD symptom, 24,
92
Sexuality, obsessional concern, 58, 124
Shaman, 36
Shame
childhood development, 168
OCD, 4
OCD treatment, 194
Shammai, Rabbi, 55
Show Trial, 70-71
Signaling, 28
Sin, concept of, 93, 119
"Sinners in the Hands of an Angry
God," 64
Sixtus IV, Pope, 61, 62
Skinner, B. F., 195
Sky Is Falling, The, 117
Smell, early role of, 28, 32
Social differentiation, human, 30, 45

Socialization, childhood
    development, 169
Socrates, 133
Sodom and Gomorrah, 47
Somnolence, 154
St. Augustine, 179
St. Francis, 20-21, 212-213, 230
St. Martin, 5
Startle response, 18, 129-130, 132,
    140, 141, 159, 165-166, 175,
    176, 185-186, 198
  impulse control, 214-215
  PTSD, 141
Staupitz, Johann, 60-61
Stephen, stoning of, 54, 55
Story of Civilization, The, 71
Storytelling, origin of, 34
Straightener, OCD symptom, 4, 10,
    88, 191
Strep infection, 153, 159, 167
Studdert-Kennedy, G. A., 74
Subject/object split, 196-197
Suffering, reality of, 223, 233, 235,
    241
Sullivan, Harry Stack, 204
Superstition
  early childhood, 162, 168, 169
  OCD, 117-118, 120, 124
  OCD treatment, 192, 194
Support groups
  fears of members, 12-14
  for OCD, 2, 90-91, 93-94, 158, 191
  religious feelings expression, 85
Survival Feedback Loop, The, 186
Symmetry, passion for, 37-38
Symptom creep, 163-164, 189-190

Taboos, ancient Hebrews, 45-46
Tactile system, 199
Temples, of ancient Hebrews, 49-50,
    56
"Tender-minded," OCD, 63-64
Tennyson, Alfred, 240

Terror
  basis for, 198
  OCD symptom, 26, 142
Test phobia, 207
Thalmus, midbrain, 128-129
Therapy, for OCD, 84, 87-88, 89,
    139-140, 203
"There once was a man," 103-104
"There's a recession in Hell," 108
Thirty Years War, 65
"Tics," Tourette's syndrome, 80-81
Tillich, Paul, 37, 40, 201, 224-225,
    229, 242
Time, concept of, 142, 200-201
"Time was," 95-96
Toilet training, 167
"Tommy," 243-244
Tool making, 30
*Tormenting Thoughts and Secret
    Rituals,* 161
Torquemada, Fra Thomas de, 57
Touching Tree, The, 198
"Touch-minded," OCD, 63, 64
Tourette's syndrome, 13, 29, 79-80, 81
  evolutionary perspective, 151
Tower of Babel, 1, 2, 46
Toynbee, Arnold, 242
Traditional law, emergence of, 37
Trance state, 159, 190, 193, 197, 198
Transgression, 116, 120
Trauma
  early humanoid, 31-32
  OCD, 130-131
Treatment target, OCD therapy, 203
Trichotillomania, 13, 29, 136, 198
Trivialization, 165
Truth
  issue of, 237
  search for, 218-219
Twain, Mark, 119
'Twas the night before Christmas,
    parody, 104-105
Twelve Step program
  for alcoholism, 46
  healing power of, 230, 240

Twelve Step program *(continued)*
   for kleptomania, 75
   for OCD, 177

"Ultimate Concern," 40, 229
Ultimate Reality, 236, 242
Unitarians, scrupulosity in, 24-25

Valuing, 177
Van Ornum, William A., 74
Varieties of Religious Experience,
   The, 79, 172
Veterinarian, 2, 9, 16, 185, 188-189
Violence
   obsessional concerns, 124
   origins of, 30-31, 36-37
Von Taylor, Joey, scenario, 201-202
Vulcan, 229

Walker, Alan, 30, 32
"Wash bear," 16
Washer, animal behavior, 16

Washers, OCD symptom, 25, 57,
   191, 198
"Way of the Heart, The," 215
Weaning, 167
Wesley, John, 121, 136, 216
"When your judgment time has
   come," 110
Whitehead, Alfred North, 19, 25-26,
   142, 220, 221, 244
Wilson, Edmund, 176, 220
Wisdom, gained from OCD,
   208-209, 217-218
Witchcraft, among Hebrews, 37
Witness, as compulsion, 237
Women, brain usage, 134-135
"Word salad," 150
Working memory, OCD, 9, 131-132
Worry, basis for, 24, 137, 198

Yaryura-Tobias, José A., 60, 63
Young Man Luther, 59

"Zoning out," 171, 175, 198, 200

Order Your Own Copy of
This Important Book for Your Personal Library!

THE OBSESSIVE-COMPULSIVE DISORDER
Pastoral Care for the Road to Change

_____ in hardbound at $49.95 (ISBN: 0-7890-0707-X)

_____ in softbound at $19.95 (ISBN: 0-7890-0862-9)

COST OF BOOKS _____	☐ **BILL ME LATER:** ($5 service charge will be added) (Bill-me option is good on US/Canada/Mexico orders only; not good to jobbers, wholesalers, or subscription agencies.)
OUTSIDE USA/CANADA/ MEXICO: ADD 20% _____	
POSTAGE & HANDLING_____ *(US: $3.00 for first book & $1.25 for each additional book) Outside US: $4.75 for first book & $1.75 for each additional book)*	☐ Check here if billing address is different from shipping address and attach purchase order and billing address information. Signature_____
SUBTOTAL_____	☐ **PAYMENT ENCLOSED: $**_____
IN CANADA: ADD 7% GST_____	☐ **PLEASE CHARGE TO MY CREDIT CARD.**
STATE TAX_____ *(NY, OH & MN residents, please add appropriate local sales tax)*	☐ Visa ☐ MasterCard ☐ AmEx ☐ Discover ☐ Diner's Club
FINAL TOTAL_____ *(If paying in Canadian funds, convert using the current exchange rate. UNESCO coupons welcome.)*	Account # _____ Exp. Date _____ Signature _____

Prices in US dollars and subject to change without notice.

NAME _____

INSTITUTION _____

ADDRESS _____

CITY _____

STATE/ZIP _____

COUNTRY _____ COUNTY (NY residents only) _____

TEL _____ FAX _____

E-MAIL_____
May we use your e-mail address for confirmations and other types of information? ☐ Yes   ☐ No

Order From Your Local Bookstore or Directly From
The Haworth Press, Inc.
10 Alice Street, Binghamton, New York 13904-1580 • USA
TELEPHONE: 1-800-HAWORTH (1-800-429-6784) / Outside US/Canada: (607) 722-5857
FAX: 1-800-895-0582 / Outside US/Canada: (607) 772-6362
E-mail: getinfo@haworthpressinc.com
PLEASE PHOTOCOPY THIS FORM FOR YOUR PERSONAL USE.

BOF96